Developing Jini™ Applications Using J2ME™ Technology

Developing Jini™ Applications Using J2ME™ Technology

Hinkmond Wong

♦♦ Addison-Wesley

Boston • San Francisco • New York • Toronto • Montreal
London • Munich • Paris • Madrid
Capetown • Sydney • Tokyo • Singapore • Mexico City

The publisher offers discounts on this book when ordered in quantity for special sales. For more information, please contact:

Pearson Education Corporate Sales Division
201 W. 103rd Street
Indianapolis, IN 46290
(800) 428-5331
corpsales@pearsoned.com

Visit Addison-Wesley on the Web: www.aw.com/cseng/

Library of Congress Cataloging-in-Publication Data

Wong, Hinkmond.
    Developing Jini™ applications using J2ME™ technology / Hinkmond Wong.
        p.   cm.
Includes bibliographical references and index.
    ISBN 0-201-70244-4
    1. Electronic data processing--Distributed processing. 2. Jini.
3. Java (Computer program language)   I. Title.
QA76.9.D5 W66 2002
004'.36--dc21

                                                        2002025359

For information on obtaining permission for use of material from this work, please submit a written request to:

Pearson Education, Inc.
Rights and Contracts Department
75 Arlington Street, Suite 300
Boston, MA 02116
Fax: (617) 848-7047

ISBN 0-201-70244-4

Text printed on recycled paper

1 2 3 4 5 6 7 8 9 10—MA—0605040302

First printing, March 2002

To Jenn and Fridgie

Contents

Preface

The world of Java technology is quickly changing from the world of the desktop computer and back-end servers to that of small consumer electronics and embedded devices. During the next few years small devices that connect to the Internet will far outnumber larger personal computers. Consumer products such as PDAs (personal digital assistants), cellular phones, game consoles, television set-top boxes, and car navigation systems will be the new launching pad for the Web.

The Java 2 Platform, Micro Edition (J2ME) technology from Sun Microsystems addresses the needs of this new environment. This book explains the concepts of profiles and configurations to help simplify the required pieces of technology for smaller Java technology-enabled devices targeted for the consumer and the embedded market.

With Jini network technology, any small device can connect to the network in a simple manner. New mechanisms have been designed for software and hardware to automatically join together into a federation of devices and services. This is a natural progression because Jini technology uses a Java distributed computing platform architecture.

Joining the J2ME environment and Jini technology is an easy fit. Jini network technology enables small Java technology-enabled devices to talk with each other, and the J2ME environment enables the simple programming of small devices using the Java computing platform.

This book teaches you how to use both J2ME technology and Jini network technology to design and implement consumer and embedded devices. It is intended for software developers and Java hobbyists. The reader will discover the world of the J2ME environment and Jini network technology through detailed explanations and programming examples. Before starting, the reader should have a good sense of Java programming and a fair understanding of computer networking. This book does not require specific knowledge of embedded systems development, only a fair understanding of the Java programming language.

This book focuses on the concepts of J2ME technology and Jini network technology. The reader will learn about the different network architectures that are available for small devices. Finally, code examples are included and described to show how programming small devices using Jini technology is done in the Java programming language.

This book will help the reader get a good start in the design and development of the next generation of connected Java technology-enabled small devices that will take the world beyond the personal computer.

Acknowledgments

I would like to thank the many people who helped in the creation of this book. First the J2ME and Jini team members (both past and present) at Sun Microsystems. It's been quite a journey, but Moore's Law is proving that small devices are viable in a distributed computing environment.

I'd like to especially thank Ken Arnold and Laird Dornin for their help in outlining this book and giving me valuable comments during the preliminary stage. I'd like to also thank Kevin Russell and Mark Fulks, my past and present managers, who gave full support in seeing this book through. Rob Patten helped me maneuver around the hazards and roadblocks of getting it published.

The entire team at Addison-Wesley was extremely helpful in teaching this new author about how a book gets from manuscript to bound pages. I'm very grateful to Tracy Russ; Mike Hendrickson; Julie DiNicola; Ross Venables; and, last but not least, Marilyn Rash and her team—Nancy Crumpton, Rob Mauhar, Susan Riley, and Dianne Wood—who helped me in innumerable ways in organizing and scheduling the final production of my book.

Finally, I'd like to thank my co-workers on the J2ME CDC/Foundation Profile and CVM teams. You guys are fun to work with and make it all worthwhile.

1

Introduction

Over the past several years, Java technology has matured on the desktop and in servers into a powerful and efficient computing platform. Businesses have quickly adopted and implemented this new platform in many ways, from database connectivity to application servers. Developers have been impressed by the language's ease of use and its platform independence.

Now, smaller generations of the Java programming language platform have been introduced—ones created for specialized markets. The concept of just one Java technology for large server systems no longer applies; there is commonality now among embedded devices.

These new devices are small, mobile, and able to be networked. They include cell phones and personal digital assistants (PDAs) and household appliances that are becoming more connected through the use of home networks these days (see Figure 1.1). With all these types of devices distributed over a wide network, it's natural to use Java technology to standardize on a common programming environment and to use Jini network technology to enable these systems to communicate with each other. Java technology provides the shared application programming interfaces (APIs), while Jini technology provides a seamless way for various devices to be integrated and to interact.

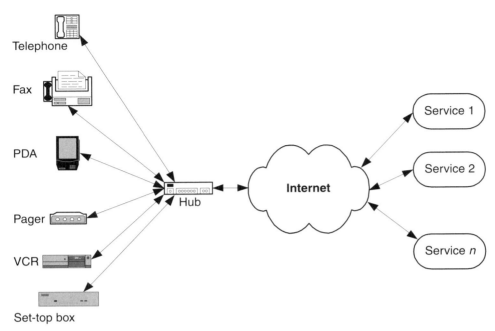

Figure 1.1   New small devices on the network

Having these technologies on a small device provides a way for embedded systems to be a part of the growing trend toward distributed computing, where many devices that are powerful enough to behave as individual computers can also work in a collaborative effort to achieve greater distributed computing power.

Small devices running these technologies can also access many different types of back-end services on the Internet. Web services delivered to the various devices provide flexibility and power to small computing systems.

1.1   Distributed Computing and Embedded Devices: A Natural Fit

This book uses Jini network technology with the Java 2 Platform, Micro Edition (J2ME™) to show how to connect embedded devices using a distributed computing model (see Figure 1.2). With distributed computing, all devices on a network can participate in a collaborative effort in achieving a computing goal. Lots of tiny computers working together trying to solve a big problem provides robustness and the ability to evolve. The robustness comes from the Jini technology's ability to

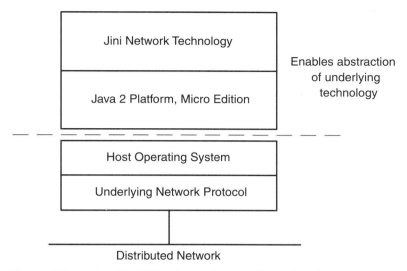

Figure 1.2   Jini and J2ME technologies hide the underlying network protocol.

enable clients and services to come and go from a distributed network. Because Jini technology is not restricted to one particular underlying protocol, it provides the ability to evolve a distributed network.

The consumer and embedded devices of the future need a way to easily connect together and to distribute computing resources appropriately. The network of these devices must be able to scale to large numbers and to handle the administrative complexity of these large numbers of new devices. Jini network technology is a perfect fit for adding connectivity to network devices and solving the problem of how best to integrate a quickly growing number of Internet appliances to the network of humans who will use them.

J2ME and Jini technologies on these devices provide many benefits:

- *Simple-to-use devices:* Connections are automatically made; behavior is the same across vendors.

- *Robust applications:* The devices can use intermittent connections.

- *Little or no administration:* Administration is handled behind the scenes.

- *Direct interaction:* Devices can communicate easily with other devices.

- *Intermittent connectivity:* Devices can handle lost connections.

1.2   How Traditional Networks Have Failed

Traditional networks have used fixed protocols that have caused major problems when a new and better protocol is developed. When upgrading a network that is dependent on fixed protocols, many changes are needed in many different places—in the network, on all the existing devices, on all new devices, and so on. This system is prone to errors and is "fragile" as technological advancements are made.

Here are some examples of the failure of fixed protocols:

- *Cell phones:* With new area codes popping up and old area codes being split, it is no wonder that many people become confused and their lists of phone numbers become out of date. Area codes should be hidden from the user as an underlying protocol. The proper abstraction layer should be the name of the person or business that one is trying to contact.

- *Postal addresses:* People and offices often relocate, and their mail must somehow get forwarded to new addresses. A better way is to abstract the physical address to a simple interface to specific postal addresses.

- *Web servers:* Out-of-date Web addresses cause broken links. Uniform Resource Locators (URLs) are notorious for changing rapidly and/or becoming obsolete. There should be a way to use an abstract reference to the content of a Web page—for example, a television schedule listing for Monday night instead of having to remember a URL to the *TV Guide* Web page for Monday night.

- *Web browsers:* When a Web browser tries to load specially formatted content for the first time, such as a Shockwave Flash or RealAudio file, a new plug-in must be loaded, but these plug-ins are not available for all computers, especially for newer PDAs. A better way is to use Java technology programs, instead of plug-ins, which guarantee that the program will execute within the Java runtime environment that is present on the device.

- *Personal computers:* Software is notorious in its failure to provide an easy way for users to install programs on a computer. Users have to contend with CD-ROMs, Web downloads, and drivers. A better way is to use self-installing software, which is possible with the use of J2ME and Jini technologies.

J2ME and Jini technologies do away with these types of failures. Devices using J2ME and Jini technologies can evolve over time with new data and new protocols, without requiring the user to manually update a specific device. Jini technology provides the abstraction layer for devices to hide protocols and fixed information.

Abstract interfaces to protocols, such as area codes, postal addresses, URLs, and software programs, are the only requirement. The underlying complexity is hidden by the use of that simple interface, freeing the user and developer from having to know the exact protocol to use.

1.3   Benefits of Using Java Technology

In general, Java technology implements the benefits of abstraction and addresses specific failures of the past such as those discussed in the previous section. The benefits of using J2ME technology are the same benefits of using Java technology. J2ME technology simply implements the Java technology in smaller devices. The major advantages of using Java technology are the following:

- *Reliability:* Embedded devices cannot tolerate reboots and crashes, which Java technology eliminates.

- *No memory pointers:* C programming–type memory allocations and management are not needed.

- *Security*: Built-in Java technology security keeps data safe from unauthorized access.

- *No viruses:* Built-in Java technology security also prevents occurrences of viruses and worms.

- *Automatic memory garbage collection:* Memory garbage collection minimizes memory leaks.

- *Object orientation:* The objected-oriented nature of the Java programming language makes software design much easier.

As one can see, Java technology concentrates on security and ease of programming to enable the user of an embedded device to keep data from being harmed and to enable developers to program efficiently. These benefits have enabled Java technology to catch on quickly. Because they apply to large computer systems, the advantages of Java technology can also apply to the embedded world through J2ME technology.

1.4   Advantages of Jini Network Technology

With access to Java technology in many devices, the benefits of Jini network technology become apparent for connecting a device with its service provider network, which may be at best a 3GB or 2.5GB wireless connection (much slower than Ethernet capabilities) or at worst an intermittent or spotty connection. An environment where reliability and speed are problems requires robustness. Jini technology addresses that need in the following ways:

- *Service discovery:* The ability to automatically find and use available services on a network.

- *Extensibility model:* The ability to add new protocols and services on a network without affecting current use.

- *Changing network:* The ability of networks to evolve to use future standards without being tied to a fixed set of protocols for compatibility.

- *Leasing:* Increasing the longevity of the network as clients are automatically updated to connect using new protocols after current leases expire.

- *Handling of failures and intermittent connectivity:* The ability to fail over to other services on a network when the initially requested service is not available.

The Jini network technology creates an abstraction layer to hide the faulty and unreliable aspects of a data network, which is beneficial to the user because an embedded device should turn on and work correctly with little effort.

The Jini technology takes J2ME technology a step further with robustness and the ability to evolve on the network.

1.5   How Java and Jini Technologies Work Together in Embedded Devices

Java and Jini technologies can enable embedded devices to do many things. The two technologies together address the problems of reliability and ease of use. One builds on the other as the programming efficiencies of Java technology are used as springboards for extending the network beyond computer servers and desktops to reach small hand-held devices.

The following are highlights of how Java and Jini technologies are able to work together:

- *Java technology based:* Jini technology builds on the existing advantages of Java technology because Jini technology is written in the Java programming language.

- *Network extensions:* Jini technology enables the power of Java technology to extend to the network by addressing how services are offered to client devices.

- *Servers and desktop computers:* Jini technology can be used with larger computer systems connecting to smaller devices. Java objects are transferable between all Java technology-enabled systems.

- *Small devices:* Applications enabled with Jini technology can now run on small devices using J2ME technology and/or Jini surrogate architecture.

- *J2ME technology:* The footprint matters more in small devices, and J2ME technology addresses that by providing smaller profiles and configurations.

- *Flexibility:* Java and Jini technologies enable embedded systems to use many different types of services and to interact with many different types of devices. The common base is Java technology.

- *Service and device interaction:* Devices can teach each other new behavior by exchanging Java objects via Jini networking technology.

The pairing of Java and Jini technologies provides an advanced, easy-to-use programming environment with a service discovery and connection model. This opens the network to incorporate devices, from servers to hand-held PDAs, enabling systems to seamlessly communicate with each other and to exchange data and behavior, evolving into the future along the way.

1.6 Summary

This chapter described how the failures of the past have led to new technologies that solve those past problems for the small devices of today. J2ME and Jini technologies address the failures of past systems that relied on ever-changing underlying information such as area codes, postal addresses, URLs, and computer programs. Using abstract interfaces to shelter ever-changing underlying protocols enables both J2ME and Jini technologies to hide complexity from the developer and user.

The additional benefits of the J2ME and Jini environments being Java technologies, and the flexibility of Jini technology, provide a full set of features to solve many of the problems of the fast-changing protocols of today. This is important for the next generation of consumer devices that must meet the needs of an ever-evolving network of services and service providers.

2

The Power of Java Technology in Small Devices

The advantages of the power of Java technology in small devices are apparent when you look at the many problems inherent in the current set of devices. Many different service providers for small devices are in existence today, each on its own private network or on a network with standards incompatible with other protocols.

Many of the devices have had no way of communicating with other devices until recently. Java technology provides a common language among all types of devices.

Instead of relying on a fixed protocol to enable these devices to intercommunicate, an evolving standard can be put in place—a standard that relies on a common technology base, which allows for interdevice connections. This common technology base is the Java programming language, which provides all the benefits of a modern computing language's ease of programming. The added benefit of a true object-oriented environment is also provided—where not just data but also functional program behavior is transferred in the programming objects.

Object-oriented programming has existed for many years but has not been widely used for embedded devices. Devices were previously not powerful enough to handle it. The new J2ME technology enables Java technology to be scaled down to small devices (see Figure 2.1) and enables objects to be passed back and forth among devices.

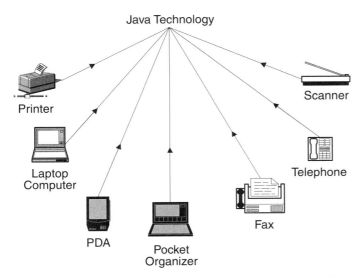

Figure 2.1 Java technology provides a common language for small devices.

A lot of complexity is hidden when devices are designed using object-oriented techniques. Distributed computing, which depends on object-oriented programming, is easy to implement, especially with Jini network technology layered on top of the Java technology as a common base.

2.1 Java Technology Addresses the Problems of Small Devices

The common problems of devices center mainly around the fact that devices use proprietary communication methods. Manufacturers failed to foresee the need for all types of devices to communicate with each other, and in many cases they purposely used proprietary systems to ensure lock-in to their specific brand. Today, the benefit of enabling all devices to intercommunicate is apparent—it enables users to interact with one another and with different services across a network.

The existing problems of small devices and their networks can be itemized as follows:

- *Proprietary device architectures:* Each device had its own way to communicate with other devices. Java technology creates the common language between devices.

- *Proprietary network protocols:* Each device had its own network protocol. Jini technology hides the need to know about fixed protocols.

- *Minimal network effect:* By hiding the proprietary aspects of networks, devices can easily communicate with each other.

The preceding list demonstrates the need for a solution to enable greater interoperability. It also shows how Java technology is addressing the problems. Manufacturers are finding it easier to port Java virtual machines (JVMs) to their devices, so Java technology is becoming more available on many types of consumer electronics. With more Java technology available, better interoperability is realized by standardizing on a runtime environment where write once, run anywhere (WORA) can occur.

2.2 J2ME Technology

Java 2 Platform, Micro Edition (J2ME) addresses the needs of disparate devices and the desire to have them easily intercommunicate. J2ME technology provides a solid base for device development because millions of developers write programs in Java, and many sources of information are available on the Web and in books. The following are some specific advantages that J2ME technology gives to device development:

- *Common application base:* The WORA concept can apply to programs written for all devices.

- *Diversity of devices:* The heterogeneous nature of devices makes it important to have WORA.

- *Dynamic class loading:* Using dynamic class loading hides protocol proliferation.

- *Forward reference:* Abstract interfaces hide the complexity of devices.

Much is to be gained by hiding the complexity of a device. The developer sees a simpler way to program the device by using a well-known abstract interface. For example, when exchanging a message between two cell phones, fixed protocols, such as Simple Message Service (SMS) or AOL Instant Messaging (AIM), hard-coded into a device aren't necessary. A Java programming interface can hide that from the developer. A simple call to a `sendMessage()` method means the developer has to remember only one API and doesn't have to look up the right interface for SMS versus AIM. The underlying protocol remains hidden.

2.3   The Increasing Power of Small Devices

The functionality of small devices is increasing as "gadgets" get smaller, acquire more memory, and use better processors. This increased power turns these embedded devices into powerful computers that one can hold in one's hand. Not only do small devices now have many of the same abilities as large computers, they are also highly networkable. The following are some points about the increased power of small devices:

- *Increased functionality:* Java and Jini technologies provide more types of services to all different types of devices.

- *Better connection to the network:* Java technology enables better networking APIs to be used.

- *Ability to interoperate:* Java programs on one device can talk directly with Java programs on another.

- *Enhanced applications:* Java technology enables developers to use the latest object-oriented programming techniques.

- *Increased security:* Java technology has built-in protection for devices.

The new generation of devices enables people to move data and access services in ways that never could be used before. This new power has its drawbacks—one of these is: Greater functionality usually means greater complexity. The way to manage this complexity (especially complexity due to new networking capabilities to back-end services) is to use technologies such as J2ME and Jini to push down the intricacies to a lower level, thus enabling the developer to work at a more abstract, higher level. Abstraction frees the mind of the developer to concentrate on more important issues such as what types of services should be available to devices and the implementation of an easy-to-use interface.

The problems presented by the next generation of devices are addressed by J2ME technology (see Figure 2.2). The specifics of J2ME technology are explored in the next sections.

2.4   J2ME CLDC

The Connected Limited Device Configuration (CLDC) uses the K virtual machine (KVM), which is a specialized Java virtual machine targeted at consumer devices with limited resources. The typical devices that use a KVM include cell phones,

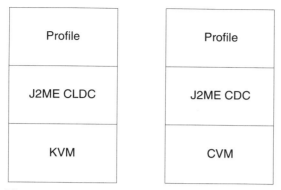

Figure 2.2   J2ME CLDC and CDC stacks

pagers, PDAs, and mobile point-of-sale (POS) terminals. KVM was built from the start with small devices in mind. It makes efficient use of a small memory footprint and can fit just in the range of kilobytes of memory (thus the "K" in its name).

For operation, the KVM needs 128KB of total available memory and is best suited for a 16- or 32-bit RISC or CISC processor. It has been optimized to work within this type of environment and has been proven to work on a device such as the Palm Pilot.

2.4.1   Technical Overview

The KVM was written to the Java virtual machine specification with the exception of bytecode verification. Having a bytecode verifier on a small device is too cumbersome in most cases. The KVM follows a modular design to allow for different device configurations.

The static memory footprint for just the virtual machine part of the KVM is about 40KB. It reads Java class files and supports class loading. The full Java bytecode set is supported with a 32-bit word size. Multithreading is supported in the form of Java threads, which are platform-independent. The multithreading capabilities of the KVM may be disabled if the device does not require multiple-thread processing.

2.4.2   New Features

The KVM was written in the C programming language in about 16,000 lines of code (about half of those lines are comments). The size of an executable for the KVM can range from 30KB to 55KB, depending on the options and libraries that have been compiled in it. The typical executable on the KVM for Palm OS is about 45KB, which includes graphics with event handling. The typical runtime heap size is about 60KB on the KVM for Palm OS. The minimum heap size is 4KB. It is recommended that the device have 128KB available for memory.

The total memory footprint can be calculated as VM + *libraries* + *heap space*. This formula works out to be about 80KB to 128KB for the minimum KVM total memory footprint and about 160KB to 256KB for the typical case. The speed of the KVM is about 30 percent to 80 percent of a Java Development Kit (JDK) version 1.1 JVM without the use of a just-in-time (JIT) compiler, which is speedy, considering that the devices that it runs on are typically battery-powered portable devices that are much smaller than desktop computers.

Sun Microsystems is currently maintaining sample implementations of the KVM for Palm OS, Solaris, and Windows. Twenty ports of the KVM have been completed so far, and the feedback has been very good.

2.4.3   Unsupported Features

The unsupported features of the KVM include the following:

- *Bytecode verification:* An off-device verifier can be used instead.

- *Java Native Interface (JNI):* This feature is too costly for limited devices. Instead, native code can be linked directly in the virtual machine.

- *Graphics support for Abstract Windowing Toolkit (AWT):* This feature is too costly for limited devices.

- *Advanced Java 2 features:* Reflection, RMI, and other features are too costly.

Even with these unsupported features, the KVM adds value to a small device by providing a common platform among different types of devices with different environments. A common platform provides the advantages of the Java programming language such as object-oriented technology, a large developer community, downloadable bytecodes, and local processing. With these advantages, the KVM becomes a great solution for small devices with limited capabilities.

The following are the J2ME CLDC resource requirements:

- *Memory:* 512KB ROM

- *Processor:* 16-bit CPU

- *Network connection:* No networking required

- *User interface:* No graphical user interface (GUI) is bundled with the CLDC and KVM. However, a finalized Java Specification Request (JSR), JSR 37, called the Mobile Information Device Profile (MID Profile or MIDP), adds APIs to the CLDC and enables the implementor to add a GUI.

2.5   J2ME Connected Device Configuration

The J2ME Connected Device Configuration (CDC) is a new subset of Java technology APIs that has been targeted for more powerful embedded devices. It comes with the minimal core set of libraries that is needed to build a device based on the Java technology.

It also is fully compatibile with a regular JVM, providing needed interoperability with the Java virtual machines running on much larger computers such as back-end servers.

J2ME CDC concentrates on the following benefits:

- *Advanced networking:* The J2ME CDC provides the latest Java technology APIs for socket-based networks.

- *Jini technology requirements:* The J2ME CDC-based Remote Method Invocation (RMI) optional package enables fully Jini technology-enabled devices to run.

- *J2SE developers:* J2ME leverages the existing knowledge of Java 2 Platform, Standard Edition (J2SE) programmers.

- *Easy porting:* The core classes of the J2ME CDC-based Foundation Profile include the well-known packages of `java.lang`, `java.net`, `java.io`, `java.util`, `java.security`, and `java.text`.

- *No deprecated methods:* J2ME CDC removes deprecated methods to make programming safer and easier.

- *Advanced packages:* Future profiles, which are logical groupings of APIs, address the specific needs of small devices. Examples include Personal Basis Profile (PBP), Personal Profile (PP), and more.

The J2ME CDC opens a vast amount of Java 2 technology functionality for small devices, paving the way for Jini technology. The ability of Java and Jini technologies to run in a small space on embedded systems opens new ways to make services available for greater numbers of users. Flexibility, interoperability, and the ability to evolve are present on consumer devices in a way that has never been seen before.

The following are the resource requirements of the J2ME CDC:

- *Memory:* 2MB ROM, 512KB RAM

- *Processor:* 32-bit CPU

- *Network connection:* At minimum User Datagram Protocol (UDP)—a full TCP/IP stack may be added by the profile

- *User interface:* No GUI—a GUI may be added by the profile

2.6   Summary

Small electronic devices are becoming powerful, networked, hand-held computers. The way they can exchange and process data makes them more functional than ever before and at the same time more complex. J2ME and Jini technologies address the new power of these devices and push the complexity down to a lower level, leaving the developer with a simple abstract interface.

Developers can concentrate on better programming techniques and not have to worry about the low-level protocols when programming for J2ME technology-enabled devices. This frees manufacturers from wallowing in the details, allowing them to focus on flexibility and interoperability, and it enables a device to grow and learn new standards over time.

3

The Jini Network Technology Vision

The vision for Jini technology started with a vision of the integration of network services based on various research projects such as Oberon. The Oberon system was invented by Niklaus Wirth, who was the inventor of the Pascal computing language. A lightweight system, Oberon was written in one programming language and uses knowledge-based objects that spans the gap between the operating system and an application. This was key to building a unified, integrated network of services such as that found in Jini technology.

The Oberon system relies on a single-user system that enables a single-threaded, multitasking operating system to run in a single window. The system enables the extension of persistent objects that build a graphical user interface (GUI), which is a tree of many objects that export abstract data types.

In the Oberon system, applications are modules that reuse the abstract data types of the GUI objects and are not exposed to their implementation. The Oberon system embodies the strength that Jini network technology developers wanted to emulate: extensibility that isn't tied to an underlying implementation. (More information about the Oberon system, which spurred the initial concepts of Jini technology, can be found at *www.oberon.ethz.ch/white.html*.)

3.1   Wire Protocols: Constricting and Fragile

The concept of abstracting the underlying implementation is important because of how constricting and fragile an underlying protocol can be. A wire protocol, such as that found in the communications layer of a computer network, has many restrictions, including the following:

- All participants must implement all protocol versions for full compatibility. For example, when features are added to sendmail and a new sending protocol is established, it is difficult to upgrade all servers at once.

- Improved functionality implies increased complexity. For example, when a new compression scheme is added to the File Transfer Protocol (FTP), existing clients cannot understand the new scheme.

These types of restrictions only make it harder to evolve a network. The Jini network technology hides the protocol to provide more flexibility.

3.2   Objects on the Network

In Jini technology, data objects should not be transferred to and from nodes on a network. Instead, they should be part of the network itself, which means that the objects' data and behavior are accessed through interfaces by other objects on the network. The protocol is hidden, and the network objects are not restricted by the wire protocol.

3.3   The API Defines the Network Interface

The API, not the low-level technical details, should define the network. The developer needs to remember only one API call on any environment where J2ME and Jini technologies exist. It is not necessary to keep references to all the different protocols—for example, cell phone protocols such as Code Division Multiple Access (CDMA), Time Division Multiple Access (TDMA), and Global System for Mobile Communications (GSM)—available to devices and their service providers.

3.3.1   Byte-Level Protocols Are Irrelevant

With Jini technology, byte-level protocols are an implementation detail and are irrelevant for the purpose of designing software for a network service. The software architect of small devices is freed from the details of the network and can concentrate on the details of delivering a quality service that meets customers' needs.

3.4   Late Binding Insulates Developers

Jini technology promotes late binding of APIs so that developers are insulated from the API implementation. Late binding occurs when an interface that is used during programming doesn't have to know the actual implementation that will bind to that interface during runtime. The implementation is said to be *late binding* to the interface. The use of late-binding interfaces to underlying protocols means that protocols are unnecessary at the application programming level, which frees the developer from the complexity of keeping the protocol layer up to date.

3.5   The Power of Write Once, Run Anywhere

The concept of WORA does not apply just to application portability. It also enables the portability of new programming behavior, which is sent on the fly as part of class loading with Java technology. This power enables devices to take part in distributed computing. The automatic update of new class files enables the behavior of small devices to continuously evolve.

3.6   Capitalizing on the Simplifying Assumptions of Java Technology

Jini technology leverages many aspects of Java technology. This leveraging capitalizes on the Java technology simplifications which include making the network homogenous, checking and converting class types, not requiring Java technology on every device, not having to worry about byte order, and writing programs just once for many types of devices.

Java technology simplifications eliminate the burden of the mundane parts of software development for the programmer and make automatic checking part of the platform. It lessens the risk of introducing bugs due to the easy oversight inherent in routine programming tasks. The following list describes simplifications of Java technology in greater detail:

- *Makes the network homogenous:* The devices on a network are heterogeneous by nature. Java technology is the equalizer, enabling all the disparate devices on a network to have a common API set.

- *Creates a uniform communications model using class type checking:* Automatic class type checking ensures that the classes of two programs running on two different devices are compatible. This gives a uniform base of programming behavior among all devices on a network.

- *Converts complex class types automatically:* The complex class types represented on one device are automatically converted by the Java technology layer. This advantage means that the developer does not have to worry about how one representation of a class looks on another device on the network. All devices see program classes, even complex class types, the same way.

- *Allows Java technology to be present somewhere on the network, not necessarily on every machine:* For uniformity in communication, Java technology is key in enabling classes to interoperate. However, it is not necessary that the Java technology be present in all devices. The technology can exist somewhere on the network, and devices can access it by proxy.

- *Makes byte order unimportant:* The byte order of data becomes unimportant with Java technology because the format of the data is abstracted below the programming classes. The classes and their instantiated objects need not know whether the byte order of the underlying data is big endian or little endian. Classes and their objects are concerned only with access to that data through common APIs.

- *Enables write once, run anywhere:* With WORA, developers need not worry about porting applications or classes from one platform to another. The programs and classes written in the Java programming language work on other platforms.

3.7   Objects on the Network

The objects on the network that transfer back and forth between services and devices (also between devices themselves) have additional advantages when used with Java technology; two of them are summarized next.

- *Avoidance of versioning problems:* Vast reduction in problems with regard to versioning occurs when dynamically sending new behavior via class loading. This allows integration of new functionality and automatic bug fix updates.

- *Facilitates the interoperability of different vendors:* Each vendor provides its own interface implementations that can interoperate with other vendors' devices.

Objects are used in the protocols that are transferred between disparate devices and servers.

3.8 Jini Technology Matters in Small Devices

Once the base of Java technology is established, the next logical layer on small devices is Jini technology. The advantages of having Jini technology on top of Java technology for small devices can be summarized as follows:

- *Installation:* One infrastructure is used to accommodate unforeseen change.

- *Network administration:* Simple or nonexistent administration happens across the network.

- *Edges of the network:* The devices on a network are seamlessly able to adapt to change.

- *Uniform communications model:* All devices and services standardize on using Java and Jini technologies as the means for communication.

- *Not specifically for embedded devices:* Jini technology is not designed specifically for small devices; however, full Jini technology-enabled devices are enabled by J2ME technology.

- *Broadly applicable:* Applications can span from devices to enterprise systems.

- *Originally for the office environment:* Although Jini technology was originally designed for the office environment, it now can also be applied to wireless devices in offices.

3.9 Summary

The Jini technology vision incorporates many of the preexisting advantages of Java technology and extends them to the network. Java and Jini technologies on small devices provide more flexibility and room for growth. Software is made up of class types on a network which interoperate using common interfaces.

The abstraction of the implementation enables the devices from different vendors to interoperate. Devices can be updated on the fly with new information to keep devices from becoming stale. The devices on the edges of the network can continue to participate with services and other devices by taking part in the Jini technology framework and using Java technology's dynamic class loading to the fullest extent.

4

J2ME Basics

$\mathbf{T}$he J2ME environment starts with designing the base of the target platform. Choosing the right configuration and profiles is important. The developer must first decide what functionality is required in the device. The functionality requirement sets the memory and processing requirements.

Greater cost is associated with a device that has a more complicated functionality, such as GUI interaction or a TCP/IP network connection to the Internet. The J2ME environment is designed so that one can incorporate only what is needed from the Java platform to support the requirements of the system.

With a closer look at the J2ME technology market, one can divide devices into two sectors. One sector is the *mobile information device* group. The characteristics of the devices in this group are

- *Personal-type devices:* Pagers, cell phones, PDAs, and so on

- *Connection to a network:* Usually a low bandwidth connection and not necessarily over TCP/IP

- *Small amount of available memory:* In the range of 256KB to 512KB

Another sector of J2ME devices is the *advanced information device* group. The characteristics of this group are

- *Fixed-type devices:* The more advanced PDAs, TV set-top boxes, Web phones, automobile console systems, and so on

- *Higher bandwidth connection to a network:* Persistent TCP/IP connection

- *More available memory:* 2MB to 16MB

- *Advanced user interface:* More capability than is found on small LCD screens of pagers and cell phones

The two different sectors of devices require two sets of functionality from the J2ME environment. The mobile information device is best suited to use the KVM as defined by the CLDC. The advanced information device is best suited for the CVM as defined by the CDC.

The choice of configuration is an important starting point when designing a device. The configuration represents the standard specification of the Java environment and the Java virtual machine (JVM) functionality for the device itself. Choosing a JVM means that you need to choose an implementation for it that conforms to either the CLDC or CDC specification for a device. The implementation that is chosen can be one from Sun Microsystems (KVM for CLDC or CVM for CDC), or it can be a compatible JVM from another company.

The details of a J2ME configuration are covered in the next section in order to provide an understanding of how the J2ME Java VM and configuration fit together.

4.1   Java Technology for Consumer and Embedded Devices

Before the Java 2 Platform, Micro Edition technology was developed, two technologies from Sun Microsystems addressed the consumer and embedded market: PersonalJava and EmbeddedJava. PersonalJava is an environment that was pared down from the original Java for desktops and servers to fit into approximately 2MB of ROM and 2MB of RAM. EmbeddedJava was designed to fit into even smaller environments but filtered out library functionality until all that was left was just the application programming interfaces (APIs) and dependencies that were needed to run a specific application.

PersonalJava has continued in J2ME, while EmbeddedJava has turned into a licensing agreement with Sun Microsystems. The way that PersonalJava has been folded into J2ME is that licensees can continue to develop using the PersonalJava application environment, but when they are ready to upgrade they must use the J2ME CDC and the J2ME Personal Profile.

EmbeddedJava licensees can continue to develop filtered environments for their devices but must not expose their APIs to third-party developers; instead, they must keep the device as a "black box."

4.2 J2ME PersonalJava

PersonalJava was developed as the environment targeted for consumer and embedded devices using Java technology. It became obsolete when J2ME CDC was developed because J2ME CDC is a fully functioning Java 2 virtual machine. PersonalJava applications can run on a J2ME CDC system with the Personal Profile.

While the compatibility of PersonalJava and Personal Profile enables the development of legacy devices dependent on PersonalJava to continue, it is most advantageous to switch to J2ME CDC and the Personal Profile completely. The advantages of doing so are

- Full compatibility with the Java 2 virtual machine specification
- Java 2 fine-grained security
- Floating point
- User-defined dynamic class loading
- Java Native Interface (JNI)
- Reflection
- Full threads
- Finalization
- Weak references
- Error handling
- Full Java 2 class file verification

Once a migration is made to J2ME CDC and Personal Profile from PersonalJava, the major advantages become clear with the ability to create new J2ME profiles. With additional J2ME profiles, new APIs can be defined by leveraging the existing J2ME configurations and profiles.

The use of profiles is easier than relying on the confusing sets of optional functionality in PersonalJava. By using profiles to control optional sets of APIs, there is less complexity in the build environments, more fine control down to the method level, and better logical groupings of APIs along vertical markets.

In the next sections, an overview of J2ME technology is provided. The basic components of J2ME, namely configurations and profiles, are discussed.

4.3 J2ME Configurations and Profiles

J2ME technology consists of two basic configurations: J2ME Connected Device Configuration (CDC) and J2ME Connected Limited Device Configuration (CLDC). J2ME CLDC is the base technology for small devices with limited resources. J2ME CDC is also a base technology for small devices that have greater resources than required by J2ME CLDC. J2ME RMI Optional Package (Remote Method Invocation Optional Package) is an additional technology that enables full Jini technology participation.

The J2ME configuration is the minimal set of core Java classes that the JVM requires to operate. It is the support base of Java classes for the JVM. The two JVMs covered in this chapter are the KVM, which operates with less than 256KB of RAM, and the CVM, which operates with more than 256KB of RAM. These two JVMs are contributed implementations from Sun Microsystems. They are looked at in this chapter, but keep in mind that any corresponding CLDC- or CDC-compatible JVM will work with your device.

4.4 The Migration Path from PersonalJava to J2ME

The migration path from PersonalJava to J2ME technology has been made as seamless as possible. Two Java Specification Requests (JSRs) currently deal with PersonalJava technology support in J2ME: the J2ME Personal Basis Profile and the J2ME Personal Profile.

The J2ME Personal Basis Profile (PBP) is a subset of the J2ME Personal Profile. The PBP contains all the core libraries of the J2ME Foundation Profile (JFP) plus the added limited GUI components of the Abstract Windowing Toolkit (AWT) based on the Java Developer's Kit (JDK) version 1.1.x. The set of limited graphical user interface (GUI) components include only lightweight components, such as `Container` and `Component`, which can be extended into other more complicated components.

The J2ME Personal Profile adds the rest of the AWT components of the GUI. So every AWT component that is found in JDK 1.1.x is also found in the J2ME Personal Profile.

4.5   Programming Issues

The following are the programming issues that must be addressed when considering J2ME technology:

- *Choosing the right target environment:* Decide which configuration is best, J2ME CLDC or J2ME CDC.

- *Choosing full Jini technology or Jini surrogate architecture support:* Depending on the level of Jini technology support, RMI Optional Package or a design based on the Jini surrogate architecture should be used.

- *Choosing the host development environment:* Currently J2ME CDC-based profiles are best suited for Linux systems.

4.6   Summary

J2ME technology has two configurations for use with small devices. It is up to the developer to decide which is best for the target device. PersonalJava technology is supported with a migration path to J2ME technology.

The environments of J2ME CDC and CLDC address different resource limitations. The RMI Optional Package adds full Jini technology support.

5

Developing with J2ME

This chapter is a quick-start guide to developing with J2ME technology. The two starting points are Connected Device Configuration (CDC) and Connected Limited Device Configuration (CLDC). The decision of which of these base technologies to use is based on the needs of the device itself.

Several profiles, on top of these configurations, must also be considered in deciding which to use; the most popular profiles are Mobile Information Device Profile (MIDP) for CLDC and Foundation Profile and Personal Profile for CDC.

5.1 Preliminary Steps

Before choosing which profiles to use for device development, one must take the vital step of recognizing a device's requirements. The steps for developing with J2ME technology are

1. Collect the device requirements—memory, graphics support (GUI), CPU, storage, and so forth.

2. Choose the configuration, either J2ME CDC or CLDC.

3. Choose the profile—MIDP for CLDC, Personal Profile or Foundation Profile for CDC.

4. Download the development environment.

5. Port the development environment to the device platform.

6. Build a test application for the device.

7. Test the application on the device.

5.2   Deciding Which Profile to Choose

When looking at the different profiles from which to choose, the developer should always keep in mind the requirements of the target device, which are the overriding guide. This chapter discusses three of the J2ME profiles: Mobile Information Device Profile, Foundation Profile, and Personal Profile. Each of the profiles has its advantages and disadvantages for different devices. Each profile is best-suited for a specific device.

- MIDP is for cell phone devices. The basic underlying technology is very lightweight and is limited in functionality. It is based on the J2ME CLDC.

- Foundation Profile is meant for non-GUI embedded devices. The basic purpose of the Foundation Profile is to be the application environment for embedded devices without GUI support. This profile is also intended to be the starting set of core APIs needed for other J2ME CDC-based profiles (such as Personal Profile) that add APIs such as `java.awt`.

- Personal Profile is meant for more powerful hand-held computing devices. It continues the evolutionary path of the older PersonalJava technology from Sun Microsystems. This profile maintains the intent of the Foundation Profile (and all J2ME CDC-based profiles) to give full Java 2 support on the virtual machine level; in addition, the Personal Profile adds a GUI toolkit (`java.awt` based on JDK 1.1).

5.3   Mobile Information Device Profile

To quickly start developing with J2ME MIDP technology, download the J2ME Wireless Toolkit, versions of which are available for Windows, Solaris, and Linux. (For more information, see *java.sun.com/products/j2mewtoolkit/*.) The J2ME Wireless Toolkit for Linux is used in the examples in this chapter.

5.3.1 Download and Installation

To download the J2ME Wireless Toolkit, first point a browser at *developer.java.sun.com/ developer/releases/j2mewtoolkit/*. Next read the "System Requirements" and the instructions for "Installing the J2ME Wireless Toolkit." Make sure a version of the Java 2 Platform, Standard Edition is already loaded on the Linux system (see the instructions). Then go to the bottom of the Web page and choose the Linux version to download. (*Note:* Free registration to the Java Developers Connection is required.)

To install, just place the downloaded .bin file in the directory of your choice. Make sure to become root if the directory requires root permission. Run the installation script with the following steps:

1. Change the bin script to execute permission: `chmod u+x <downloaded_bin_script>`.

2. Execute the bin script: `./<downloaded_bin_script>`.

3. Agree to the licensing terms.

4. Choose the Java interpreter to use from the Linux system.

5. Choose the installation directory.

6. Choose to set standalone.

7. Change the directory to the bin subdirectory: `cd j2mewtk/bin`.

8. Run the startup shell: `./ktoolbar.sh`.

5.3.2 Building

The next step involves creating a new project and writing a MIDlet. First, in the GUI window of the J2ME Wireless Toolkit, do the following:

1. Click New Project.

2. Enter a project name and the name of the MIDlet class file:
   ```
   Project Name: helloworld
   MIDlet Class Name: HelloWorldMIDlet
   ```

3. Click Create Project.

4. Click OK for the settings for the project.

5. Edit in the `j2mewtk/apps/helloworld/src` directory (using your favorite Linux editor, such as vi) a new Java source file named `HelloWorldMIDlet.java`.

The source code follows:

```
/* HelloWorldMIDlet.java */
import javax.microedition.rms.*;
import javax.microedition.lcdui.*;
import javax.microedition.midlet.*;
import javax.microedition.io.*;

/**
 * The MIDlet application class for HelloWorldMIDlet.
 */
public class HelloWorldMIDlet extends MIDlet implements CommandListener {

    // Commands available for this MIDlet
    private Command exitCommand;
    private Command doneCommand;
    private Command infoCommand;


    private Display display;
    private javax.microedition.lcdui.TextBox hello = null;
    private javax.microedition.lcdui.TextBox info = null;

    public HelloWorldMIDlet() {

      // Get the display that was created for this MIDlet
      display = Display.getDisplay(this);

      exitCommand = new Command("Exit", Command.EXIT, 1);
      doneCommand = new Command("Done", Command.OK, 2);
      infoCommand = new Command("Info", Command.OK, 2);
    }

    /**
     * Start up the HelloWorld MIDlet by creating the TextBox
     * and associating the exit command and listener.
     */
    public void startApp() {
      hello = new
       javax.microedition.lcdui.TextBox("Hello World Demo",
                 "HelloWorld from J2ME MIDP!", 40, 0);
      hello.addCommand(exitCommand);
      hello.addCommand(infoCommand);
      hello.setCommandListener(this);

      display.setCurrent(hello);
```

```
    info = new
    javax.microedition.lcdui.TextBox
      ("Info for Hello World Demo", "This is the
      HelloWorld MIDlet", 40, 0);
    info.addCommand(exitCommand);
    info.setCommandListener(this);
}

/**
 * Pause: nothing needed because there are no background
 * activities or record stores that need to be closed.
 */
public void pauseApp() {
}

/**
 * Nothing to cleanup.
 */
public void destroyApp(boolean unconditional) {
}

/*
 * Handle commands
 */
 public void commandAction(Command c, Displayable s) {
    /* On the exit command, cleanup and notify
     * MIDlet has been destroyed.
     */
    if (c == exitCommand) {
        destroyApp(false);
        notifyDestroyed();
     }
    // Done
    else if (c == doneCommand) {
      display.setCurrent(hello);
    }
    // Info
    else if (c == infoCommand) {
      display.setCurrent(info);
    }
 }
}
```

5.3.3   Running an Example Program

The new source file is ready to be built and run. In the J2ME Wireless Toolkit window, click the Build button and then click the Run button. You should see your Hello World MIDlet run in its own window.

5.4   Foundation Profile

The best environment in J2ME technology for non-GUI embedded systems is the J2ME Foundation Profile.

5.4.1   Download and Installation

A free implementation for Linux/x86 platforms can be downloaded from the Sun Micro-systems community source Web site at *www.sun.com/software/communitysource/ j2me/cdc/download.html.* This software is free to download, but registration is required. After logging in with free registration, agree to the licensing terms and follow these instructions:

1. Unzip the download bundle. You will see nested zip bundles for the source and documents.

2. Unzip the zip bundle. Choose the installation directory. The source tree for building the Foundation Profile is ready.

5.4.2   Building

You must first build the Foundation Profile environment itself to provide the proper J2ME Java virtual machine and the library Java archive (JAR) files. To build the J2ME Foundation Profile environment, follow these instructions:

1. Make sure you have the correct Linux and Java environments on your system (RedHat Linux 6.2 and Java 2 Platform, Standard Edition version 1.3.1 are recommended).

2. Change the directory to the Linux build directory: `cd build/linux`.

3. Use the following `make` command to build:

```
make CVM_JAVABIN=<your_java_bin> CVM_DEBUG=true
    J2ME_CLASSLIB=foundation
```

For example:

```
make CVM_JAVABIN=/usr/java/jdk1.3.1/bin CVM_DEBUG=true
    J2ME_CLASSLIB=foundation
```

If you have a later RedHat Linux 7.x system, make sure to build with the following `make` command instead:

```
make CC=egcs CVM_JAVABIN=<your_java_bin> CVM_DEBUG=true
   J2ME_CLASSLIB=foundation
```

For example:

```
make CC=egcs CVM_JAVABIN=/usr/java/jdk1.3.1/bin CVM_DEBUG=true
   J2ME_CLASSLIB=foundation
```

(*Note:* Refer to Linux instructions for how to install the `egcs` package.)
You are now ready to run an example program (see the next section).

5.4.3 Running an Example Program

To run an example program, follow these instructions:

1. Start with a simple Java program, such as the following:
   ```
   /* HelloWorldFoundation.java */
   /**
    * The J2ME CDC/Foundation Profile application class
    * for HelloWorldFoundation.
    */
   public class HelloWorldFoundation {

       public static void main(String args[]) {
          System.out.println("Hello World from J2ME Foundation Profile!");
       }
   }
   ```

2. Compile using the J2SE javac compiler against the J2ME Foundation Profile build-time classes and foundation classes:
   ```
   javac -bootclasspath <toplevel>/build/linux/btclasses.zip:<toplevel>
      /build/lib/foundation.jar HelloWorldFoundation.java
   ```

3. Run using the J2ME Foundation Profile CVM:
   ```
   cd <toplevel>/build/linux/bin
   ./cvm -Djava.class.path=<path_to_HelloWorldFoundation>
      HelloWorldFoundation
   ```

You should see the HelloWorld message printout.

5.5 Personal Profile

The Personal Profile is a superset of the J2ME Personal Basis Profile.

5.5.1 Download and Installation

Go to *wireless.java.sun.com/personal* and follow the downloading instructions. (*Note:* At the ime of this writing, the download site was still being developed. Check back at this URL periodically if the download is still not available when you first go to look for it.)

5.5.2 Building

First build the J2ME Personal Profile environment itself to provide the proper J2ME Java virtual machine and the library JAR files. To build the J2ME Personal Profile environment, follow these instructions:

1. Make sure you have the correct Linux and Java environments on your system (RedHat Linux 7.x and Java 2 Platform, Standard Edition version 1.3.1 are recommended).

2. Change the directory to the Linux build directory: `cd build/linux`.

3. Use the following make command to build:
   ```
   make CVM_JAVABIN=<your_java_bin> CVM_DEBUG=true
      J2ME_CLASSLIB=personal AWT_PEERSET=personal
   ```

   For example:
   ```
   make CVM_JAVABIN=/usr/java/jdk1.3.1/bin CVM_DEBUG=true
      J2ME_CLASSLIB=personal AWT_PEERSET=personal
   ```

You are now ready to run an example program (see the next section).

5.5.3 Running an Example Program

To run an example program, follow these instructions:

1. Start with a simple Java program, such as the following:
   ```
   /* HelloWorldPersonal.java */
   /**
      * The J2ME CDC/Personal Profile application class
      * for HelloWorldFoundation.
      */
   ```

```
import java.awt.*;
import java.awt.event.*;

public class HelloWorldPersonal extends Frame {

public void start() {
  // Add a Component
  Label label = new Label("HelloWorld from J2ME Personal Profile!");

  add("Center", label);
  validate();
}

  public static void main(String argv[]) {
    HelloWorldPersonal app = new HelloWorldPersonal();
    app.start();
    app.setSize(220, 200);
    app.validate();
    app.show();
  }
}
```

2. Compile using the J2SE javac compiler against the J2ME Personal Profile build-time classes and foundation classes:

```
javac -bootclasspath <toplevel>/build/linux/lib/
  btclasses.zip:<toplevel>/build/lib/personal.jar
  HelloWorldPersonal.java
```

3. Run using the J2ME Personal Profile CVM:

```
cd <toplevel>/build/linux/bin
./cvm -Djava.class.path=<path_to_HelloWorldPersonal>
  HelloWorldPersonal
```

You should see the HelloWorld message in a J2ME Personal Profile window.

5.6 Summary

In this chapter, J2ME technology was discussed in detail and basic instructions were provided for developing with J2ME technologies such as J2ME CLDC/MIDP, CDC/Foundation Profile, and CLDC/Personal Profile.

6

Jini Technology Basics

Jini network technology is the new basis for networking in the J2ME. It was developed at Sun Microsystems as a way for software and hardware components to be integrated into one network, known as a *Jini technology-enabled network* (or *Jini network*).

6.1   Jini Network Terminology

A Jini network brings together many different types of devices with Java technology as the common base. In the past, electronic devices and computer programs had no easy way of networking together. Now, with the use of Jini technology, devices, such as cell phones, pagers, PDAs, and TV set-top boxes, can speak a common language.

Jini technology has four basic parts, making it simple to use:

- *Plug-and-Work model:* The power of Jini network technology to enable devices to connect to a network and interact with services without human administration

- *Lookup service*: Where Jini services announce their availability

- *Discovery protocol:* A process used to find the required lookup services in a local network

- *Proxy object:* Part of a Jini service that runs on the client

With these four simple parts, one can understand how an entire Jini federation operates. With the exception of the Plug-and-Work model, the parts are self-explanatory. The next section describes the Plug-and-Work model in detail.

6.2   The Plug-and-Work Model

The concept of a Plug-and-Work network is simple: A device should be able to connect to a network of services without human intervention, which is easier said than done in most cases. However, Jini network technology enables devices to break the ties to a human administrator. Instead, it enables a device to discover for itself what is on a network.

The Plug-and-Work model is based on two concepts: code downloading and remote interfaces:

- *Code downloading:* The ability of data and functionality to be automatically downloaded to a device so that it does not require updating by a human. Also, code downloading extends Java technology class type checking, enabling subclassing to extend functionality far into the future and into many subtypes that may not be designed or developed yet.

- *Remote interfaces:* Java technology interfaces negate the need for strict dependency on a service implementation. Instead, the well-known interface describes the dynamically downloaded code, which enables a device to dynamically learn how to use a new service.

With code downloading and remote interfaces, a device can go about its business of utilizing a service without being tightly coupled to an implementation or relying on a human to program it correctly to access the service.

When a device can download code on its own, there is no need to upgrade it manually with the latest software off the Web. Each time a device uses a service, it gets the service's most up-to-date implementation, containing all the bug fixes and enhancements available up to that moment. The data and behavior are downloaded together, enabling a late binding to occur from the device to the service at the last minute. This enables a device to evolve as the services it uses are improved over time, and it enables the device to get the latest updated service.

In the case of a stock quote service, the device needs to know only the interface to the service to access the stock price. If the Yahoo! stock quote service, for example, is temporarily disconnected, the device can automatically discover a new stock quote service with the same interface and use it without having to be reprogrammed.

The strengths of the Plug-and-Work model are in the way it handles network failures and its ability to switch over to any service that uses a well-known interface on the network.

6.3 Object Protocol

With Jini network technology, one deals with an object exchange protocol; this means that software objects are passed back and forth between entities. With older protocols, only data is passed back and forth. In all other communication protocols, data is used as the flow of information. The objects that transfer with Jini technology contain the encapsulation of data and methods to interact with the object's data, which is a more faithful implementation of the object-oriented distributed computing model. With objects being passed back and forth, encapsulated data and methods are conveniently grouped together no matter where they show up on the network.

When a computer system on one side of the world gets a proxy object from a Jini lookup service on the other side, all the data and method interfaces that the system needs to interact with that object have been completely transferred to it.

A true distributed computing environment cannot exist without being able to easily transport objects on a network. With Jini technology, for the first time, all the objects of a programming language like Java are distributed to any system in the Jini federation.

6.4 Dynamic Network Edges

The dynamic nature of Jini network technology is a great way for devices on the "edge" of a network to handle change. The *edge* of a network is where the end-user exists and is the point farthest away from where services originate.

An example of an end-user on the edge of a network is a cell phone user. He or she is the endpoint of the services that the cell phone provider makes available. Being so far away from the service provider means that the end-user on the edge of a network is isolated from provider-assisted intervention if something goes wrong. In addition, the edge of a network is far away in network distance from updates to the cell phone. A cell phone user is usually resistant to having anything manually done to the device itself because a cell phone should be a self-contained unit and should be able to maintain the connection to the service provider in a robust manner without hassle.

The infrastructure of Jini network technology enables a cell phone to be deployed once without requiring constant service provider intervention to update software or to fix bugs. Jini network technology enables code to be downloaded (for example, through Remote Method Invocation—RMI) without interfering with client code already on the phone.

When older legacy devices are mixed with new devices (as on many cell phone networks today), and robust interaction is required between these devices, Jini network technology really shines. It is not necessary to know all the possible edges of the network nor to intervene or administer the client code of those edges. It is necessary only to be able to download proxy code to the edges, so less knowledge is embedded in the edges, enabling the creation of a network that does not break down and can scale expeditiously at the edges.

Dynamic network edges are the reality of a quickly evolving environment such as the world of cell phone users. When a cell phone or a PDA that links to back-end wireless services needs to know what the service can do and can access that service by downloading it, much complexity is hidden from the device. This is the main advantage of Jini network technology.

6.5 Leases

Another aspect of Jini network technology is service leases. When one creates a Jini service, one must register it and request a lease from the lookup service. The lease returned from the lookup service identifies the amount of time left before the registry entry expires for that particular service, which prevents a Jini service from becoming stale as an invalid entry in the lookup service registry. An invalid registry entry can occur when the service goes down or when the network connection is lost.

Leased Jini services enable a robust network in a Jini federation. Failure of services on the network does not cause the entire network to fail. Leasing is part of the general programming model of Jini technology. One can also use leases to manage other resources on the network.

6.6 Attributes

The robustness of the Jini federation is also enhanced by the lookup service's ability to use matching for service lookup, which adds flexibility to the system, in addition to its inherent reliability.

Each Jini proxy object has one or more attributes. These attributes are type/value pairs used to distinguish one Jini service from another. For example, one can have a Jini service attribute with a value that describes the location of the service it represents, such as "second floor, building #1."

The Jini client can set a matching pattern with the Jini lookup service of a set of attributes or of service types with the values specifically defined or intentionally left blank (the latter means that the client does not care what the value is). The Jini lookup service finds the matching services according to that set of attributes and/or service types and returns them to the client. This is a powerful way for Jini clients to match on generic services (for example, a fax service) or on very specific services (for example, a fax service on a certain floor of a specific building).

6.7 Groups

A Jini lookup group is a way to categorize Jini services. If a network has many lookup services, one may want to select a particular one. Doing this enables specific lookup services to be limited to only a small number of specialized services.

For example, consider a service for a television in a house. One may want to register it with the entertainment group on a certain lookup service of a home network. Another lookup service that is assigned to the heating and ventilation group can ignore the service requests from the entertainment group, and the entertainment group can ignore the announcements coming from the heating and ventilation lookup service. Groups facilitate an organized service structure. Enhanced organization provides efficiency in terms of client interactions with the specific services.

6.8 Lookup and Discovery

Figure 6.1 shows the basic parts of a Jini federation as it first begins to connect. Initially, a service must be created with a public API—for example, a pager acting as a client and connecting to a created `StockQuote` service. Once the public API is established for the `StockQuote` service, an implementation can be made based on its specification. For the example in this chapter, the `StockQuote` service is implemented as wireless. In Figure 6.1, one sees a Jini service proxy object (`WirelessStockQuoteProxy`) being registered with the Jini lookup service through the `JoinManager()` constructor method. The lookup service keeps the `WirelessStockQuoteProxy` object in its registry for later download by a Jini client. The `WirelessStockQuoteService` is the implementation of the `Wireless-StockQuoteProxy` interface.

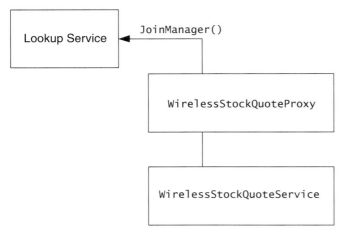

Figure 6.1 Registration of a Jini service proxy object

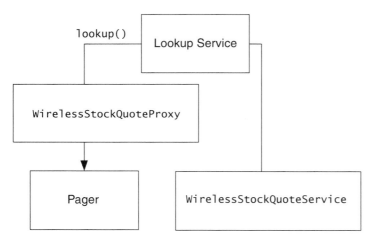

Figure 6.2 Lookup service is discovered, and proxy is downloaded from the lookup
service by a Jini client.

For Jini technology, code downloading is crucial because that is how dynamic
behavior is formed. With code mobility, there is not just one computer system but
a network of computer systems that run a program.

In Figure 6.2, one can see how a Jini client (`Pager`) first discovers the Jini
lookup service and then is able to download the Jini proxy object with a lookup

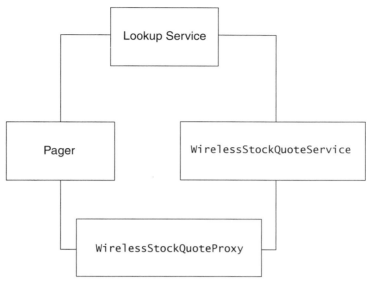

Figure 6.3   The Jini client can use the proxy object directly to communicate
back to the Jini service.

service `lookup()` method. `WirelessStockQuoteProxy` is downloaded to interact
with `WirelessStockQuoteService`. A coding example is given in Section 6.9,
along with the details of this process. For now, the basic idea is presented in the
figures shown here.

In Figure 6.3, the `Pager` object can use the `WirelessStockQuoteProxy` object
to communicate directly to `WirelessStockQuoteService`. The Jini lookup service has finished its job at this point by providing the correct proxy object to the
Jini client that requested a connection to the Jini stock quote service. The `Pager`
object calls the methods in the `WirelessStockQuoteProxy` object to retrieve the
specified stock prices from the `WirelessStockQuoteService` object that can
exist across the network on some other computer.

The Jini lookup service behaves as a control center that matches client
requests with the registered proxy object for the requested service. This simple
process frees the J2ME device developer from reinventing shared communication
functionality, which makes writing Jini technology software much easier when
dealing with distributed objects that wish to communicate with each other.

6.9   Simple Code Example

The following simple code example starts a service on a J2ME technology-enabled device and allows it to be a full RMI service that can be called from anywhere on the network by an RMI client.

```
import java.io.*;
import java.lang.*;

import java.rmi.*;
import java.rmi.server.UnicastRemoteObject;

import jini.net.JoinManager;
import net.jini.core.discovery.*;
import net.jini.core.entry.*;
import net.jini.core.lookup.*;
import net.jini.lookup.entry.*;
import com.sun.jini.lookup.entry.BasicServiceType;

//
// To create a RMI service, make sure to do the following:
//  1. Extend the class using java.rmi.server.UnicastRemoteObject
//  2. Implement your own remote interface which in turn extends
//          Remote (in this case WirelessStockInterface)
//  3. Implement the RMI Service class using Serializable interface
//  4. Add your functionality to the implementation of the remote
//          interface (in this case getStockQuote())
//  5. Register this RMI Service with a Jini lookup service
//          (in this case see main())
//
public class WirelessStockQuoteService extends UnicastRemoteObject
    implements WirelessStockInterface, Serializable {

    public WirelessStockQuoteService() throws RemoteException {
    super();
    }

    public String getStockQuote(String symbolName) {
    String retStr = null;

        // Set RMI security manager if there isn't one
    if (System.getSecurityManager() == null) {
        System.setSecurityManager(new RMISecurityManager());
    }
```

```
// Functionality here to retrieve the stock quote
//      of symbolName
// ...

return(retStr);
}

public static void main (String[] args) {
WirelessStockQuoteService wStockQuoteService = new
    WirelessStockQuoteService();
ServiceInfo serviceInfo = new ServiceInfo("PRODUCT", "MANUFACTURER",
                        "VENDOR", "VERSION", "","");
BasicServiceType basicServiceType = new
    BasicServiceType("WirelessStockQuoteService");
Entry entry[] = new Entry[] {serviceInfo, basicServiceType};
try {
    JoinManager joinManager = new JoinManager
        (wStockQuoteService, entry,
        new ServiceIDHandler(), new LeaseRenewalManager());
} catch (java.io.IOException ioe) { }
}
}
```

The first step is to register the RMI service using RMI Optional Package, which is done by calling the following Jini technology API:

```
JoinManager joinManager = new JoinManager
    (wStockQuoteService, entry,
    new ServiceIDHandler(), new LeaseRenewalManager());
```

6.10 Proxy

The term *proxy* is used in many ways in discussions of computer programming. In the context of RMI technology, the term *proxy* means a computer programming object that contains data and programming behavior that enables it to run on a computer system separate from the originating calling object. This enables many computer systems to run in distributed programming environments instead of running a single program on just one computer system.

Quick-Start Guide for the Jini Technology Environment

Here is a quick-start guide for how to run the most important pieces of the Jini technology environment. First, make sure to download the most recent version of the Jini Technology Starter Kit from *www.sun.com/software/communitysource/jini/download.html*.

This book uses the Jini Technology Kit version 1.2. Follow the instructions for how to install the kit for a Linux system. Note that you must also have a J2SE version 1.3 environment on your system. After those two environments are installed, bring up the Jini technology environment with the following instructions:

1. Start the HTTPD server:

   ```
   java -jar <toplevel>/jini1_2/lib/tools.jar -port 8080 -dir
     <toplevel>/jini1_2/lib &
   ```

2. Remove the RMI daemon log if it exists:

   ```
   rm -rf ~/log
   ```

3. Start the RMI daemon:

   ```
   rmid -J-Dsun.rmi.activation.execPolicy=none &
   ```

4. Start the Jini lookup service:

   ```
   java -jar -Djava.security.policy=<toplevel>/jini1_2/example/
     lookup/policy.all <toplevel>/jini1_2/lib/reggie.jar http://
     <your_web_server>:8080/reggie-dl.jar <toplevel>/jini1_2/
     example/lookup/policy.all /tmp/reggie_log public &
   ```

5. Start the RMI registry (optional if running RMI services)

   ```
   rmiregistry &
   ```

6. Run the Jini services browser example:

   ```
   java -cp <toplevel>/jini1_2/lib/jini-core.jar:<toplevel>/
     jini1_2/lib/jini-examples.jar:<toplevel>/jini1_2/lib/
     reggie.jar -Djava.security.policy=<toplevel>/jini1_2/example/
     browser/policy -Djava.rmi.server.codebase=http://
     <your_web_server>:8080/jini-examples-dl.jar
     com.sun.jini.example.browser.Browser &
   ```

7. Start a service (for example, `PrintService`):

```
cd <your_example_workspace>/work/jini/src/PrintService
java -cp .:<your_example_workspace>/work/jini/src/
   PrintService:<toplevel>/jini1_2/lib/jini-core.jar:<toplevel>/
   jini1_2/lib/sun-util.jar:<toplevel>/jini1_2/lib/jini-
   ext.jar:<toplevel>/jini1_2/lib/reggie.jar -
   Djava.rmi.server.codebase=http://<your_web_server>/
   <your_example_workspace>/jini/src/PrintService/ -
   Djava.security.policy=<your_example_workspace>/work/jini/src/
   PrintService/po.policy Print |& tee ~/jini_printservice.log &
```

6.11 Summary

This chapter gave a brief overview of the Jini network technology. The basics of Jini technology were covered, including the Plug-and-Work model lookup service, the discovery protocol, and the proxy object. How leases work and how attributes can be used to define a Jini service were also covered. Finally, this chapter described how lookup groups logically organize Jini services.

Other materials are available for more information on RMI and how to best use RMI Optional Package with J2ME technologies. One place to start is the Web page at *java.sun.com/products/jdk/rmi/index.html*, where you will find information regarding the larger version of RMI for J2SE technology. The Web site relates to J2ME technology in that it enables a J2ME technology-enabled device to run as a full RMI client.

7

Jini Technology in Small Devices

7.1   Plug-and-Work in Small Devices

Plug-and-Work is the concept of having a device connect to a network automatically. Jini technology provides for the Plug-and-Work model by addressing the dynamic nature of a device network. Drivers are automatically downloaded and distributed to all devices. The network of devices can grow and learn new behavior. The reach of computing power spreads over a large number of systems, and limited-resource devices can still participate with more powerful systems.

The following are the key points about how Plug-and-Work addresses better device behavior using Jini technology:

- *Better device driver distribution:* Devices and services teach each other new capabilities. There is no longer a dependency on the underlying protocol.

- *Powerful adaptive architectures:* Devices adapt to each other with minimal a priori knowledge.

- *Compute server:* Multiple vendor implementations of the same interface can all work on a single processing task.

- *Leasing:* Devices can come and go as they please.

- *Resource constraints:* Devices don't need numerous resources to follow the Jini technology Plug-and-Work model.

- *Class loading:* New device behavior is loaded on-the-fly.

- *Intermittent connectivity:* Devices don't have to be fully networked all the time.

The next sections contain more detail about the Jini technology Plug-and-Work model's key points.

7.2 Better Device Driver Distribution

Device drivers for PCs usually have been made available either on computer media, such as CD-ROMs and floppy disks, or over the Web. Both ways have problems because computer media can easily be misplaced or lost and Web downloads usually involve the user hunting for the right driver at a specific URL.

Jini technology alleviates this problem by automatically downloading device drivers from a Jini lookup service each time the service is needed. The downloading happens over the network from wherever the device's service originates, such as an Internet service provider. There is no need to keep track of what software version a device has because the service provider does that using Jini technology. The device is guaranteed to have the latest service because the download is automatic.

7.3 Powerful Adaptive Architectures

Jini technology in small devices enables networks to adapt to change. Each device has changeable classes that evolve with the network. An adaptive architecture allows devices on a network to grow over time. A cell phone user, who can run a movie ticket purchasing program on his or her phone, might want to be able to run an updated movie preview viewing program.

Jini technology allows this to happen online because the new program itself is automatically downloaded from a Jini lookup service when the latest movie previews become available to the cell phone user. The architecture of the network adapts to the user's needs and to the service provider's latest applications available over the network.

7.4 Compute Server

Devices become a part of an overall compute server. Compute servers embody the distributed computing model, where a device on a Jini network can perform a small part of an overall computing goal.

A network of devices can become a large distributed system in which each device runs a small task that is part of a bigger process. For example, a network of sensors could each report back temperature readings, which in turn could be used by a large mainframe computer to compute weather predictions.

The Jini technology can automatically have each sensor be a service that reports data back to any other device on the network that needs the information.

7.5 Leasing

Leasing in Jini technology enables devices to connect and disconnect from the network without a direct protocol. If a device becomes unplugged, its lease simply runs out. Services can disconnect the device and check in at a later time.

Having devices disconnected when they become inactive allows the network to be efficient. All devices on the network are guaranteed to be within their lease times, which means that the data on the network does not go stale.

An example is a chat application that networks cell phone users with Jini technology. When users turn off their phones, the leasing model in Jini technology will gracefully terminate their service after the lease runs out and let the other chat users know that they are not available.

7.6 Resource Constraints

There are two resource constraint options for participation in a Jini network. One option is full Jini technology capabilities with a J2ME Foundation Profile environment and the Remote Method Invocation Optional Package (RMI Optional Package). This option requires about 2.2MB of space and a 32-bit processor. The second option is the Jini surrogate architecture, which enables a Jini surrogate to run on another system while no Java or Jini technology is needed on the device itself.

A full Jini technology-enabled device the first option needs to have at least RMI Optional Package to run RMI services that register with a Jini lookup service. An example of a full Jini technology-enabled device is a network router that is running a service to report on its status. The router, through an RMI service running with the RMI Optional Package, can automatically report any errors or network problems to any other device or system on the network. This router needs to have at least 2.2MB of memory available and a 32-bit processor. Many new routers already have this requirement, so they are fully able to run the complete Jini technology.

The second option—using the Jini surrogate architecture—uses a system with at least a 32-bit processor and 2.2MB of memory to act as a surrogate for a limited-resource device. An example is a light sensor that is connecting via a serial port to a PC. The light sensor itself has no memory and only a small microcontroller that is not capable of running Jini technology. The PC, however, has enough resources to run a Jini service on behalf of the light sensor. This allows the light sensor to appear as if it were a full Jini technology-enabled service on the network that offers data about the light detected in a certain room or office.

7.7   Class Loading

Class loading is a strong point of having Java technology on a device or nearby for a device to use. With classes dynamically loaded, behavior can change—new functionality can be downloaded and new bug fixes can be updated.

Applications and services are not statically loaded on a device, so there is no lock-in to only one version of software. The advantage becomes apparent when looking at a music-playing device using Jini technology. The current music devices can play MP3 music files, but there may be a new standard for music files in the future. Jini technology allows the music device to automatically download new music-playing software through class loading and then can handle any future file standard changes.

7.8   Intermittent Connectivity

With Jini technology, the main point is not having to rely on a connection all the time. Intermittent connections can be made from the device to the network, and Jini technology takes care of managing the times when devices show up and disappear.

Intermittent connectivity is important because network technology (especially for wireless devices) can be spotty, particularly when a device is moving rapidly, such as in a car or on a train. Jini network technology enables devices to sync up when necessary and disconnect when a full connection is not available or momentarily not required.

The network is vital in Jini technology in order to share services among devices and systems, but it is not necessary to have a device connected to the network all the time.

7.9   Summary

In this chapter, the use of Jini technology on small devices was described. The Plug-and-Work model was detailed and the advantages of driver distribution, adaptive architectures, distributed compute servers, leasing, resource constraints, class loading, and intermittent connections were outlined.

Having a network of small devices that can grow and adapt is powerful. There is no lock-in to one version of software or one protocol. Data can move to all devices in a more efficient manner and allow even limited-resource devices to interact with other more robust systems on a network.

8

J2ME RMI Optional Package

The Remote Method Invocation Optional Package (RMI Optional Package) for J2ME was created to provide a lightweight version of RMI for small devices.

8.1 RMI Optional Package for the J2ME CDC

RMI Optional Package was created with the J2ME Connected Device Configuration (CDC) in mind. The J2ME CDC environment makes all the Java 2 core libraries available. These packages include `java.lang`, `java.net`, `java.io`, `java.util`, `java.security`, and `java.text`.

With these core libraries, the full functionality of RMI is realized. J2ME Connected Limited Device Configuration (CLDC), on the other hand, does not have such a feature-rich set of libraries. With the basic CDC core libraries, RMI Optional Package can function on a device by offering unicast remote objects, which can be registered with RMI to allow other Java objects to remotely call RMI Optional Package objects running on the CDC device. As long as the RMI Optional Package service calls only core library APIs in common with CDC and J2SE, there is no difference if the service runs on a J2SE or CDC device. This is important because it allows cross-compatibility of RMI services, which can run on large systems or small devices. Also, it is easier for the developer since the RMI service needs to be written only once.

8.2   RMI Optional Package Design Goals

The design goals of RMI Optional Package are

- *Full Jini technology support:* The ability for a J2ME CDC-based device to participate in a Jini network.

- *Full RMI client-side support:* The ability to interact with an RMI server somewhere on the network.

- *Interoperability with J2SE:* The ability to exchange RMI objects with a Java 2 Platform, Standard Edition (J2SE) server.

8.3   J2SE Features

The RMI Optional Package was developed by the Java Community Process expert group for Java Specification Request (JSR) 66. The goal of JSR 66 was to create a specification for small devices. The APIs of the specification center on the J2SE Java RMI API.

The RMI Optional Package features include full RMI support for J2SE compatibility, including dynamic code downloading; distributed garbage collection (DGC); unicast remote object export; the client-side activation protocol; and the RMI registry.

Dynamic code downloading allows a device to load new classes over the network or from local file storage. DGC frees the developer from having to manage the manual allocation and clean-up of remote objects. The client-side activation protocol gives a device with RMI Optional Package the ability to start and stop remote objects running on another system in order to free resources on the server when the client is done. Finally, the RMI registry is the central location where RMI services are managed. These features on a device provided by RMI Optional Package allow it to behave exactly like a J2SE system invoking methods using RMI.

8.3.1   The Security of the Java Programming Model

The security of RMI Optional Package is inherited from the Java 2 security model, which enables only a restricted set of actions for untrusted classes. This provides security by only allowing safe actions (e.g., ones that do not include disk access or memory modification) for untrusted classes such as those downloaded from the Web.

8.3.2   Dependency Considerations for Downloading Code

There are dependencies on underlying APIs when code is dynamically downloaded. If API A depends on API B, the core libraries of the device running A must guarantee that B is available, which becomes more difficult in subsetted environments such as J2ME. A *subsetted environment* means there are certain groups of APIs that have been taken out, such as `java.awt`, from CDC. This is done to reduce the memory footprint. It is difficult for a downloaded application to know if a particular dependency is missing, so this is a problem when using the J2ME environment. The application developer can avoid it with careful planning using APIs that are common to the lowest platform.

8.4 Serving Java Code in a Small Environment

When RMI Optional Package exists on a small device, several considerations govern how classes are downloaded to it. Will there be enough room for the class to download? Will the processor be fast enough to do the processing required? These are just a couple of the questions that must be considered when designing a device to use RMI Optional Package.

8.4.1 Interoperability with J2SE

Another important consideration concerns what type of interoperability is needed with J2SE. Does the server that the device connects to have the right version of J2SE with which to interoperate? What library calls will the RMI methods use? The developer must decide which version is the lowest common platform required by the service and then use the `System.getProperty("java.version")` API to check if it is running on a compatible system. The library calls are determined by which packages, such as `java.lang`, `java.net`, `java.io`, and `java.util`, are needed by each call. These packages must be present on all platforms on which the service runs. The developer can check for each package in the platform specifications.

8.5 Java Card RMI Technology

A Java Card also can participate using RMI technology, which is a more difficult situation because RMI on Java Card is very limited. Java Card is the specification of Java technology running on a *smart card*—a card the size of a credit card in which an embedded chip allows a limited Java virtual machine (JVM) to run. Because a Java Card contains a limited JVM due to size and resource constraints of the smart card, the RMI technology that can run on it is also limited by the Java Card virtual machine's functionality. For more information, the developer of a Java Card RMI service should check the Java Card 2.2 specification (see *java.sun.com/ products/javacard/* and *javacardforum.org*), which contains Java Card RMI support.

8.6   J2ME CDC/CLDC Client Method Invocation Semantics

The semantics of J2ME method invocation involve understanding the underlying dependencies of the client calls.

Consideration must be given to the services as well as the client calling the RMI methods on those services. The developer must decide what common packages will be included by the client call dependencies and which platforms will have those packages. If the lowest common platform is J2SE, then the client call can only run on a system with at least J2SE. If the developer creates client calls that use packages available on both J2SE and J2ME technologies, then that RMI client call can run on those platforms. To have the remote method work correctly, the developer must keep the least common denominator for client calls in mind and program to that platform.

8.6.1   Java Card Side-Server Implementation

On a Java Card, an RMI server can be implemented that enables other RMI clients that connect to the Java Card to perform simple method calls, such as a request for an encrypted password or for authentication for identification purposes. This functionality is made available in the Java Card 2.2 specification, which is still in process at the time of this book's writing. For more information, see *javacardforum.org*.

8.7   Other Considerations

Another consideration of RMI Optional Package is the use of RMI in special circumstances, such as when the RMI calls across a slow or intermittent network connection. This situation can be difficult when the RMI client is caught waiting for the RMI server to come back online.

8.8   Summary

This chapter described the considerations for RMI Optional Package along with design goals and features. J2ME RMI Optional Package enables RMI calls to originate from small devices, which means more types of devices can become RMI clients. It also opens the network to more functionality that is available as on-demand services to client devices.

9

J2ME RMI Optional Package Example

This chapter continues the discussion about RMI Optional Package, which was described in the previous chapter, and includes an example of how to use J2ME RMI Optional Package. Instructions for downloading and building RMI Optional Package are covered. In addition, sample code for writing a simple RMI Optional Package service is provided.

The J2ME RMI Optional Package can be downloaded from *http://www.sun.com/software/communitysource/j2me/*.

9.1   Building the J2ME RMI Optional Package

To build the J2ME RMI Optional Package, one must first be familiar with building the J2ME Foundation Profile. To become familiar with building the J2ME profile, see the section on "Building the Implementations" in the Foundation Profile online documentation at *java.sun.com/j2me/docs/pdf/CDCFoundation_Porting_Guide.pdf*. Once you have done this, it is simple to add the right build flags to build the J2ME RMI Optional Package (see the following).

Note: At the time of the writing of this book, the J2ME RMI Optional Package specification was still being defined, so the URL to download the reference implementation source bundle may change. Search the *java.sun.com* Web site if the URL given here does not give a link to the J2ME RMI Optional Package site.

The sample implementation that comes with the J2ME Foundation Profile includes the Linux version for the x86 CPU. The RMI Optional Package is layered on top of the Foundation Profile by downloading the reference implementation source code bundle for Linux x86 platforms from the URL given in this book's introduction. Follow the download instructions for RMI Optional Package. The build options to include the package in the J2ME Foundation Profile build are as follows:

```
make CVM_DEBUG=true J2ME_CLASSLIBS=foundation OPT_PKGS=rmi
```

For more information, see the RMI Optional Package documentation, which comes with the RMI Optional Package download.

9.2   A Simple RMI Service

As a simple RMI service, the HelloWorld service is a good place to start. It sends the string "Hello World!" to any RMI client that calls the right API to the simple service.

In the code that follows, the class HelloWorldService extends UnicastRemoteObject, which enables this class to be an RMI service. Next, the interface for HelloWorldInterface is implemented in the getHelloWorld() method. This method simply returns the "Hello World!" string to the RMI client calling this service. This code shows how simple it is to set up any RMI service:

```
import java.rmi.*;
import java.rmi.server.UnicastRemoteObject;

//
// To create a RMI service, make sure to do the following:
// 1. Extend the class using java.rmi.server.UnicastRemoteObject
// 2. Implement your own remote interface which in turn extends
//         Remote (in this case HelloWorldInterface)
// 3. Implement the RMI Service class using Serializable interface
// 4. Add your functionality to the implementation of the remote
//         interface (in this case getHelloWorld())
//
public class HelloWorldService extends UnicastRemoteObject
    implements HelloWorldInterface, Serializable {

    public HelloWorldService() throws RemoteException {
        super();
    }
```

```
public String getHelloWorld() {
String retStr = null;

    // Set RMI security manager if there isn't one
if (System.getSecurityManager() == null) {
    System.setSecurityManager(new RMISecurityManager());
}

// Functionality for the service goes here
// ...

return("HelloWorld!");
}
public static void main(String args[]) {
        // Create and install a security manager
        if (System.getSecurityManager() == null) {
            System.setSecurityManager(new RMISecurityManager());
        }
        try {
            HelloWorldService hws = new HelloWorldService();
            // Register this service to the RMI registry
            Naming.rebind("//hostname/HelloWorldService", hws);
        } catch (Exception e) {
        e.printStackTrace();
        }
    }
}

public interface HelloWorldInterface extends Remote {

    public String getHelloWorld() throws RemoteException;

}
```

9.3 Connecting the RMI Service

The RMI service for `HelloWorldService` can be started by simply calling the registration API (`java.rmi.Naming.bind()`) for the RMI object. This is done in the `main()` method of the preceding code and allows the program to look on the network for any RMI registry that may be running and then register the given RMI service. The RMI registry can be started on the system by the user with the command `rmid`. Run the code as a Java application to start the service. For more information about getting started with RMI, see *java.sun.com/j2se/1.3/docs/guide/rmi/getstart.doc.html*.

9.4   Using RMI Optional Package with Jini Technology

It is a simple transition to use RMI Optional Package with Jini technology. The HelloWorld RMI service described in the last section (HelloWorldService) can be used as a Jini technology-enabled service. First, discover a Jini lookup service on a network. Next, use that lookup service for registering the HelloWorld service. The service can be used by a Jini technology-enabled client.

This is done with the JoinManager class in Jini. The sample code for the main() method to get the HelloWorldService registered with a Jini lookup service would look like this:

```
public static void main(String[] args) {
    HelloWorldService hws = new HelloWorldService();
    ServiceInfo serviceInfo = new ServiceInfo("PRODUCT", "MANUFACTURER",
                                "VENDOR", "VERSION", "","");
    BasicServiceType basicServiceType =
                                new BasicServiceType("HelloWorldService");
    Entry entry[] = new Entry[] {serviceInfo, basicServiceType};
    try {
        JoinManager joinManager = new JoinManager
            (hws, entry,
             new ServiceIDHandler(), new LeaseRenewalManager());
    } catch (java.io.IOException ioe) { }
```

By replacing the other main() method with the preceding main() method, the call to the JoinManager constructor initiates a lookup of the Jini registry on the network and, once found, the HelloWorldService object is registered with it.

9.5   Summary

This chapter described how the RMI Optional Package can be downloaded and built. It then described how RMI Optional Package can be used both on a RMI technology-enabled network and also on a Jini technology-enabled network. On both networks, a vast amount of resource and computing power can be gained by remotely calling methods across computer systems.

10

Jini Surrogate Architecture

In Chapter 6, several ways to construct a Jini network were described. One way is to use a network proxy to translate the Jini lookup and discovery protocol for a particular device that may not have enough resources to handle a Java virtual machine (JVM) and/or Jini proxy objects.

The Jini technology surrogate architecture can exist in the home, office, or any physical location where the connection from a back-end services hub is required to a local area within both Jini- and non-Jini-enabled client devices.

This type of situation—where a device is resource-constrained and must rely on a host system to act on its behalf in a Jini federation—is ideal for the Jini surrogate architecture. The surrogate architecture was conceived by Jim Waldo, an engineer at Sun Microsystems, and is an open project at the *jini.org* Web site. The working group that developed the specification for the surrogate architecture was led by Keith Thompson at Sun Microsystems.

The surrogate architecture enables devices that have limited resources to take advantage of Jini technology and to fully participate with other Jini technology-enabled services and devices. These limited devices can then get to services from anywhere on the network by using the simple approach of delegating a Jini surrogate to act on behalf of the device.

The basics of the Jini surrogate architecture are covered in this chapter.

10.1   Benefits

The primary motivation for developing the surrogate is to enable resource-limited devices to fully participate in a Jini network. Taking part as a simple client (that is, a consumer of information) of Jini services is sufficient in many cases. An example of a simple client is a wireless PDA that accesses limousine service information at an airport from a Jini service. An additional benefit is when a limited device such as that can also make available its own full Jini service that can run on another system unhindered by memory or processor constraints. Providing Jini services from a device presents a more feature-rich networking environment where small devices are producers of information (that is, they provide services) and are not just simple consumers (clients).

For example, consider a simple Mobile Information Device Profile/Connected Limited Device Configuration (MIDP/CLDC) device such as a cell phone with a small LCD display. Simple MIDP/CLDC devices are, by definition, limited in resources, so running a full Java 2 virtual machine is not appropriate or feasible. Even if this type of device were able to run a full Java 2 virtual machine, it would find itself out of memory when it tried to download more than one Jini service proxy. The surrogate architecture enables a device to be an MIDP/CLDC cell phone with its resource limitations, while leveraging a more powerful system—the surrogate host of the surrogate architecture—somewhere on the network to act on its behalf.

The surrogate host runs a full Java 2 virtual machine and has full Jini technology support, which enables any small device that can talk to a surrogate host to become a fully Jini technology-enabled client *and* service in the Jini network. For example, the MIDP/CLDC cell phone, which before was just a simple client downloading limousine service information from a back-end airport Jini service, can become a full Jini service through an airport surrogate host, broadcasting the location of its owner who is looking for a ride from the airport. Via this broadcasted Jini service on the Jini network, the cell phone can find a limousine driver who also has a Jini technology-enabled cell phone that discovers the customer broadcasting the requested service and determines the specific gate where the customer is waiting.

10.2   Functional Requirements

The functional requirements of the surrogate architecture specify three basic points that define the operation of the Jini network. The requirements are modified here to apply to a case in which a device needs a surrogate to participate in the Jini network:

- *Discovery and join protocols:* A device must be able to delegate to a surrogate participation in the Jini discovery and join protocols.

- *Download and execute classes:* A device must be able to delegate how and where classes are downloaded and executed using the Java programming language.

- *Export classes:* A device must be able to delegate from where optional Java classes are exported.

By meeting these three requirements, participation in a Jini network is ensured. With the aid of a third party (that is, a surrogate), a device that cannot receive a Jini proxy object, that cannot directly connect with a Jini network, or that cannot run a Java virtual machine can become Jini technology-enabled.

The surrogate architecture has three goals that are met through the specification:

- *Device type independence:* Through use of a surrogate, a device is not tied to any specific type of software or hardware.

- *Network type independence:* Through use of a surrogate, a device is not tied to any specific type of network.

- *Plug-n-work:* Through use of a surrogate, a device must be able to discover a Jini network, have code downloaded on its behalf, and lease distributed resources.

10.3 Overview

Figure 10-1 depicts the surrogate architecture. The large box represents a system that can run one or more surrogate hosts. This system is called the *host-capable machine* and is the environment in which a surrogate can run. It contains the host resources, which are isolated from other surrogate hosts to provide security and protection from the corrupt behavior of malicious surrogates. It also provides isolation to manage resources such as memory and input/output device access. The host-capable machine may directly connect to the Jini network, and a device may indirectly connect to the host-capable machine over an interconnect. The interconnect may be a specific connection between a surrogate and the device, such as a Universal Serial Bus (USB) connection.

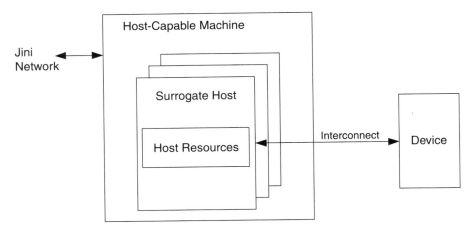

Figure 10.1 Surrogate architecture

10.4 Discovery

In the Jini discovery process, there are two ways in which the device and surrogate host can find each other:

- Device broadcast

- Surrogate host device detection

In the first case, a device broadcasts its existence on the network and waits for a surrogate host to find it, which is comparable to the way the Dynamic Host Configuration Protocol (DHCP) works on a TCP/IP network. A device keeps broadcasting that it is new on the network until a server gives it the information it needs to start its network participation. In the case of the Jini surrogate architecture, the device broadcasts until a surrogate host gives it the information it needs to run a surrogate for that device.

In the case where the surrogate host detects devices on the network, the surrogate host blocks or polls for devices that appear on its network, which is similar to the USB way of finding devices. The surrogate host keeps listening for new connections of devices, and, when the host detects such a device, it initiates the procedure to allow that device to begin participation in the Jini network.

10.5   Surrogate Retrieval

The first part of incorporating a device into the Jini network is for the surrogate host to retrieve the surrogate, which is done in one of three ways:

- Device uploads surrogate.

- Surrogate host extracts surrogate from device.

- Surrogate host downloads surrogate from elsewhere.

An example of the first way, for a device to upload the surrogate to the surrogate host, is for the device to open a socket to the surrogate host and write the host the bytecodes that represent the surrogate's Java class or JAR files.

Another method in which surrogate retrieval can be done is for the surrogate host to extract the surrogate from the device. For example, if the device has an embedded Web server on board, the surrogate host can make an HTTP request to download the surrogate class or JAR files.

An example of the final way is for the surrogate host to use a URL provided by the device to download the surrogate off the Internet. Or the device, using some other protocol, may indicate where the surrogate exists, so that the host may find it to download.

10.6   Activation

After the surrogate is retrieved, the next step is activation. The requirements for activation are

- *Manifest check:* The surrogate host must check the manifest for the `Surrogate-Class` header in the JAR file for the surrogate.

- *Resource extraction:* The surrogate host must look for the `Surrogate-Codebase` header in the JAR file for the surrogate.

- *Execution environment:* A new thread and class loader are created for the surrogate.

- *Object instantiation:* The surrogate object becomes initiated.

- *Get codebase:* The codebase annotation is set if the interface is available.

- *Activate:* The surrogate object is activated.

Four issues regarding activation must be considered:

- *Keep service ID:* The unique service ID should be kept for future registrations.

- *Resources:* The resource usage of the surrogate must be monitored to prevent denial of service (DoS).

- *Liveness:* The surrogate host is responsible for making sure there is a live connection to the device. If not, the surrogate should be deactivated.

- *Logging:* The surrogate might want to log its errors and events. It is up to the surrogate host to decide how to handle this issue.

10.7 Deactivation

In deactivation, three unordered actions take place:

- *Deactivate:* The surrogate is deactivated by calling its `deactivate()` method.

- *Release:* The resources that the surrogate was using should be released.

- *Destroy:* The execution environment may be destroyed at this point.

10.8 Specifications

The following are the specifications needed when conforming to the surrogate architecture:

- *Jini technology surrogate architecture specification:* The overall requirements

- *Interconnect specification:* The specific requirements for a given type of connection between a surrogate host and the device

In the interconnect specification, requirements are given for the discovery protocol (where the device or host initiates and whether it is a push or pull action), the retrieval process (how and where the surrogate is retrieved), liveness (how to check for a live connection), APIs (any new methods needed), context (additional information needed), and security (how encryption and authentication are handled).

10.9 Surrogate Interfaces

This section contains a list of interfaces and classes that are used in the surrogate architecture with brief descriptions of them. For more information, check the Jini technology surrogate architecture specification (see *jini.org/standards/sa.pdf*).

- Surrogate: Interface for activating and deactivating the surrogate
- GetCodebase: Interface for setting the codebase
- HostContext: Interface for accessing the execution environment
- DeactivationListener: Interface for getting notifications when a child surrogate is deactivated
- SurrogateController: Interface for allowing a parent to deactivate a child surrogate
- SurrogateCreationException: Class thrown when a failure occurs during execution of the newSurrogate method of the HostContext interface
- KeepAliveManagement: Interface for defining a live connection for the interconnect
- KeepAliveHandler: Interface for responding to a query about the liveness of a connection

10.10 Surrogate Packaging

In packaging a surrogate, you must use a JAR file that contains a manifest with the following:

- *Surrogate-class header:* Specifies the name of the surrogate class in the JAR file
- *Surrogate-codebase header:* Specifies the resources of the surrogate's codebase

The actual surrogate Java class created by the developer that implements the Surrogate interface must be present as well as all support resources, including data, Web pages, and images.

10.11 Security

The security of the surrogate host must be assured. Security includes isolation of surrogates from other surrogates to prevent malicious attacks. The isolation model follows the Java 2 Platform Runtime Environment model. The surrogate host also must manage the permissions granted for thread creation and storage access. This again prevents malicious attacks on system resources and keeps a system from being overwhelmed with processing too many surrogates. Finally, the need for encryption and authentication must be considered.

Special considerations must be taken when working with the Jini surrogate architecture:

- Use the surrogate architecture only when you cannot download a Java object.

- A JVM must be somewhere on the network.

- Services don't have to be aware of Jini technology at all since a proxy is used as an intermediary.

- The Jini surrogate architecture is a stewardship architecture—where Jini technology is adapted to unaware devices.

- There are protocol advantages to having an architecture optimized for a specific network.

- Protocol disadvantages are avoided because lock in to a fixed network is not required.

10.12 Downloading the Jini Surrogate Architecture

To download code related to the Jini surrogate architecture project, access this Web site (free registration required): *developer.jini.org/exchange/projects/surrogate/*.

The *developer.jini.org* Web site is a free resource for developers wishing to explore different topics related to Jini network technology. One of the more popular projects is the Jini surrogate architecture project because of its ability to fold many types of devices into the world of Jini network technology.

10.13 Summary

The Jini surrogate architecture provides a way for resource-limited devices to participate in a Jini network.

This chapter provided the basics of the surrogate architecture. The concepts of a Jini surrogate host, surrogate object, and device were introduced.

The Jini surrogate architecture is flexible and powerful in being able to fold in devices that were once thought to be too limited to participate fully in a dynamic network such as a Jini federation.

11

Jini Surrogate Architecture Example

The preceding chapter introduced the Jini surrogate architecture. This chapter contains an example using it. The steps in creating a client and a surrogate are given in the first section, followed by detailed explanations of each step plus code listings of the client and surrogate.

The information here should help you map what is needed to create your own client and surrogate for a device.

11.1   Guide to Developing the Example

In order to develop an example for the Jini surrogate architecture, the following steps must be taken:

1. Decide on the protocol to use between the client and the surrogate.

2. Write the client program.

3. Write the surrogate program.

4. Make sure to have the Jini environment running correctly (see the Jini environment quick-start guide sidebar in Chapter 6).

5. Start the client program.

6. Verify that the surrogate is running correctly.

The remainder of this chapter walks you through the process step by step.

11.2 Decide on the Client/Surrogate Protocol

In deciding on the client/surrogate protocol, the developer must first consider the resource limitations of the device. The easiest type of minimal connection is usually the best solution. Most of the time, this means a simple connection, such as RS-232, Universal Serial Bus (USB), or IEEE 1394 (Firewire), to a PC. An alternative would be to use a wireless technology, such as Bluetooth, as the device's network connection.

Another way for the Jini surrogate architecture to work is to use TCP/IP to connect a limited-resource system to a system that can handle a full Java 2 virtual machine and Jini technology. These types of interconnects are described as projects at *developer.jini.org/exchange/projects/surrogate/rellinks.html*.

For the interconnect in this example, a simple UDP socket is used to deliver a surrogate to the surrogate host to be run on behalf of an MIDP device. This case will be explored in the next sections.

11.3 Write the Client Program

The following code has an implementation of an MIDP MIDlet that opens a UDP socket to a known surrogate host. The MIDlet then requests that the host start a Jini service on its behalf. The beginning part of the code sets up the GUI of the MIDlet to let the user choose to join the Jini network. The latter part of the code sends a UDP datagram to the known surrogate host with a URL-to-surrogate code that is later used by the surrogate host to start as a Jini service. This code assumes that the MIDP device is on a network that allows UDP datagrams to be sent.

```
import javax.microedition.rms.*;
import javax.microedition.lcdui.*;
import javax.microedition.midlet.*;
import javax.microedition.io.*;

/**
 * The MIDlet application class for JiniSurrogateDeviceMIDlet.
 */
```

```
public class JiniSurrogateDeviceMIDlet extends MIDlet implements
CommandListener {

    // Commands available for this MIDlet
    private Command exitCommand;
    private Command doneCommand;
    private Command jiniCommand;


    private Display display;
    private javax.microedition.lcdui.TextBox hello      = null;
    private javax.microedition.lcdui.TextBox jini       = null;

    public JiniSurrogateDeviceMIDlet() {

    // Get the display that was created for this MIDlet
        display = Display.getDisplay(this);

        exitCommand = new Command("Exit", Command.EXIT, 1);
            doneCommand = new Command("Done", Command.OK, 2);
            jiniCommand = new Command("Connect Jini", Command.OK, 2);
    }

    /**
     * Start up the JiniSurrogateDevice MIDlet by creating the TextBox and
     * associating the exit command and listener.
     */
    public void startApp() {
        hello = new
        javax.microedition.lcdui.TextBox("Hello World Demo",
                            "JiniSurrogateDevice!", 40, 0);
        hello.addCommand(exitCommand);
        hello.addCommand(jiniCommand);
        hello.setCommandListener(this);

        display.setCurrent(hello);

        jini = new
        javax.microedition.lcdui.TextBox
            ("Connecting Jini Surrogate",
             "Jini surrogate has been started",
             40, 0);
        jini.addCommand(exitCommand);
        jini.setCommandListener(this);
    }
```

```java
/**
 * Pause is a no-op since there are no background activities or
 * record stores that need to be closed.
 */
public void pauseApp() {
}

/**
 * Destroy must cleanup everything not handled by the garbage collector.
 * In this case there is nothing to cleanup.
 */
public void destroyApp(boolean unconditional) {
}

/*
 * Respond to commands, including exit
 * On the exit command, cleanup and notify that the MIDlet has
 * been destroyed.
 */
public void commandAction(Command c, Displayable s) {
    if (c == exitCommand) {
        destroyApp(false);
        notifyDestroyed();
    }
    // Done
    else if (c == doneCommand) {
        display.setCurrent(hello);
    }
    // Jini
    else if (c == jiniCommand) {
        requestJiniSurrogate();
        display.setCurrent(jini);
    }

}

//
// Request a MIDP Jini surrogate host start a surrogate for this device
//
    public void requestJiniSurrogate() {
        boolean waitingMsgPrinted = false;

        DatagramPacket packetSend = null;
        DatagramPacket packetReceive = null;
        byte[] bufSend = null;
        byte[] bufReceive = null;
        String msg = null;
        String msgReceiveExpected = null;
```

```
    String strReturn = null;
    int timeSleepBeforeSend = 0;

    // send command
    if (jiniRequest == null) {
        msg = MSGID_END;
        msgReceiveExpected = MSGID_END;
    } else {
        msg = MSGID_SURROGATE_REQUEST +
                jiniRequest +
                "|" + " <URL to surrogate class>";
        msgReceiveExpected = MSGID_SURROGATE_STARTED +
                jiniRequest +
                "|";
    }
    bufSend = msg.getBytes();

// Send request to surrogate host via UDP to start a surrogate with code
// from <URL to surrogate class>
    packetSend = new DatagramPacket(bufSend, bufSend.length,
                addressUdpServer, portServer);

    bufReceive = new byte[256];
    packetReceive = new DatagramPacket(bufReceive, bufReceive.length);

    while (true) {
        if (timeSleepBeforeSend > 0) {
        try {
                Thread.sleep(timeSleepBeforeSend);
                System.out.print(".");
         } catch (Exception eAny) {
            System.out.println("sleep excep" + eAny);
        }
        }

        try {
            // attempt to send
            socketUdpServer.send(packetSend);
        } catch (IOException eSend) {
            if (waitingMsgPrinted) {
                System.out.print(".");
            } else {
                System.out.print("Waiting for server (send) " +
                    hostServer + " at  port " + portServer);
                waitingMsgPrinted = true;
            }
        }
```

```
     try {
            // get reply
            socketUdpServer.receive(packetReceive);
            strReturn = new String(packetReceive.getData());
            if (strReturn.startsWith(msgReceiveExpected)) {
                timeSleepBeforeSend = 0;
                break;
            }

     } catch (IOException eReceive) {
            String eMsg = eReceive.toString();
            if (waitingMsgPrinted) {
                System.out.print(".");
            } else {
                System.out.print("Waiting for server (receive) " +
                    hostServer + " at  port " + portServer +
                    " (" + eMsg + ")");
                waitingMsgPrinted = true;
            }
          if (eMsg.equals("java.net.SocketException: socket closed")) {
                // Server is not there
                timeSleepBeforeSend = SLEEPBEFORESEND;
            } else
            if (eMsg.equals(
                "java.io.InterruptedIOException: Receive timed out")) {
                if (packetReceive.getAddress() == null) {
                    // Server was up, but is no longer there
                    timeSleepBeforeSend = SLEEPBEFORESEND;
                    continue;
                }
                timeSleepBeforeSend = 0;
                int timesRetry = 50;
                for (int retry = 1; retry < timesRetry; retry++) {
                    packetReceive.setLength(bufReceive.length);
                    try {
                        // get reply
                        socketUdpServer.receive(packetReceive);
                      strReturn = new String(packetReceive.getData());

                        if (strReturn.startsWith(msgReceiveExpected)) {
                            timeSleepBeforeSend = 0;
                            break;
                        }

                    } catch (IOException eReceiveRetry) {
                        eMsg = eReceiveRetry.toString();
                        if (eMsg.equals(
```

```
                                "java.net.SocketException: socket closed")) {
                                    timeSleepBeforeSend = SLEEPBEFORESEND;
                                    break;
                                } else
                                if (eMsg.equals(
                        "java.io.InterruptedIOException: Receive timed out"
                                        )) {
                                    if (packetReceive.getAddress() == null) {
                                        // Server was up, but is no longer there
                                        timeSleepBeforeSend = SLEEPBEFORESEND;
                                        break;
                                    }
                                    continue;
                                } else {
                                    break;
                                }


                        }
                    }
                }


                packetReceive.setLength(bufReceive.length);
            }

        }

        // Display response

        System.out.println(1, "From host " + hostServer +
        "->" + strReturn , packetReceive);

            return strReturn;
        }
}
```

11.4   Write the Surrogate Program

Next, a surrogate program must be written for the surrogate host to download
code from the given URL to run as a Jini service. This is done according to how
the specific interconnect is being used—in this case, using a simple UDP request
protocol. The surrogate must follow the Jini Technology Surrogate Architecture
Specification (see *developer.jini.org/exchange/projects/surrogate/sa.pdf*). For purposes of this example, the specification is simplified to use the surrogate interface
without the use of a HostContext.

```
package net.jini.surrogate;
public interface Surrogate {
    void activate(HostContext hostContext,
            Object context)
            throws Exception;
    void deactivate();
}
```

The following code represents the surrogate that will run on the surrogate host. It implements the surrogate interface, which means it has an `activate()` and a `deactivate()` method. The `activate()` method in this example starts up the Jini service and registers it with the Jini lookup service on the network. This service then provides a way for other clients on the network to ping the MIDP device using the remote method `pingMIDPDevice()`.

```
import java.rmi.*;
import java.rmi.server.UnicastRemoteObject;
import net.jini.surrogate.*;

public class JiniSurrogate extends UnicastRemoteObject
    implements net.jini.surrogate.Surrogate, Serializable {

    public JiniSurrogate() throws RemoteException {
        super();
    }

    public String pingMIDPDevice(String deviceName) {
        // Set RMI security manager if there isn't one
    if (System.getSecurityManager() == null) {
        System.setSecurityManager(new RMISecurityManager());
    }

    return("Alive");
    }

    public void activate(HostContext hostContext,
                Object context) throws Exception {
        JiniSurrogate jiniSurrogate = new
            JiniSurrogate();
        ServiceInfo serviceInfo = new ServiceInfo("PRODUCT", "MANUFACTURER",
                            "VENDOR", "VERSION", "","");
        BasicServiceType basicServiceType = new
            BasicServiceType("JiniSurrogate");
        Entry entry[] = new Entry[] {serviceInfo, basicServiceType};
        try {
            JoinManager joinManager = new JoinManager
```

```
            (jiniSurrogate, entry,
              new ServiceIDHandler(), new LeaseRenewalManager());
    } catch (java.io.IOException ioe) { }
    }
    public void deactivate() {
    }
}
```

11.5   Run the Jini Technology Environment

To test this system, the developer must start the Jini technology environment on his or her network (see the quick-start sidebar in Chapter 6). This allows the system to behave as a surrogate host.

11.6   Start the Client Program

The client program must then be started on the MIDP device. It looks for a UDP server and sends a request message that starts a surrogate on its behalf. A surrogate host program must be running to accept the client's connection and to download the code from the specified URL in the request message. Then, the downloaded code is instantiated as a Java object and the `activate()` method is called to start it as a service on the Jini network. The surrogate host code for this example can be found at *developer.jini.org/exchange/projects/gateway/*.

11.7   Verify the Surrogate Is Running

The last step is to make sure the surrogate is running correctly. One way is to have a separate Jini client call the `pingMIDPDevice()` remote method to see if there is a response. For sample code that can act as a test client, see *developer.jini.org/exchange/projects/gateway/*. Once a response is received, it verifies that the surrogate is running correctly.

11.8   Summary

This chapter showed how easy it is to create a Jini surrogate architecture example. Following the example of the Jini technology interconnect specification is the best way to learn this process. Once learned, it is easy to carry this concept further to other devices with limited resources that can be allocated to Jini technology.

Other Java Technology Environments

Using other Java environments with Jini technology is important. Other Java environments, such as J2EE and J2SE, are used by most back-end servers today. Tying those legacy systems together with Jini technology is important to maintain server access to existing back-end data. An example of this is using Jini technology to allow access to a database through J2EE servlets. This could open J2ME devices to existing back-end data through Jini services that tunnel into servers through servlets.

The previous chapters concentrated on J2ME CDC- and CLDC-based profiles, which are good approaches for small devices on the client side. But there is also interaction on the back-end with services that connect to other systems running Java technology. These systems can be legacy systems running J2EE with Enterprise JavaBeans (EJBs) or a service that uses RMI. The back-end services of Jini network technology are able to use any type of Java technology to get the job done.

On the client side, PersonalJava and EmbeddedJava technologies are legacy environments that have their own issues, such as the following:

- *Compatibility:* PersonalJava and EmbeddedJava technologies are compatible with JDK 1.1 technology. This is a problem because the new Java 2 environment has better features, such as fine-grained security, weak references, collection classes, and so on.

- *Cannot support full Jini devices:* Since PersonalJava and EmbeddedJava technologies don't have full Java 2 technology compatibility, they cannot run as full Jini technology-enabled devices. They need to use the Jini surrogate architecture to participate in a Jini network.

- *Missing features in JDK 1.1:* PersonalJava and EmbeddedJava technologies do not have these specific features: enhanced garbage collection, fine-grained security, and RMI enhancements.

These reasons make it difficult for older Java technologies, such as PersonalJava and EmbeddedJava environments, to work well in a Jini network. If a device already has these older technologies, the Jini surrogate architecture can help bridge it into a Jini network; otherwise, it is best to start fresh, applying J2ME technology to new devices.

12.1   Local Application Servers

The back-end legacy processing can be handled by local application servers. Instead of having a PC on every office worker's desk, smaller devices can be used to access the connection to local application servers.

Local application servers can run everything from word processors to e-mail applications, but the applications are run on the back-end application server itself, freeing up small hand-held devices to handle only incoming data and outgoing user commands.

With J2ME devices, the limited resources on a small device can take full advantage of the Java programming environment. A J2ME device, such as a network-connected PDA or computer terminal, can have enough power to run a color touch-screen and enough memory to run local processing. At the same time, a J2ME device can connect to a back-end application server that runs the more complex database and enterprise applications. A back-end server frees up resources that would normally be tied up on high-performance PCs. Instead, the lower-power devices are easier to use and can be easily replaced.

12.2   External Application Servers

With external application servers, many in-house applications can be farmed out to third parties that can maintain programs such as payroll, purchasing, and accounting. This way, the third party can make money by charging fees and the enterprise can save money by not having to provide for the upkeep of so many software applications.

Another advantage of external application servers is that they eliminate the need for a single location for a business. A business can be virtual with many workers scattered around the globe. Application servers can be located in one place, while the workers who need to access them can be located anywhere.

Globally distributed workers enable round-the-clock production and development of a product as some workers begin their day in one time zone while others end their day in another time zone. The application server runs 24 hours a day, 7 days a week.

With a J2ME device, speed and reliability will be greater than with PCs that connect to external application servers. This is because small devices are built more like consumer electronics with easy-to-operate user interfaces and their reliability is more like that of household appliances than PCs, which are known to be crash-prone. An example is a very reliable telephone that does not crash versus a PC, which may have to be rebooted frequently when running many applications for long periods of time. A device with J2ME technology can access an application server for expanded functionality, in addition to having the reliability of a consumer electronic device.

12.3   Integrating J2ME Devices with the Enterprise

When integrating J2ME devices with the enterprise, a few issues must be considered:

- *Types of services needed by the enterprise:* The more complex services will require more memory on a device. Typical PDAs today have up to 32MB of memory. This would be typical for enterprise applications on J2ME devices running on high-end PDAs.

- *Number of people who will connect J2ME devices to the server:* When more people are connecting to one server, a more powerful processing system is needed. The use of clustering can help alleviate delays when a server becomes overburdened with connections.

- *Type of bandwidth needed:* Many of today's high-end devices can connect using IEEE 802.11b wireless technology, which allows up to 11Mbps of bandwidth. This is equivalent to a wired Ethernet connection to desktop PCs—plenty of bandwidth for today's enterprise applications.

- *Type of connectivity—full-time or intermittent:* A mobile worker will probably want an intermittent connection from his or her J2ME device. This means the enterprise software should be able to efficiently handle users who spontaneously appear and disappear from the network.

By considering these issues, it is easy to narrow down what types of functionality are needed on the device and what CPU and memory requirements are required to meet that functionality. One can also see that Jini technology helps address these issues by off-loading many of these requirements to the back-end server instead of the J2ME device itself.

In Figure 12.1, a group of wireless PDAs with J2ME can access an application server running Jini services, which can then access data from an enterprise database. This off-loads all the heavy processing to the application server instead of the PDA devices.

The application server design pattern can be applied to a real-world situation. The client part of the design pattern is in the wireless PDAs running the J2ME platform. Clients of an application server are lightweight and specifically handle the presentation and interaction of data with the user. The central part of the design pattern is in the local application server, where the bulk of the application runs. The final part is in the back-end database where the data is kept.

This three-tier system keeps the processing at a minimum in the lightweight clients (wireless PDAs), which is exactly what one wants in mobile device computing. The enterprise office environment makes the three-tier system easy compared to a system with heavyweight clients, since it is sitting piggyback on the most common office network protocol, namely Ethernet (TCP/IP).

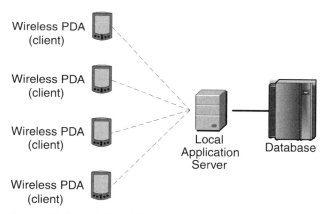

Figure 12.1   Wireless PDAs connect to a LAN application server.

12.4 Sun Open Net Environment

To extend the TCP/IP network, one can look at an open standard proposed by Sun. Early in 2001, Sun Microsystems announced the Sun Open Net Environment (Sun ONE) initiative. This new architecture is based on open network computing using smart Web services. These smart Web services enable customers to create new Internet services using an open architecture, roadmap, and product base.

The main point of Sun ONE is the connection from devices to a multiple array of available services, which extends the TCP/IP network with open standards. This is achieved through

- Open architectural standards based on Java technology, LDAP, XML, and other open standards

- Roadmap for Web services

- Tools that provide support for design, creation, and deployment of Web services

With Sun ONE, companies can tie together all of their devices and services under an open architecture. For the J2ME and Jini technologies, Sun ONE is just another way to represent the connections and data representation.

One example of using Sun ONE is supply-chain integration, where businesses can communicate with each other to access procurement software from any type of device. Another example of using Sun ONE is the ability to create an online auction easily, such as a commodities broker being able to bid on multiple suppliers of futures contracts.

The TCP/IP network is the underlying support of Sun ONE. It is easy to see how interoperability of devices and services are linked together. Sun ONE introduces a layer of standards that glues the communication between devices and services together.

Figure 12.2 shows how the standards, such as XML and LDAP, can be used to translate from device to service and back over the TCP/IP network as the carrier. Different implementors of these standards can compete with each other to provide different levels of support. The companies that implement the Sun ONE architecture include iPlanet, a division of Sun Microsystems. It does not matter which company provides the glue layer as long as the open standard is followed.

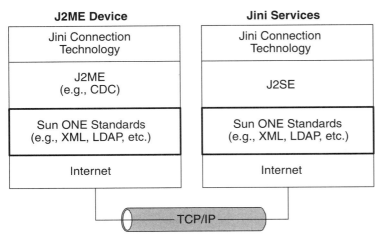

Figure 12.2   Sun ONE extends open standards on top of TCP/IP networking.

12.5   Integrating with CRM

In today's e-commerce world, Customer Relationship Marketing (CRM) is important in terms of getting information to a customer directly, such as knowing what types of sales item he or she prefers. CRM enables companies to direct-market specifically at a certain target.

When CRM is applied to the J2ME world, a salesperson in the field has an advantage when making a customer call because he or she has a wireless J2ME device with all the customer's preferences and dislikes downloaded from a server onto the screen.

In Figure 12.3, a salesperson with a wireless PDA or laptop computer with the J2ME environment can remotely log in to his or her company's application server

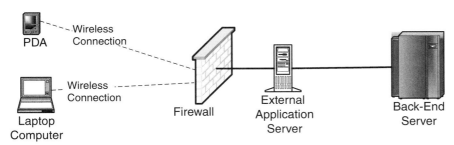

Figure 12.3   Wireless connection of J2ME devices to a Jini CRM application server
behind a firewall

and access Jini services that provide information, such as customer names, addresses, and customized data, that help the salesperson personalize the service between the client and the company.

12.6   Integrating with ERP

In many companies, various strategic planning tasks are now accomplished over the internal network using Enterprise Resource Planning (ERP) applications. These types of applications can be used to run all areas of a company: logistics, supply chain, human resources, and any other type of corporate planning. Companies such as Oracle and SAP specialize in ERP software.

The current trend is to make all ERP data available on the network from large databases. The databases are accessed by middleware that serves the information to data terminals. In the past, the data terminals were PCs and desktop computers. Now, the wire connection to large desktop systems can be eliminated by serving the data to small hand-held wireless devices. The typical model follows that of the multitier software environment: many lightweight clients connecting through transaction-based software to the actual data on a back-end server. Lightweight clients can be wireless devices that tunnel through ERP software to get to the database (see Figure 12.4). This allows J2ME and Jini technology to be used as the glue between the wireless device and the ERP software layers.

12.7   Integrating with a Sales Organization

The same types of devices that help with ERP can help the sales force of an enterprise. Vendors can record sales using a wireless PDA that connects directly to a company database. The data can reflect up-to-the-minute information on sales; having timely data makes projections into the future possible and more reliable.

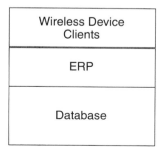

Figure 12.4   ERP software model

Mobile access to data can give any company a big advantage over competitors by enabling employees to know, in real-time, what the sales of different product lines look like and to make adjustments as they see fit.

Today companies such as Siebel are supporting different mobile devices, including phones, hand-held PDAs, and notebook PCs. The information is synchronized with the company's headquarters.

With J2ME and Jini technologies, this synchronization can be automated instead of manual. An example is having a J2ME technology-enabled PDA that has the IEEE 802.11b wireless technology. Once a user with this type of PDA walks back into his or her office, the device's J2ME software automatically finds the nearest Jini lookup service and requests an update of data through the wireless connection. The user does not need to do anything manually because the J2ME and Jini technologies take care of network detection and software startup using the discovery protocol.

12.8 Summary

This chapter showed how other Java technology environments can be used with Jini technology. It is important to note that the Jini surrogate architecture enables Jini services to be easily connected to other environments where Java technology already exists.

Legacy environments, such as J2SE and J2EE, run in many enterprises, linking application servers to databases. Also, other environments, such as Sun ONE, use Java technology to enable enterprise systems—for example, CRM, ERP, and sales applications—to run smoothly in a corporation. There are many reasons why one should want to use J2ME and Jini network technology to link with other Java technology environments in the enterprise, including increasing productivity by breaking away from the PC model (having a computer on everyone's desk) and decreasing cost by having an application server do the bulk of the processing because workers use J2ME devices.

The use of mobile computing enables enterprise workers to be untethered from desks and to move freely outside companies' offices to attend to tasks in the field and with their customers.

13

Another Java Technology Example

In the previous chapter, other Java technologies were discussed. This chapter provides an example, using a Jini surrogate connecting with a J2SE application, to show how to connect a legacy Java application with a Jini network. The information here can be used as a template to connect other Java technology legacy applications to the world of Jini technology.

13.1   Guide to Developing the Example

In order to develop an example for other Java technology environments, the following steps must be taken:

1. Decide on which type of Java technology environment to use (for example, J2EE, J2SE, applet, servlet, PersonalJava, and so on).

2. Decide on the protocol to use to interact with the other type of environment.

3. Write the client program.

4. Write the surrogate program.

5. Make sure the Jini environment is running correctly (see the Jini environment quick-start guide sidebar in Chapter 6).

6. Start the client program.

7. Verify that the surrogate is running correctly.

The remainder of this chapter walks you through the process step-by-step.

13.2 Decide on which Java Technology Environment to Use

This part depends on the requirements of the legacy application. If a legacy application is already using J2EE or J2SE technology, one can easily create a surrogate to bridge it to a Jini network. This is more cost-effective than converting the entire legacy application to a full Jini technology-enabled service because less code has to be rewritten in it. Instead, only a messaging process needs to be added (such as a TCP/IP socket) to the legacy application in order to communicate with the surrogate.

13.3 Decide on the Protocol to Use to Interact with the Other Type of Environment

In deciding on the client/surrogate protocol between a legacy Java application and a surrogate, the developer must first consider the resource limitations of the device. The easiest type of minimal connection between a J2EE or J2SE application and a surrogate is a TCP/IP socket. One way to make a TCP/IP surrogate is to use the IP surrogate interconnect specification found as a project at *developer.jini.org/exchange/projects/surrogate/rellinks.html*.

For the interconnect in this example, a simpler TCP/IP socket is used to deliver a surrogate to the surrogate host to be run on behalf of a J2SE legacy application instead of the IP surrogate interconnect. This case will be explored in the next sections.

13.4 Write the Client Program

The following code has an implementation of a J2SE legacy application that opens a TCP/IP socket to a known surrogate host. The legacy application then requests that the host start a Jini service on its behalf. The beginning part of the code is where the legacy functionality exists, and the latter part of the code sends a TCP/IP message to the known surrogate host with a URL-to-surrogate code that is used later by the surrogate host to start as a Jini service. This code assumes that the J2SE legacy application is on a network that allows socket messages to be sent.

```
/**
 * The J2SE legacy application to Jini network using Jini surrogate.
 */
import java.io.*;
import java.net.Socket;

public class J2SELegacyApp {

//...
// Legacy functionality of application
//...


//
// Connect to a Jini surrogate host to start a surrogate for this J2SE
//  legacy app via TCP/IP socket to a known port on a known Jini
//  surrogate host.
//
    public void connectJiniSurrogate() {
    // Fill-in your system-specific information here
    int         port = PORT_NUM;
    String      hostname = HOSTNAME;

    BufferedOutputStream outputStream;
    BufferedInputStream  inputStream;

    byte[]   dataBuffer = new byte[DATA_BUFFER_MAX];
    String   dataString = null;

    String   JINI_SURROGATE_OKAY_MSG = "OKAY_SURROGATE_STARTED: ";

    // Fill-in your URL to your surrogate JAR here
    String   JINI_SURROGATE_REQ_MSG =
        "START_SURROGATE: <URL_to_surrogate_JAR>";

    // Open a socket to the known Jini surrogate host
    try {

        System.out.println("Opening Jini surrogate host "+hostname+
                        " port # "+port);
        socket = new Socket(hostname, port);

    } catch (Exception e) {
        e.printStackTrace();
    }

    try {
```

```java
// Get the input and output streams of socket to surrogate host
outputStream = new BufferedOutputStream(socket.getOutputStream());
inputStream = new BufferedInputStream(socket.getInputStream() );

// Convert surrogate request message to socket message
dataBuffer = JINI_SURROGATE_REQ_MSG.getBytes();

// Send the surrogate request message to the surrogate host
try {
    outputStream.write(dataBuffer, 0, dataBuffer.length);
    outputStream.flush();
    System.out.println("Sent: "+JINI_SURROGATE_REQ_MSG);
} catch (Exception e) {
    e.printStackTrace();
}

// Listen for Jini surrogate host reply
System.out.println
    ("Listening for messages from Jini surrogate...");

// Loop to get status and commands from Jini surrogate which is
//    running in the surrogate host
while (inputStream.read(dataBuffer, 0, DATA_BUFFER_MAX)
        != -1) {
    dataString = new String(dataBuffer);

    // Print received message
    System.out.println("Received Jini surrogate message: "+
                dataString);

    // Check for type of message received
    if (dataString.indexOf(JINI_SURROGATE_OKAY_MSG) != -1) {
        // Process okay message
    } else if
        (dataString.indexOf
          (JINI_SURROGATE_LEGACY_APP_CMD1) != -1) {
        // Process this legacy command
        // Send back message to surrogate with outputStream.write()
    } else if
        (dataString.indexOf
          (JINI_SURROGATE_LEGACY_APP_CMD2) != -1) {
        // Process this legacy command
        // Send back message to surrogate with outputStream.write()
    }
    // Other commands go here
    // ...
}
```

```
            // Cleanup and close
            inputStream.close();
            outputStream.close();
            socket.close();

        } catch (IOException ioe) {
            ioe.printStackTrace();
        }

    }
```

13.5 Write the Surrogate Program

The surrogate program must allow the surrogate host to download the code from a JAR file to run on behalf of the J2SE legacy application. This is done according to the specific interconnect being used—in this case, a simplified TCP/IP socket request protocol. The surrogate must follow the Jini Technology Surrogate Architecture Specification (see *developer.jini.org/exchange/projects/surrogate/sa.pdf*). For purposes of this example, the specification is simplified to the use of the surrogate interface without the use of a `HostContext`. Here is the code to use:

```
package net.jini.surrogate;
public interface Surrogate {
    void activate(HostContext hostContext,
            Object context)
            throws Exception;
    void deactivate();
}
```

The following code represents the surrogate that will run on the surrogate host. It implements the surrogate interface; this means that it has an `activate()` and a `deactivate()` method. The `activate()` method in this example starts the Jini service and registers it with the Jini lookup service on the network. This service then provides a way for other clients on the network to interact with the J2SE legacy application through the `sendJ2SELegacyApp()` remote method.

```
import java.rmi.*;
import java.rmi.server.UnicastRemoteObject;
import net.jini.surrogate.*;

public class JiniJ2SELegacyAppSurrogate extends UnicastRemoteObject
    implements net.jini.surrogate.Surrogate, Serializable
{
```

```java
public JiniJ2SELegacyAppSurrogate() throws RemoteException {
    super();
}

// Interface API for J2SELegacyApp service
public String sendJ2SELegacyApp(String message) {

    // Set RMI security manager if there isn't one
if (System.getSecurityManager() == null) {
    System.setSecurityManager(new RMISecurityManager());
}

// Process messages here by sending to J2SE legacy app via
//     TCP/IP Socket outputStream.write()
// ...

// Process reply from J2SE legacy app via TCP/IP Socket
//     inputStream.read()
// ...

return(returnMesg);
}

public void activate(HostContext hostContext, Object context)
throws Exception {

    JiniJ2SELegacyAppSurrogate jiniSurrogate =
        new JiniJ2SELegacyAppSurrogate();

    ServiceInfo serviceInfo = new ServiceInfo("PRODUCT",
                                "MANUFACTURER",
                                "VENDOR", "VERSION",
                                "", "");

    BasicServiceType basicServiceType =
        new BasicServiceType("JiniSurrogate");

    Entry entry[] = new Entry[] {serviceInfo, basicServiceType};

    try {
        JoinManager joinManager = new JoinManager
            (jiniSurrogate, entry, new ServiceIDHandler(),
             new LeaseRenewalManager());
```

```
        } catch (java.io.IOException ioe) { }
    }

    public void deactivate() {

    }
}
```

For the full source code for this example, see *developer.jini.org/exchange/ projects/gateway/*.

13.6 Run the Jini Technology Environment

To test this system, the developer needs to start the Jini technology environment on his or her network (see the quick-start sidebar in Chapter 6). This allows the system to behave as a surrogate host.

13.7 Start the Client Program

The client program is the J2SE legacy application in this example; it must be started on the J2SE system on the same network. It looks for a Jini surrogate host with the known TCP/IP socket port and sends a request message to start a surrogate on its behalf. A surrogate host program must be running to accept the client's connection and to download the code from the URL specified in the request message. Then, the downloaded code is instantiated as a Java object and the `activate()` method is called to start it as a service on the Jini network. The surrogate host code for this example can be obtained from *developer.jini.org/exchange/projects/ gateway/*.

13.8 Verify that the Surrogate Runs Correctly

The last step is to make sure that the surrogate is running correctly. One way to do so is to have a separate Jini client call the `sendJ2SELegacyApp()` remote method to see if there is a response. For sample code that can act as a test client, see *developer.jini.org/exchange/projects/gateway/*. Once a response is received, this is verification that the surrogate is running correctly.

13.9 Summary

An example using another type of Java environment was given in this chapter. The Jini surrogate architecture is simple to use and can easily be applied to J2SE legacy applications. The interconnect that bridges the information from the J2SE legacy application to the Jini network is important as it allows old software to work with new Jini network technology. This expands the reach of Jini technology to the many systems that need it.

14

Jini Technology
Design Ideas

Jini technology can be applied to many future environments. The potential for evolution on the network is a definite advantage for systems that use Jini network technology. Devices and systems can grow and learn as a distributed network of computers should do.

14.1 New Ideas for Jini Technology

Here are just a few introductory ideas for new Jini technology development:

- *Distributed computing among small devices:* With so many small devices in existence, there should be a way to harness the computing power of each. Jini technology ties together all the separate, tiny devices to make a large-scale computing system.

- *Network-aware devices:* Devices should be able to discover services on the network for themselves instead of a service provider having to hard-code fixed services into a device.

- *Code mobility among intermittently connected devices:* Code and data should move freely to devices so that when they are out of range of a network or momentarily disconnected, they can still operate. One example is having games that download to a device so that one can still play even when the network signal is lost.

- *Location-based applications:* With Global Positioning System (GPS) information available to electronic devices, it should be easy to transmit location data back to the Jini technology services that run on a network so that services can adapt to a device based on where the user is. For example, if a cell phone user wants to know where the closest gas station is, a Jini technology service will be able to provide that information automatically.

- *Peer-to-peer applications with JXTA technology:* Jini technology allows a bridge to form for peer-to-peer applications. For example, a Jini technology service can be a wrapper around a JXTA peer application that runs on the network system. All Jini technology-enabled devices could use it because it is visible to them on the Jini lookup service.

14.2 J2ME Future Enhancements

The future enhancements of J2ME will concentrate on size reduction, security, and flexibility. These key features will enable both Java technology and Jini network technology to grow and to be robust on many different types of devices. The security enhancements have a fine-grained way of controlling the security on different devices when code is downloaded to them. An example of the size reduction is the ability to change Java class files to read-only mode, which compresses the file size. This is also known as ROMizing—or turning code into formats that can be burned into read-only memory (ROM). One example of future Jini technology fine-grained security may be the ability to authenticate a user by having a smart card attached to the device.

14.3 Jini Future Enhancements

The Jini technology enhancements that are expected in the future include the following:

- *Size reduction:* By reducing the Java class dependencies, the total size of Java class files will be smaller; this can be done primarily in the profiles for J2ME.

- *Security:* Increased security for communication, authentication, and delegation.

- *Helper utilities:* Utilities to lessen the number of method calls needed to perform routine operations.

- *Helper services:* Services to lessen the source code needed to perform certain service tasks.

14.4   Existing Peer-to-Peer Technology

The J2ME and Jini technology environment is well suited for the latest advances in peer-to-peer (P2P) architectures. P2P, which has been around for a long time, enables disparate computer systems to collaborate on a task.

Two recent examples of P2P distributed computing are the Gnutella music file-sharing program and the NASA SETI@home project. Both of these projects have taken advantage of the computing power that is available (mostly MP3 music files) across the Internet. These programs enable local computer files to be shared with other users of the same program or protocol (see Figure 14.1).

The difference between the programs is apparent in their communication protocol. The NASA SETI@home approach to process sharing is to use the classic client-server model. A group of centralized servers sitting on the network somewhere enables clients to connect and register the music files each PC has to share. The servers control the data flow and act as the registry for all music files available to all clients. The classic client-server model makes one single system (or group of systems) the controlling point, which is not robust because it can become a single point of failure. Also, the classic client-server model is a bottleneck in terms of communications. If one NASA SETI@home client wants to go on to its next task, it must go to one central server.

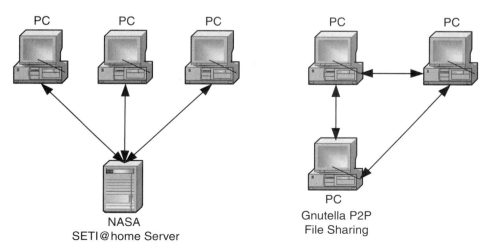

Figure 14.1   NASA SETI@home central server model and Gnutella peer-to-peer model

Gnutella follows the peer-to-peer model, in contrast to the client-server model of NASA SETI@home. There is no centralized server; instead, each computer system behaves as both a server and a client in a distributed network of PCs. Each peer has information about its own set of music (or other types of) files to share; plus, it has information about other reachable peers. The P2P model enables communication to hop from peer to peer on the distributed network. Instead of searching on a centralized server for a specific file, a search is initiated with a timeout, or distance (for example, time-to-live—TTL) of how many maximum hops are needed to go from peer to peer until the file being searched is found.

With a TTL limitation, a P2P search does not get caught in an infinite loop, trying to search for something that may not exist. The model of P2P is based on the Ethernet (TCP/IP) standard itself. Many independent distributed nodes on the Internet enable communication back and forth between any two nodes. The packets of communication, routed from peer to peer through the Internet, enable a certain amount of TTL before the packet is dropped. A distributed system can handle many independent nodes talking to one another in a P2P fashion. Otherwise, a central server or group of centralized servers would be too swamped to handle high numbers of nodes on a network.

14.5 Peer-to-Peer Strategy

A good strategy to take with P2P is to follow what Bill Joy suggests for the JXTA (pronounced "juxta") project at Sun Microsystems. The JXTA project is using the Apache license to model the primitive instructions to support P2P. This ties in with J2ME and Jini technologies in that protocols are obsolete among devices and can be made public through Open Source. It is not advantageous to keep protocols private in the Jini technology network because it is better to have as many devices share as many services as possible. Having peer devices communicate with each other easily is a good goal. J2ME and Jini technologies take steps toward that type of P2P interoperability by reducing resource requirements and eliminating the need for fixed protocols among peers.

14.6 J2ME Client Device Strategy

The strategy to use in client devices centers on the format of data that is exchanged between the device and the service. The format should be chosen based on the following:

- *From device to service:* Comma-separated fields or key value pairs

- *From service to service:* XML data following a standard document type definition (DTD) or schema

In addition, security should be considered. The easiest way to handle security in a J2ME client device is to follow the HTTPS technology between the client and service.

Messaging is the final concern. One should design messages to be batch-sent to the service in order to conserve bandwidth and not use the network for messages that are too short. Batching messages also helps when only an intermittent connection is possible. An example is when an airplane passenger uses a J2ME device to compose e-mail messages. Because he or she is not connected to the network while in flight, the messages must be queued. When the plane lands, the passenger exits the gate and walks within range of a wireless network connection in the airport; then, a Jini service can automatically process all the batched messages from the J2ME device and send them.

14.7 Further Readings and Online Resources

- *The Jini Specification, Second Edition*, Ken Arnold, Bryan O'Sullivan, Robert W. Scheifler, Jim Waldo, Ann Wollrath, Addison-Wesley, 2000.

- *Core Jini, Second Edition,* W. Keith Edwards, Prentice Hall PTR, 2000.

- Java 2 Platform, Micro Edition: *www.java.sun.com/j2me/*

- Jini network technology: *www.sun.com/jini/*

- Open Services Gateway Initiative: *www.osgi.org/*

14.8 Summary

The next generation of Jini technology-enabled devices will rely on a distributed computing model. By emphasizing code mobility, the vision of Jini technology is achieved in presenting a network that is robust and that can withstand pieces that intermittently drop out or become disconnected. This is the power of distributed systems and the promise of Jini network technology.

Legend for Appendices

The following is a condensed summary of all the classes defined in the Jini specifications, listed alphabetically. It is done in the style introduced by Patrick Chan in his excellent book, *Java Developers Almanac*. Where a term is broken in an unusual spot for page fit, such as in the middle of a word or after a period, a special continuation character (¬) is used to denote this break.

1. The name of the class.
2. The name of the package containing the class
3. The chain of superclasses. Each class is a subclass of the one above it.
4. The names of the interfaces implemented by each class.
5. Icon column. Icons that may occur in this column are:

   ❏   static method
   ✳   constructor
   ○   abstract
   ●   final
   ■   static final
   ◆   protected
   ✍   field

6. The version number (i.e., the version of Java technology where the class member was first introduced).
7. The return type of a method or the declared type of an instance variable.
8. The name of the class member (in bold type). If it is a method, the parameter list and optional *throws* clause follows. Members are arranged alphabetically.

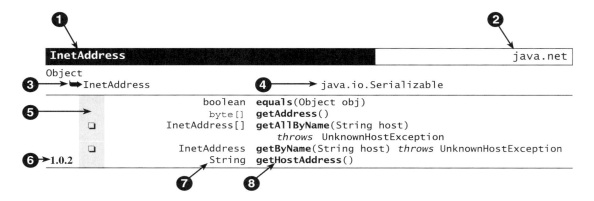

J2ME CDC/Foundation Profile Almanac

AbstractCollection
java.util

Object
   ➥AbstractCollection   Collection

✳◆		**AbstractCollection**()
	boolean	**add**(Object o)
	boolean	**addAll**(Collection c)
	void	**clear**()
	boolean	**contains**(Object o)
	boolean	**containsAll**(Collection c)
	boolean	**isEmpty**()
○	Iterator	**iterator**()
	boolean	**remove**(Object o)
	boolean	**removeAll**(Collection c)
	boolean	**retainAll**(Collection c)
○	int	**size**()
	Object[]	**toArray**()
	Object[]	**toArray**(Object[] a)
	String	**toString**()

AbstractList
java.util

Object
   ➥AbstractCollection   Collection
      ➥AbstractList   List

✳◆		**AbstractList**()
	void	**add**(int index, Object element)
	boolean	**add**(Object o)
	boolean	**addAll**(int index, Collection c)
	void	**clear**()
	boolean	**equals**(Object o)
○	Object	**get**(int index)
	int	**hashCode**()
	int	**indexOf**(Object o)
	Iterator	**iterator**()
	int	**lastIndexOf**(Object o)
	ListIterator	**listIterator**()
	ListIterator	**listIterator**(int index)
✍◆	int	**modCount**
	Object	**remove**(int index)
◆	void	**removeRange**(int fromIndex, int toIndex)
	Object	**set**(int index, Object element)
	List	**subList**(int fromIndex, int toIndex)

AbstractMap   java.util

```
Object
    ➡AbstractMap                              Map
```

✳◆		**AbstractMap**()
	void	**clear**()
	boolean	**containsKey**(Object key)
	boolean	**containsValue**(Object value)
○	Set	**entrySet**()
	boolean	**equals**(Object o)
	Object	**get**(Object key)
	int	**hashCode**()
	boolean	**isEmpty**()
	Set	**keySet**()
	Object	**put**(Object key, Object value)
	void	**putAll**(Map t)
	Object	**remove**(Object key)
	int	**size**()
	String	**toString**()
	Collection	**values**()

AbstractMethodError   java.lang

```
Object
    ➡Throwable                        java.io.Serializable
        ➡Error
            ➡LinkageError
                ➡IncompatibleClassChangeError
                    ➡AbstractMethodError
```

❊		AbstractMethodError()
❊		AbstractMethodError(String s)

AbstractSequentialList   `java.util`

```
Object
    ➥AbstractCollection              Collection
        ➥AbstractList                List
            ➥AbstractSequentialList
```

❊◆		AbstractSequentialList()
	void	add(int index, Object element)
	boolean	addAll(int index, Collection c)
	Object	get(int index)
	Iterator	iterator()
○	ListIterator	listIterator(int index)
	Object	remove(int index)
	Object	set(int index, Object element)

AbstractSet   `java.util`

```
Object
    ➥AbstractCollection              Collection
        ➥AbstractSet                 Set
```

❊◆		AbstractSet()
	boolean	equals(Object o)
	int	hashCode()
	boolean	removeAll(Collection c)

AccessControlContext   `java.security`

```
Object
    ➥AccessControlContext
```

❊		AccessControlContext(AccessControlContext acc, DomainCombiner combiner)
❊		AccessControlContext(ProtectionDomain[] context)
	void	checkPermission(Permission perm)
		throws AccessControlException
	boolean	equals(Object obj)
	DomainCombiner	getDomainCombiner()
	int	hashCode()

AccessControlException   `java.security`

```
Object
    ➥Throwable                       java.io.Serializable
        ➥Exception
```

➥RuntimeException
  ➥SecurityException
    ➥AccessControlException

✲		**AccessControlException**(String s)
✲		**AccessControlException**(String s, Permission p)
	Permission	**getPermission**()

AccessController   `java.security`

Object
  ➥AccessController

❑	void	**checkPermission**(Permission perm)
		throws AccessControlException
❑	Object	**doPrivileged**(PrivilegedAction action)
❑	Object	**doPrivileged**(PrivilegedAction action,
		AccessControlContext context)
❑	Object	**doPrivileged**(PrivilegedExceptionAction action)
		throws PrivilegedActionException
❑	Object	**doPrivileged**(PrivilegedExceptionAction action,
		AccessControlContext context)
		throws PrivilegedActionException
❑	AccessControlContext	**getContext**()

AccessibleObject   `java.lang.reflect`

Object
  ➥AccessibleObject

✲◆		**AccessibleObject**()
	boolean	**isAccessible**()
❑	void	**setAccessible**(AccessibleObject[] array,
		boolean flag) *throws* SecurityException
	void	**setAccessible**(boolean flag)
		throws SecurityException

Adler32   `java.util.zip`

Object
  ➥Adler32   Checksum

✲		**Adler32**()
	long	**getValue**()
	void	**reset**()
	void	**update**(byte[] b)
	void	**update**(byte[] b, int off, int len)
	void	**update**(int b)

AlgorithmParameterGenerator	java.security

Object
   ➡AlgorithmParameterGenerator

❊◆		**AlgorithmParameterGenerator(**
		    AlgorithmParameterGeneratorSpi paramGenSpi,
		    Provider provider, String algorithm)

●	AlgorithmParameters	**generateParameters()**
●	String	**getAlgorithm()**
❏	AlgorithmParameter¬ Generator	**getInstance(**String algorithm) *throws* NoSuchAlgorithmException

❏	AlgorithmParameter¬
	Generator
		getInstance(String algorithm, String provider)
		    throws NoSuchAlgorithmException,
		    NoSuchProviderException

●	Provider	**getProvider()**
●	void	**init(**spec.AlgorithmParameterSpec genParamSpec) *throws* InvalidAlgorithmParameterException

●	void	**init(**spec.AlgorithmParameterSpec genParamSpec,
		    SecureRandom random)
		    throws InvalidAlgorithmParameterException

●	void	**init(**int size)
●	void	**init(**int size, SecureRandom random)

AlgorithmParameterGeneratorSpi	java.security

Object
   ➡AlgorithmParameterGeneratorSpi

❊		**AlgorithmParameterGeneratorSpi()**
○◆	AlgorithmParameters	**engineGenerateParameters()**

○◆	void	**engineInit(**spec.AlgorithmParameterSpec genParamSpec,
		    SecureRandom random)
		    throws InvalidAlgorithmParameterException

○◆	void	**engineInit(**int size, SecureRandom random)

AlgorithmParameters	java.security

Object
   ➡AlgorithmParameters

❊◆		**AlgorithmParameters(**AlgorithmParametersSpi paramSpi, Provider provider, String algorithm)
●	String	**getAlgorithm()**
●	byte[]	**getEncoded()** *throws* java.io.IOException
●	byte[]	**getEncoded(**String format) *throws* java.io.IOException
❏	AlgorithmParameters	**getInstance(**String algorithm) *throws* NoSuchAlgorithmException

❏	AlgorithmParameters	**getInstance(**String algorithm, String provider)
		    throws NoSuchAlgorithmException,
		    NoSuchProviderException

●	spec.Algorithm¬ ParameterSpec	**getParameterSpec**(Class paramSpec) *throws* spec.InvalidParameterSpecException
●	Provider	**getProvider**()
●	void	**init**(spec.AlgorithmParameterSpec paramSpec) *throws* spec.InvalidParameterSpecException
●	void	**init**(byte[] params) *throws* java.io.IOException
●	void	**init**(byte[] params, String format) *throws* java.io.IOException
●	String	**toString**()

AlgorithmParametersSpi   java.security

Object
   ➥AlgorithmParametersSpi

✳		**AlgorithmParametersSpi**()
○◆	byte[]	**engineGetEncoded**() *throws* java.io.IOException
○◆	byte[]	**engineGetEncoded**(String format) *throws* java.io.IOException
○◆	spec.Algorithm¬ ParameterSpec	**engineGetParameterSpec**(Class paramSpec) *throws* spec.InvalidParameterSpecException
○◆	void	**engineInit**(spec.AlgorithmParameterSpec paramSpec) *throws* spec.InvalidParameterSpecException
○◆	void	**engineInit**(byte[] params) *throws* java.io.IOException
○◆	void	**engineInit**(byte[] params, String format) *throws* java.io.IOException
○◆	String	**engineToString**()

AllPermission   java.security

Object
   ➥Permission   Guard, java.io.Serializable
      ➥AllPermission

✳		**AllPermission**()
✳		**AllPermission**(String name, String actions)
	boolean	**equals**(Object obj)
	String	**getActions**()
	int	**hashCode**()
	boolean	**implies**(Permission p)
	PermissionCollection	**newPermissionCollection**()

Annotation   java.text

Object
   ➥Annotation

✳		**Annotation**(Object value)
	Object	**getValue**()
	String	**toString**()

ArithmeticException   java.lang

```
Object
  ➥Throwable                        java.io.Serializable
     ➥Exception
        ➥RuntimeException
           ➥ArithmeticException
```

✲	**ArithmeticException**()
✲	**ArithmeticException**(String s)

Array   java.lang.reflect

```
Object
  ➥Array
```

❏	Object	**get**(Object array, int index) *throws* IllegalArgumentException, ArrayIndexOutOfBoundsException
❏	boolean	**getBoolean**(Object array, int index) *throws* IllegalArgumentException, ArrayIndexOutOfBoundsException
❏	byte	**getByte**(Object array, int index) *throws* IllegalArgumentException, ArrayIndexOutOfBoundsException
❏	char	**getChar**(Object array, int index) *throws* IllegalArgumentException, ArrayIndexOutOfBoundsException
❏	double	**getDouble**(Object array, int index) *throws* IllegalArgumentException, ArrayIndexOutOfBoundsException
❏	float	**getFloat**(Object array, int index) *throws* IllegalArgumentException, ArrayIndexOutOfBoundsException
❏	int	**getInt**(Object array, int index) *throws* IllegalArgumentException, ArrayIndexOutOfBoundsException
❏	int	**getLength**(Object array) *throws* IllegalArgumentException
❏	long	**getLong**(Object array, int index) *throws* IllegalArgumentException, ArrayIndexOutOfBoundsException
❏	short	**getShort**(Object array, int index) *throws* IllegalArgumentException, ArrayIndexOutOfBoundsException
❏	Object	**newInstance**(Class componentType, int length) *throws* NegativeArraySizeException
❏	Object	**newInstance**(Class componentType, int[] dimensions) *throws* IllegalArgumentException, NegativeArraySizeException
❏	void	**set**(Object array, int index, Object value) *throws* IllegalArgumentException, ArrayIndexOutOfBoundsException

❏	void	**setBoolean**(Object array, int index, boolean z) *throws* IllegalArgumentException, ArrayIndexOutOfBoundsException
❏	void	**setByte**(Object array, int index, byte b) *throws* IllegalArgumentException, ArrayIndexOutOfBoundsException
❏	void	**setChar**(Object array, int index, char c) *throws* IllegalArgumentException, ArrayIndexOutOfBoundsException
❏	void	**setDouble**(Object array, int index, double d) *throws* IllegalArgumentException, ArrayIndexOutOfBoundsException
❏	void	**setFloat**(Object array, int index, float f) *throws* IllegalArgumentException, ArrayIndexOutOfBoundsException
❏	void	**setInt**(Object array, int index, int i) *throws* IllegalArgumentException, ArrayIndexOutOfBoundsException
❏	void	**setLong**(Object array, int index, long l) *throws* IllegalArgumentException, ArrayIndexOutOfBoundsException
❏	void	**setShort**(Object array, int index, short s) *throws* IllegalArgumentException, ArrayIndexOutOfBoundsException

ArrayIndexOutOfBoundsException   java.lang

```
Object
  ➥Throwable                          java.io.Serializable
    ➥Exception
      ➥RuntimeException
        ➥IndexOutOfBoundsException
          ➥ArrayIndexOutOfBoundsException
```

✳	**ArrayIndexOutOfBoundsException**()
✳	**ArrayIndexOutOfBoundsException**(int index)
✳	**ArrayIndexOutOfBoundsException**(String s)

ArrayList   java.util

```
Object
  ➥AbstractCollection                 Collection
    ➥AbstractList                     List
      ➥ArrayList                      List, Cloneable, java.io.Serializable
```

	void	**add**(int index, Object element)
	boolean	**add**(Object o)
	boolean	**addAll**(Collection c)
	boolean	**addAll**(int index, Collection c)
✳		**ArrayList**()
✳		**ArrayList**(Collection c)
✳		**ArrayList**(int initialCapacity)

```
        void  clear()
      Object  clone()
     boolean  contains(Object elem)
        void  ensureCapacity(int minCapacity)
      Object  get(int index)
         int  indexOf(Object elem)
     boolean  isEmpty()
         int  lastIndexOf(Object elem)
      Object  remove(int index)
 ♦      void  removeRange(int fromIndex, int toIndex)
      Object  set(int index, Object element)
         int  size()
    Object[]  toArray()
    Object[]  toArray(Object[] a)
        void  trimToSize()
```

Arrays   java.util

```
Object
  ➜Arrays
```

```
❑        List  asList(Object[] a)
❑         int  binarySearch(byte[] a, byte key)
❑         int  binarySearch(char[] a, char key)
❑         int  binarySearch(double[] a, double key)
❑         int  binarySearch(float[] a, float key)
❑         int  binarySearch(int[] a, int key)
❑         int  binarySearch(long[] a, long key)
❑         int  binarySearch(Object[] a, Object key)
❑         int  binarySearch(Object[] a, Object key, Comparator c)
❑         int  binarySearch(short[] a, short key)
❑     boolean  equals(boolean[] a, boolean[] a2)
❑     boolean  equals(byte[] a, byte[] a2)
❑     boolean  equals(char[] a, char[] a2)
❑     boolean  equals(double[] a, double[] a2)
❑     boolean  equals(float[] a, float[] a2)
❑     boolean  equals(int[] a, int[] a2)
❑     boolean  equals(long[] a, long[] a2)
❑     boolean  equals(Object[] a, Object[] a2)
❑     boolean  equals(short[] a, short[] a2)
❑        void  fill(boolean[] a, boolean val)
❑        void  fill(boolean[] a, int fromIndex, int toIndex,
                    boolean val)
❑        void  fill(byte[] a, byte val)
❑        void  fill(byte[] a, int fromIndex, int toIndex, byte val)
❑        void  fill(char[] a, char val)
❑        void  fill(char[] a, int fromIndex, int toIndex, char val)
❑        void  fill(double[] a, double val)
❑        void  fill(double[] a, int fromIndex, int toIndex,
                    double val)
❑        void  fill(float[] a, float val)
```

		void	fill(float[] a, int fromIndex, int toIndex, float val)
❏		void	fill(int[] a, int val)
❏		void	fill(int[] a, int fromIndex, int toIndex, int val)
❏		void	fill(long[] a, int fromIndex, int toIndex, long val)
❏		void	fill(long[] a, long val)
❏		void	fill(Object[] a, int fromIndex, int toIndex, Object val)
❏		void	fill(Object[] a, Object val)
❏		void	fill(short[] a, int fromIndex, int toIndex, short val)
❏		void	fill(short[] a, short val)
❏		void	sort(byte[] a)
❏		void	sort(byte[] a, int fromIndex, int toIndex)
❏		void	sort(char[] a)
❏		void	sort(char[] a, int fromIndex, int toIndex)
❏		void	sort(double[] a)
❏		void	sort(double[] a, int fromIndex, int toIndex)
❏		void	sort(float[] a)
❏		void	sort(float[] a, int fromIndex, int toIndex)
❏		void	sort(int[] a)
❏		void	sort(int[] a, int fromIndex, int toIndex)
❏		void	sort(long[] a)
❏		void	sort(long[] a, int fromIndex, int toIndex)
❏		void	sort(Object[] a)
❏		void	sort(Object[] a, Comparator c)
❏		void	sort(Object[] a, int fromIndex, int toIndex)
❏		void	sort(Object[] a, int fromIndex, int toIndex, Comparator c)
❏		void	sort(short[] a)
❏		void	sort(short[] a, int fromIndex, int toIndex)

ArrayStoreException   java.lang

```
Object
  ➡Throwable                          java.io.Serializable
     ➡Exception
        ➡RuntimeException
           ➡ArrayStoreException
```

✴		ArrayStoreException()
✴		ArrayStoreException(String s)

AttributedCharacterIterator   java.text

AttributedCharacterIterator   CharacterIterator

	java.util.Set	getAllAttributeKeys()
	Object	getAttribute(AttributedCharacterIterator.Attribute attribute)

java.util.Map	**getAttributes**()
int	**getRunLimit**()
int	**getRunLimit**(
	AttributedCharacterIterator.Attribute attribute)
int	**getRunLimit**(java.util.Set attributes)
int	**getRunStart**()
int	**getRunStart**(
	AttributedCharacterIterator.Attribute attribute)
int	**getRunStart**(java.util.Set attributes)

AttributedCharacterIterator.Attribute   java.text

Object
　➥AttributedCharacterIterator.Attribute java.io.Serializable

✳◆		**AttributedCharacterIterator.Attribute**(String name)
●	boolean	**equals**(Object obj)
◆	String	**getName**()
●	int	**hashCode**()
⚠■	AttributedCharacter¬ Iterator.Attribute	**INPUT_METHOD_SEGMENT**
⚠■	AttributedCharacter¬ Iterator.Attribute	**LANGUAGE**
⚠■	AttributedCharacter¬ Iterator.Attribute	**READING**
◆	Object	**readResolve**() *throws* java.io.InvalidObjectException
	String	**toString**()

AttributedString   java.text

Object
　➥AttributedString

	void	**addAttribute**(
		AttributedCharacterIterator.Attribute attribute,
		Object value)
	void	**addAttribute**(
		AttributedCharacterIterator.Attribute attribute,
		Object value, int beginIndex, int endIndex)
	void	**addAttributes**(java.util.Map attributes,
		int beginIndex, int endIndex)
✳		**AttributedString**(AttributedCharacterIterator text)
✳		**AttributedString**(AttributedCharacterIterator text,
		int beginIndex, int endIndex)
		AttributedString(AttributedCharacterIterator text,
		int beginIndex, int endIndex, Attributed¬
		CharacterIterator.Attribute[] attributes)
✳		**AttributedString**(String text)
✳		**AttributedString**(String text,
		java.util.Map attributes)

AttributedCharacter¬ Iterator	**getIterator**()	

AttributedCharacter¬
Iterator
	getIterator(
	    AttributedCharacterIterator.Attribute[]
	    attributes)	

AttributedCharacter¬
Iterator
	getIterator(
	    AttributedCharacterIterator.Attribute[]
	    attributes, int beginIndex, int endIndex)	

Attributes   java.util.jar

Object
   ➥Attributes   java.util.Map, Cloneable

✳		**Attributes**()
✳		**Attributes**(Attributes attr)
✳		**Attributes**(int size)
	void	**clear**()
	Object	**clone**()
	boolean	**containsKey**(Object name)
	boolean	**containsValue**(Object value)
	java.util.Set	**entrySet**()
	boolean	**equals**(Object o)
	Object	**get**(Object name)
	String	**getValue**(Attributes.Name name)
	String	**getValue**(String name)
	int	**hashCode**()
	boolean	**isEmpty**()
	java.util.Set	**keySet**()
△◆	java.util.Map	**map**
	Object	**put**(Object name, Object value)
	void	**putAll**(java.util.Map attr)
	String	**putValue**(String name, String value)
	Object	**remove**(Object name)
	int	**size**()
	java.util.Collection	**values**()

Attributes.Name   java.util.jar

Object
   ➥Attributes.Name

✳		**Attributes.Name**(String name)
△■	Attributes.Name	**CLASS_PATH**
△■	Attributes.Name	**CONTENT_TYPE**
	boolean	**equals**(Object o)
△■	Attributes.Name	**EXTENSION_INSTALLATION**
△■	Attributes.Name	**EXTENSION_LIST**
△■	Attributes.Name	**EXTENSION_NAME**
	int	**hashCode**()

⊿■	Attributes.Name	**IMPLEMENTATION_TITLE**
⊿■	Attributes.Name	**IMPLEMENTATION_URL**
⊿■	Attributes.Name	**IMPLEMENTATION_VENDOR**
⊿■	Attributes.Name	**IMPLEMENTATION_VENDOR_ID**
⊿■	Attributes.Name	**IMPLEMENTATION_VERSION**
⊿■	Attributes.Name	**MAIN_CLASS**
⊿■	Attributes.Name	**MANIFEST_VERSION**
⊿■	Attributes.Name	**SEALED**
⊿■	Attributes.Name	**SIGNATURE_VERSION**
⊿■	Attributes.Name	**SPECIFICATION_TITLE**
⊿■	Attributes.Name	**SPECIFICATION_VENDOR**
⊿■	Attributes.Name	**SPECIFICATION_VERSION**
	String	**toString**()

Authenticator   java.net

```
Object
    ➥Authenticator
```

✱		**Authenticator**()
◆	PasswordAuthentication	**getPasswordAuthentication**()
●◆	int	**getRequestingPort**()
●◆	String	**getRequestingPrompt**()
●◆	String	**getRequestingProtocol**()
●◆	String	**getRequestingScheme**()
●◆	InetAddress	**getRequestingSite**()
❏	PasswordAuthentication	**requestPasswordAuthentication**(InetAddress addr, int port, String protocol, String prompt, String scheme)
❏	void	**setDefault**(Authenticator a)

BasicPermission   java.security

```
Object
    ➥Permission                          Guard, java.io.Serializable
        ➥BasicPermission                 java.io.Serializable
```

✱		**BasicPermission**(String name)
✱		**BasicPermission**(String name, String actions)
	boolean	**equals**(Object obj)
	String	**getActions**()
	int	**hashCode**()
	boolean	**implies**(Permission p)
	PermissionCollection	**newPermissionCollection**()

BigInteger   java.math

```
Object
    ➥Number                              java.io.Serializable
        ➥BigInteger                      Comparable
```

		BigInteger	**abs**()
		BigInteger	**add**(BigInteger val)
		BigInteger	**and**(BigInteger val)
		BigInteger	**andNot**(BigInteger val)
	✳		**BigInteger**(byte[] val)
	✳		**BigInteger**(int signum, byte[] magnitude)
	✳		**BigInteger**(int bitLength, int certainty, java.util.Random rnd)
	✳		**BigInteger**(int numBits, java.util.Random rnd)
	✳		**BigInteger**(String val)
	✳		**BigInteger**(String val, int radix)
		int	**bitCount**()
		int	**bitLength**()
		BigInteger	**clearBit**(int n)
		int	**compareTo**(BigInteger val)
1.2		int	**compareTo**(Object o)
		BigInteger	**divide**(BigInteger val)
		BigInteger[]	**divideAndRemainder**(BigInteger val)
		double	**doubleValue**()
		boolean	**equals**(Object x)
		BigInteger	**flipBit**(int n)
		float	**floatValue**()
		BigInteger	**gcd**(BigInteger val)
		int	**getLowestSetBit**()
		int	**hashCode**()
		int	**intValue**()
		boolean	**isProbablePrime**(int certainty)
		long	**longValue**()
		BigInteger	**max**(BigInteger val)
		BigInteger	**min**(BigInteger val)
		BigInteger	**mod**(BigInteger m)
		BigInteger	**modInverse**(BigInteger m)
		BigInteger	**modPow**(BigInteger exponent, BigInteger m)
		BigInteger	**multiply**(BigInteger val)
		BigInteger	**negate**()
		BigInteger	**not**()
1.2	▱■	BigInteger	**ONE**
		BigInteger	**or**(BigInteger val)
		BigInteger	**pow**(int exponent)
		BigInteger	**remainder**(BigInteger val)
		BigInteger	**setBit**(int n)
		BigInteger	**shiftLeft**(int n)
		BigInteger	**shiftRight**(int n)
		int	**signum**()
		BigInteger	**subtract**(BigInteger val)
		boolean	**testBit**(int n)
		byte[]	**toByteArray**()
		String	**toString**()
		String	**toString**(int radix)
	❏	BigInteger	**valueOf**(long val)
		BigInteger	**xor**(BigInteger val)
1.2	▱■	BigInteger	**ZERO**

BindException

`java.net`

```
Object
   ➡Throwable                              java.io.Serializable
      ➡Exception
         ➡java.io.IOException
            ➡SocketException
               ➡BindException
```

✳		**BindException**()
✳		**BindException**(String msg)

BitSet

`java.util`

```
Object
   ➡BitSet                              Cloneable, java.io.Serializable
```

		void	**and**(BitSet set)
1.2		void	**andNot**(BitSet set)
	✳		**BitSet**()
	✳		**BitSet**(int nbits)
1.0		void	**clear**(int bitIndex)
		Object	**clone**()
		boolean	**equals**(Object obj)
		boolean	**get**(int bitIndex)
		int	**hashCode**()
1.2		int	**length**()
		void	**or**(BitSet set)
1.0		void	**set**(int bitIndex)
		int	**size**()
		String	**toString**()
		void	**xor**(BitSet set)

Boolean

`java.lang`

```
Object
   ➡Boolean                              java.io.Serializable
```

	✳		**Boolean**(boolean value)
	✳		**Boolean**(String s)
		boolean	**booleanValue**()
		boolean	**equals**(Object obj)
	✍■	Boolean	**FALSE**
	❏	boolean	**getBoolean**(String name)
		int	**hashCode**()
		String	**toString**()
	✍■	Boolean	**TRUE**
1.1	✍■	Class	**TYPE**
	❏	Boolean	**valueOf**(String s)

BreakIterator		java.text

Object
  ➡️BreakIterator   Cloneable

✳️◆		**BreakIterator**()
	Object	**clone**()
⭕	int	**current**()
✏️■	int	**DONE**
⭕	int	**first**()
⭕	int	**following**(int offset)
❑	java.util.Locale[]	**getAvailableLocales**()
❑	BreakIterator	**getCharacterInstance**()
❑	BreakIterator	**getCharacterInstance**(java.util.Locale where)
❑	BreakIterator	**getLineInstance**()
❑	BreakIterator	**getLineInstance**(java.util.Locale where)
❑	BreakIterator	**getSentenceInstance**()
❑	BreakIterator	**getSentenceInstance**(java.util.Locale where)
⭕	CharacterIterator	**getText**()
	BreakIterator	**getWordInstance**()
❑	BreakIterator	**getWordInstance**(java.util.Locale where)
	boolean	**isBoundary**(int offset)
⭕	int	**last**()
⭕	int	**next**()
⭕	int	**next**(int n)
	int	**preceding**(int offset)
⭕	int	**previous**()
⭕	void	**setText**(CharacterIterator newText)
	void	**setText**(String newText)

BufferedInputStream		java.io

Object
  ➡️InputStream
     ➡️FilterInputStream
        ➡️BufferedInputStream

	int	**available**() *throws* IOException
✏️◆	byte[]	**buf**
✳️		**BufferedInputStream**(InputStream in)
✳️		**BufferedInputStream**(InputStream in, int size)
	void	**close**() *throws* IOException
✏️◆	int	**count**
	void	**mark**(int readlimit)
✏️◆	int	**marklimit**
✏️◆	int	**markpos**
	boolean	**markSupported**()
✏️◆	int	**pos**
	int	**read**() *throws* IOException
	int	**read**(byte[] b, int off, int len) *throws* IOException
	void	**reset**() *throws* IOException
	long	**skip**(long n) *throws* IOException

BufferedOutputStream   java.io

```
Object
    OutputStream
        FilterOutputStream
            BufferedOutputStream
```

✍◆	byte[]	**buf**
✳		**BufferedOutputStream**(OutputStream out)
✳		**BufferedOutputStream**(OutputStream out, int size)
✍◆	int	**count**
	void	**flush**() *throws* IOException
	void	**write**(byte[] b, int off, int len) *throws* IOException
	void	**write**(int b) *throws* IOException

BufferedReader   java.io

```
Object
    Reader
        BufferedReader
```

✳		**BufferedReader**(Reader in)
✳		**BufferedReader**(Reader in, int sz)
	void	**close**() *throws* IOException
	void	**mark**(int readAheadLimit) *throws* IOException
	boolean	**markSupported**()
	int	**read**() *throws* IOException
	int	**read**(char[] cbuf, int off, int len) *throws* IOException
	String	**readLine**() *throws* IOException
	boolean	**ready**() *throws* IOException
	void	**reset**() *throws* IOException
	long	**skip**(long n) *throws* IOException

BufferedWriter   java.io

```
Object
    Writer
        BufferedWriter
```

✳		**BufferedWriter**(Writer out)
✳		**BufferedWriter**(Writer out, int sz)
	void	**close**() *throws* IOException
	void	**flush**() *throws* IOException
	void	**newLine**() *throws* IOException
	void	**write**(char[] cbuf, int off, int len) *throws* IOException
	void	**write**(int c) *throws* IOException
	void	**write**(String s, int off, int len) *throws* IOException

Byte   java.lang

```
Object
    ➡Number                              java.io.Serializable
        ➡Byte                            Comparable
```

	✳		**Byte**(byte value)
	✳		**Byte**(String s) *throws* NumberFormatException
		byte	**byteValue**()
1.2		int	**compareTo**(Byte anotherByte)
1.2		int	**compareTo**(Object o)
	❑	Byte	**decode**(String nm) *throws* NumberFormatException
		double	**doubleValue**()
		boolean	**equals**(Object obj)
		float	**floatValue**()
		int	**hashCode**()
		int	**intValue**()
		long	**longValue**()
	🔒■	byte	**MAX_VALUE**
	🔒■	byte	**MIN_VALUE**
	❑	byte	**parseByte**(String s) *throws* NumberFormatException
	❑	byte	**parseByte**(String s, int radix)
			throws NumberFormatException
		short	**shortValue**()
		String	**toString**()
	❑	String	**toString**(byte b)
	🔒■	Class	**TYPE**
	❑	Byte	**valueOf**(String s) *throws* NumberFormatException
	❑	Byte	**valueOf**(String s, int radix)
			throws NumberFormatException

ByteArrayInputStream   java.io

```
Object
    ➡InputStream
        ➡ByteArrayInputStream
```

		int	**available**()
	🔒◆	byte[]	**buf**
	✳		**ByteArrayInputStream**(byte[] buf)
	✳		**ByteArrayInputStream**(byte[] buf, int offset,
			int length)
		void	**close**() *throws* IOException
	🔒◆	int	**count**
1.1	🔒◆	int	**mark**
1.1		void	**mark**(int readAheadLimit)
1.1		boolean	**markSupported**()
	🔒◆	int	**pos**
		int	**read**()
		int	**read**(byte[] b, int off, int len)
		void	**reset**()
		long	**skip**(long n)

ByteArrayOutputStream   java.io

```
Object
  ➥OutputStream
      ➥ByteArrayOutputStream
```

⚘◆	byte[]	**buf**
✳		**ByteArrayOutputStream**()
✳		**ByteArrayOutputStream**(int size)
	void	**close**() *throws* IOException
⚘◆	int	**count**
	void	**reset**()
	int	**size**()
	byte[]	**toByteArray**()
1.1	String	**toString**()
1.1	String	**toString**(String enc)
		throws UnsupportedEncodingException
	void	**write**(byte[] b, int off, int len)
	void	**write**(int b)
	void	**writeTo**(OutputStream out) *throws* IOException

Calendar   java.util

```
Object
  ➥Calendar                              java.io.Serializable, Cloneable
```

○	void	**add**(int field, int amount)
	boolean	**after**(Object when)
⚘■	int	**AM**
⚘■	int	**AM_PM**
⚘■	int	**APRIL**
⚘◆	boolean	**areFieldsSet**
⚘■	int	**AUGUST**
	boolean	**before**(Object when)
✳◆		**Calendar**()
✳◆		**Calendar**(TimeZone zone, Locale aLocale)
●	void	**clear**()
●	void	**clear**(int field)
	Object	**clone**()
◆	void	**complete**()
○◆	void	**computeFields**()
○◆	void	**computeTime**()
⚘■	int	**DATE**
⚘■	int	**DAY_OF_MONTH**
⚘■	int	**DAY_OF_WEEK**
⚘■	int	**DAY_OF_WEEK_IN_MONTH**
⚘■	int	**DAY_OF_YEAR**
⚘■	int	**DECEMBER**
⚘■	int	**DST_OFFSET**
	boolean	**equals**(Object obj)
⚘■	int	**ERA**
⚘■	int	**FEBRUARY**

	✍■	int	**FIELD_COUNT**
	✍◆	int[]	**fields**
	✍■	int	**FRIDAY**
	●	int	**get**(int field)
1.2		int	**getActualMaximum**(int field)
1.2		int	**getActualMinimum**(int field)
	❑	Locale[]	**getAvailableLocales**()
		int	**getFirstDayOfWeek**()
	○	int	**getGreatestMinimum**(int field)
	❑	Calendar	**getInstance**()
	❑	Calendar	**getInstance**(Locale aLocale)
	❑	Calendar	**getInstance**(TimeZone zone)
	❑	Calendar	**getInstance**(TimeZone zone, Locale aLocale)
	○	int	**getLeastMaximum**(int field)
	○	int	**getMaximum**(int field)
		int	**getMinimalDaysInFirstWeek**()
	○	int	**getMinimum**(int field)
	●	Date	**getTime**()
	◆	long	**getTimeInMillis**()
		TimeZone	**getTimeZone**()
1.2		int	**hashCode**()
	✍■	int	**HOUR**
	✍■	int	**HOUR_OF_DAY**
	●◆	int	**internalGet**(int field)
		boolean	**isLenient**()
	✍◆	boolean[]	**isSet**
	●	boolean	**isSet**(int field)
	✍◆	boolean	**isTimeSet**
	✍■	int	**JANUARY**
	✍■	int	**JULY**
	✍■	int	**JUNE**
	✍■	int	**MARCH**
	✍■	int	**MAY**
	✍■	int	**MILLISECOND**
	✍■	int	**MINUTE**
	✍■	int	**MONDAY**
	✍■	int	**MONTH**
	✍■	int	**NOVEMBER**
	✍■	int	**OCTOBER**
	✍■	int	**PM**
	○	void	**roll**(int field, boolean up)
1.2		void	**roll**(int field, int amount)
	✍■	int	**SATURDAY**
	✍■	int	**SECOND**
	✍■	int	**SEPTEMBER**
	●	void	**set**(int field, int value)
	●	void	**set**(int year, int month, int date)
	●	void	**set**(int year, int month, int date, int hour, int minute)
	●	void	**set**(int year, int month, int date, int hour, int minute, int second)
		void	**setFirstDayOfWeek**(int value)

	void	**setLenient**(boolean lenient)
	void	**setMinimalDaysInFirstWeek**(int value)
●	void	**setTime**(Date date)
◆	void	**setTimeInMillis**(long millis)
	void	**setTimeZone**(TimeZone value)
✎■	int	**SUNDAY**
✎■	int	**THURSDAY**
✎◆	long	**time**
	String	**toString**()
✎■	int	**TUESDAY**
✎■	int	**UNDECEMBER**
✎■	int	**WEDNESDAY**
✎■	int	**WEEK_OF_MONTH**
✎■	int	**WEEK_OF_YEAR**
✎■	int	**YEAR**
✎■	int	**ZONE_OFFSET**

Certificate   java.security

Certificate

	void	**decode**(java.io.InputStream stream)
		throws KeyException, java.io.IOException
	void	**encode**(java.io.OutputStream stream)
		throws KeyException, java.io.IOException
	String	**getFormat**()
	Principal	**getGuarantor**()
	Principal	**getPrincipal**()
	PublicKey	**getPublicKey**()
	String	**toString**(boolean detailed)

Certificate.CertificateRep   java.security.cert

Object
➥Certificate.CertificateRep   java.io.Serializable

❋◆		**Certificate.CertificateRep**(String type, byte[] data)
◆	Object	**readResolve**() *throws* java.io.ObjectStreamException

CertificateEncodingException   java.security.cert

Object
➥Throwable   java.io.Serializable
  ➥Exception
    ➥java.security.GeneralSecurityException
      ➥CertificateException
        ➥CertificateEncodingException

❋	**CertificateEncodingException**()
❋	**CertificateEncodingException**(String message)

CertificateException	java.security.cert

```
Object
  ➡Throwable                          java.io.Serializable
      ➡Exception
          ➡java.security.GeneralSecurityException
              ➡CertificateException
```

✲	CertificateException()
✲	CertificateException(String msg)

CertificateExpiredException	java.security.cert

```
Object
  ➡Throwable                          java.io.Serializable
      ➡Exception
          ➡java.security.GeneralSecurityException
              ➡CertificateException
                  ➡CertificateExpiredException
```

✲	CertificateExpiredException()
✲	CertificateExpiredException(String message)

CertificateFactory	java.security.cert

```
Object
  ➡CertificateFactory
```

✲♦		CertificateFactory(
		CertificateFactorySpi certFacSpi,
		java.security.Provider provider, String type)
●	Certificate	generateCertificate(java.io.InputStream inStream)
		throws CertificateException
●	java.util.Collection	generateCertificates(java.io.InputStream inStream)
		throws CertificateException
●	CRL	generateCRL(java.io.InputStream inStream)
		throws CRLException
●	java.util.Collection	generateCRLs(java.io.InputStream inStream)
		throws CRLException
■	CertificateFactory	getInstance(String type)
		throws CertificateException
■	CertificateFactory	getInstance(String type, String provider)
		throws CertificateException,
		java.security.NoSuchProviderException
●	java.security.Provider	getProvider()
●	String	getType()

CertificateFactorySpi	java.security.cert

```
Object
  ➡CertificateFactorySpi
```

✳		**CertificateFactorySpi**()
○	Certificate	**engineGenerateCertificate**(java.io.InputStream inStream) *throws* CertificateException
○	java.util.Collection	**engineGenerateCertificates**(java.io.InputStream inStream) *throws* CertificateException
○	CRL	**engineGenerateCRL**(java.io.InputStream inStream) *throws* CRLException
○	java.util.Collection	**engineGenerateCRLs**(java.io.InputStream inStream) *throws* CRLException

CertificateNotYetValidException   `java.security.cert`

```
Object
  ➥Throwable                          java.io.Serializable
    ➥Exception
      ➥java.security.GeneralSecurityException
        ➥CertificateException
          ➥CertificateNotYetValidException
```

✳	**CertificateNotYetValidException**()
✳	**CertificateNotYetValidException**(String message)

CertificateParsingException   `java.security.cert`

```
Object
  ➥Throwable                          java.io.Serializable
    ➥Exception
      ➥java.security.GeneralSecurityException
        ➥CertificateException
          ➥CertificateParsingException
```

✳	**CertificateParsingException**()
✳	**CertificateParsingException**(String message)

Character   `java.lang`

```
Object
  ➥Character                    java.io.Serializable, Comparable
```

	✳		**Character**(char value)
		char	**charValue**()
1.1	✍▪	byte	**COMBINING_SPACING_MARK**
1.2		int	**compareTo**(Character anotherCharacter)
1.2		int	**compareTo**(Object o)
1.1	✍▪	byte	**CONNECTOR_PUNCTUATION**
1.1	✍▪	byte	**CONTROL**
1.1	✍▪	byte	**CURRENCY_SYMBOL**
1.1	✍▪	byte	**DASH_PUNCTUATION**

Version		Return	Member
1.1	⚹■	byte	DECIMAL_DIGIT_NUMBER
	❑	int	digit(char ch, int radix)
1.1	⚹■	byte	ENCLOSING_MARK
1.1	⚹■	byte	END_PUNCTUATION
		boolean	equals(Object obj)
	❑	char	forDigit(int digit, int radix)
1.1	⚹■	byte	FORMAT
1.1	❑	int	getNumericValue(char ch)
1.1	❑	int	getType(char ch)
		int	hashCode()
1.0.2	❑	boolean	isDefined(char ch)
	❑	boolean	isDigit(char ch)
1.1	❑	boolean	isIdentifierIgnorable(char ch)
1.1	❑	boolean	isISOControl(char ch)
1.1	❑	boolean	isJavaIdentifierPart(char ch)
1.1	❑	boolean	isJavaIdentifierStart(char ch)
	❑	boolean	isLetter(char ch)
1.0.2	❑	boolean	isLetterOrDigit(char ch)
	❑	boolean	isLowerCase(char ch)
1.1	❑	boolean	isSpaceChar(char ch)
1.0.2	❑	boolean	isTitleCase(char ch)
1.1	❑	boolean	isUnicodeIdentifierPart(char ch)
1.1	❑	boolean	isUnicodeIdentifierStart(char ch)
1.0	❑	boolean	isUpperCase(char ch)
1.1	❑	boolean	isWhitespace(char ch)
1.1	⚹■	byte	LETTER_NUMBER
1.1	⚹■	byte	LINE_SEPARATOR
1.1	⚹■	byte	LOWERCASE_LETTER
1.1	⚹■	byte	MATH_SYMBOL
	⚹■	int	MAX_RADIX
1.0.2	⚹■	char	MAX_VALUE
	⚹■	int	MIN_RADIX
1.0.2	⚹■	char	MIN_VALUE
1.1	⚹■	byte	MODIFIER_LETTER
1.1	⚹■	byte	MODIFIER_SYMBOL
1.1	⚹■	byte	NON_SPACING_MARK
1.1	⚹■	byte	OTHER_LETTER
1.1	⚹■	byte	OTHER_NUMBER
1.1	⚹■	byte	OTHER_PUNCTUATION
1.1	⚹■	byte	OTHER_SYMBOL
1.1	⚹■	byte	PARAGRAPH_SEPARATOR
1.1	⚹■	byte	PRIVATE_USE
1.1	⚹■	byte	SPACE_SEPARATOR
1.1	⚹■	byte	START_PUNCTUATION
1.1	⚹■	byte	SURROGATE
1.1	⚹■	byte	TITLECASE_LETTER
	❑	char	toLowerCase(char ch)
		String	toString()
1.0.2	❑	char	toTitleCase(char ch)
	❑	char	toUpperCase(char ch)
1.1	⚹■	Class	TYPE

| 1.1 | ✍■ | byte | UNASSIGNED |
| 1.1 | ✍■ | byte | UPPERCASE_LETTER |

Character.Subset   java.lang

Object
　➡Character.Subset

	❋◆		Character.Subset(String name)
	●	boolean	equals(Object obj)
	●	int	hashCode()
	●	String	toString()

Character.UnicodeBlock   java.lang

Object
　➡Character.Subset
　　➡Character.UnicodeBlock

✍■	Character.UnicodeBlock	ALPHABETIC_PRESENTATION_FORMS
✍■	Character.UnicodeBlock	ARABIC
✍■	Character.UnicodeBlock	ARABIC_PRESENTATION_FORMS_A
✍■	Character.UnicodeBlock	ARABIC_PRESENTATION_FORMS_B
✍■	Character.UnicodeBlock	ARMENIAN
✍■	Character.UnicodeBlock	ARROWS
✍■	Character.UnicodeBlock	BASIC_LATIN
✍■	Character.UnicodeBlock	BENGALI
✍■	Character.UnicodeBlock	BLOCK_ELEMENTS
✍■	Character.UnicodeBlock	BOPOMOFO
✍■	Character.UnicodeBlock	BOX_DRAWING
✍■	Character.UnicodeBlock	CJK_COMPATIBILITY
✍■	Character.UnicodeBlock	CJK_COMPATIBILITY_FORMS
✍■	Character.UnicodeBlock	CJK_COMPATIBILITY_IDEOGRAPHS
✍■	Character.UnicodeBlock	CJK_SYMBOLS_AND_PUNCTUATION
✍■	Character.UnicodeBlock	CJK_UNIFIED_IDEOGRAPHS
✍■	Character.UnicodeBlock	COMBINING_DIACRITICAL_MARKS
✍■	Character.UnicodeBlock	COMBINING_HALF_MARKS
✍■	Character.UnicodeBlock	COMBINING_MARKS_FOR_SYMBOLS
✍■	Character.UnicodeBlock	CONTROL_PICTURES
✍■	Character.UnicodeBlock	CURRENCY_SYMBOLS
✍■	Character.UnicodeBlock	CYRILLIC
✍■	Character.UnicodeBlock	DEVANAGARI
✍■	Character.UnicodeBlock	DINGBATS
✍■	Character.UnicodeBlock	ENCLOSED_ALPHANUMERICS
✍■	Character.UnicodeBlock	ENCLOSED_CJK_LETTERS_AND_MONTHS
✍■	Character.UnicodeBlock	GENERAL_PUNCTUATION
✍■	Character.UnicodeBlock	GEOMETRIC_SHAPES
✍■	Character.UnicodeBlock	GEORGIAN
✍■	Character.UnicodeBlock	GREEK
✍■	Character.UnicodeBlock	GREEK_EXTENDED

		Character.UnicodeBlock	**GUJARATI**
✎■		Character.UnicodeBlock	**GURMUKHI**
✎■		Character.UnicodeBlock	**HALFWIDTH_AND_FULLWIDTH_FORMS**
✎■		Character.UnicodeBlock	**HANGUL_COMPATIBILITY_JAMO**
✎■		Character.UnicodeBlock	**HANGUL_JAMO**
✎■		Character.UnicodeBlock	**HANGUL_SYLLABLES**
✎■		Character.UnicodeBlock	**HEBREW**
✎■		Character.UnicodeBlock	**HIRAGANA**
✎■		Character.UnicodeBlock	**IPA_EXTENSIONS**
✎■		Character.UnicodeBlock	**KANBUN**
✎■		Character.UnicodeBlock	**KANNADA**
✎■		Character.UnicodeBlock	**KATAKANA**
✎■		Character.UnicodeBlock	**LAO**
✎■		Character.UnicodeBlock	**LATIN_1_SUPPLEMENT**
✎■		Character.UnicodeBlock	**LATIN_EXTENDED_A**
✎■		Character.UnicodeBlock	**LATIN_EXTENDED_ADDITIONAL**
✎■		Character.UnicodeBlock	**LATIN_EXTENDED_B**
✎■		Character.UnicodeBlock	**LETTERLIKE_SYMBOLS**
✎■		Character.UnicodeBlock	**MALAYALAM**
✎■		Character.UnicodeBlock	**MATHEMATICAL_OPERATORS**
✎■		Character.UnicodeBlock	**MISCELLANEOUS_SYMBOLS**
✎■		Character.UnicodeBlock	**MISCELLANEOUS_TECHNICAL**
✎■		Character.UnicodeBlock	**NUMBER_FORMS**
❑		Character.UnicodeBlock	**of**(char c)
✎■		Character.UnicodeBlock	**OPTICAL_CHARACTER_RECOGNITION**
✎■		Character.UnicodeBlock	**ORIYA**
✎■		Character.UnicodeBlock	**PRIVATE_USE_AREA**
✎■		Character.UnicodeBlock	**SMALL_FORM_VARIANTS**
✎■		Character.UnicodeBlock	**SPACING_MODIFIER_LETTERS**
✎■		Character.UnicodeBlock	**SPECIALS**
✎■		Character.UnicodeBlock	**SUPERSCRIPTS_AND_SUBSCRIPTS**
✎■		Character.UnicodeBlock	**SURROGATES_AREA**
✎■		Character.UnicodeBlock	**TAMIL**
✎■		Character.UnicodeBlock	**TELUGU**
✎■		Character.UnicodeBlock	**THAI**
✎■		Character.UnicodeBlock	**TIBETAN**

CharacterIterator			**java.text**
CharacterIterator		Cloneable	
	Object	**clone**()	
	char	**current**()	
✎■	char	**DONE**	
	char	**first**()	
	int	**getBeginIndex**()	
	int	**getEndIndex**()	
	int	**getIndex**()	
	char	**last**()	
	char	**next**()	
	char	**previous**()	
	char	**setIndex**(int position)	

CharArrayReader   java.io

```
Object
  ➡Reader
      ➡CharArrayReader
```

✍◆	char[]	**buf**
✳		**CharArrayReader**(char[] buf)
✳		**CharArrayReader**(char[] buf, int offset, int length)
	void	**close**()
✍◆	int	**count**
	void	**mark**(int readAheadLimit) *throws* IOException
✍◆	int	**markedPos**
	boolean	**markSupported**()
✍◆	int	**pos**
	int	**read**() *throws* IOException
	int	**read**(char[] b, int off, int len) *throws* IOException
	boolean	**ready**() *throws* IOException
	void	**reset**() *throws* IOException
	long	**skip**(long n) *throws* IOException

CharArrayWriter   java.io

```
Object
  ➡Writer
      ➡CharArrayWriter
```

✍◆	char[]	**buf**
✳		**CharArrayWriter**()
✳		**CharArrayWriter**(int initialSize)
	void	**close**()
✍◆	int	**count**
	void	**flush**()
	void	**reset**()
	int	**size**()
	char[]	**toCharArray**()
	String	**toString**()
	void	**write**(char[] c, int off, int len)
	void	**write**(int c)
	void	**write**(String str, int off, int len)
	void	**writeTo**(Writer out) *throws* IOException

CharConversionException   java.io

```
Object
  ➡Throwable                        Serializable
      ➡Exception
          ➡IOException
              ➡CharConversionException
```

✳	**CharConversionException**()
✳	**CharConversionException**(String s)

CheckedInputStream		java.util.zip

Object
  ➡java.io.InputStream
    ➡java.io.FilterInputStream
      ➡CheckedInputStream

✳		**CheckedInputStream**(java.io.InputStream in, Checksum cksum)
	Checksum	**getChecksum**()
	int	**read**() *throws* java.io.IOException
	int	**read**(byte[] buf, int off, int len) *throws* java.io.IOException
	long	**skip**(long n) *throws* java.io.IOException

CheckedOutputStream		java.util.zip

Object
  ➡java.io.OutputStream
    ➡java.io.FilterOutputStream
      ➡CheckedOutputStream

✳		**CheckedOutputStream**(java.io.OutputStream out, Checksum cksum)
	Checksum	**getChecksum**()
	void	**write**(byte[] b, int off, int len) *throws* java.io.IOException
	void	**write**(int b) *throws* java.io.IOException

Checksum		java.util.zip

Checksum

	long	**getValue**()
	void	**reset**()
	void	**update**(byte[] b, int off, int len)
	void	**update**(int b)

ChoiceFormat		java.text

Object
  ➡Format   java.io.Serializable, Cloneable
    ➡NumberFormat
      ➡ChoiceFormat

	void	**applyPattern**(String newPattern)
✳		**ChoiceFormat**(double[] limits, String[] formats)
✳		**ChoiceFormat**(String newPattern)
	Object	**clone**()
	boolean	**equals**(Object obj)
	StringBuffer	**format**(double number, StringBuffer toAppendTo, FieldPosition status)

	StringBuffer	**format**(long number, StringBuffer toAppendTo, FieldPosition status)
	Object[]	**getFormats**()
	double[]	**getLimits**()
	int	**hashCode**()
■	double	**nextDouble**(double d)
❏	double	**nextDouble**(double d, boolean positive)
■	Number	**parse**(String text, ParsePosition status)
■	double	**previousDouble**(double d)
	void	**setChoices**(double[] limits, String[] formats)
	String	**toPattern**()

Class   java.lang

Object
  ➥Class   java.io.Serializable

	❏	Class	**forName**(String className) *throws* ClassNotFoundException
1.2	❏	Class	**forName**(String name, boolean initialize, ClassLoader loader) *throws* ClassNotFoundException
1.1		Class[]	**getClasses**()
		ClassLoader	**getClassLoader**()
1.1		Class	**getComponentType**()
1.1		reflect.Constructor	**getConstructor**(Class[] parameterTypes) *throws* NoSuchMethodException, SecurityException
1.1		reflect.Constructor[]	**getConstructors**() *throws* SecurityException
1.1		Class[]	**getDeclaredClasses**() *throws* SecurityException
1.1		reflect.Constructor	**getDeclaredConstructor**(Class[] parameterTypes) *throws* NoSuchMethodException, SecurityException
1.1		reflect.Constructor[]	**getDeclaredConstructors**() *throws* SecurityException
1.1		reflect.Field	**getDeclaredField**(String name) *throws* NoSuchFieldException, SecurityException
1.1		reflect.Field[]	**getDeclaredFields**() *throws* SecurityException
1.1		reflect.Method	**getDeclaredMethod**(String name, Class[] parameterTypes) *throws* NoSuchMethodException, SecurityException
1.1		reflect.Method[]	**getDeclaredMethods**() *throws* SecurityException
1.1		Class	**getDeclaringClass**()
1.1		reflect.Field	**getField**(String name) *throws* NoSuchFieldException, SecurityException
1.1		reflect.Field[]	**getFields**() *throws* SecurityException
		Class[]	**getInterfaces**()
1.1		reflect.Method	**getMethod**(String name, Class[] parameterTypes) *throws* NoSuchMethodException, SecurityException
1.1		reflect.Method[]	**getMethods**() *throws* SecurityException
1.1		int	**getModifiers**()
		String	**getName**()
		Package	**getPackage**()
1.2		java.security.¬ ProtectionDomain	**getProtectionDomain**()

1.1	java.net.URL	**getResource**(String name)
1.1	java.io.InputStream	**getResourceAsStream**(String name)
1.1	Object[]	**getSigners**()
	Class	**getSuperclass**()
1.1	boolean	**isArray**()
1.1	boolean	**isAssignableFrom**(Class cls)
1.1	boolean	**isInstance**(Object obj)
	boolean	**isInterface**()
1.1	boolean	**isPrimitive**()
	Object	**newInstance**() *throws* InstantiationException, IllegalAccessException
	String	**toString**()

ClassCastException   java.lang

```
Object
  ➥Throwable                        java.io.Serializable
    ➥Exception
      ➥RuntimeException
        ➥ClassCastException
```

✱	**ClassCastException**()
✱	**ClassCastException**(String s)

ClassCircularityError   java.lang

```
Object
  ➥Throwable                        java.io.Serializable
    ➥Error
      ➥LinkageError
        ➥ClassCircularityError
```

✱	**ClassCircularityError**()
✱	**ClassCircularityError**(String s)

ClassFormatError   java.lang

```
Object
  ➥Throwable                        java.io.Serializable
    ➥Error
      ➥LinkageError
        ➥ClassFormatError
```

✱	**ClassFormatError**()
✱	**ClassFormatError**(String s)

ClassLoader   java.lang

```
Object
  ➥ClassLoader
```

	✳◆		ClassLoader()
1.2	✳◆		ClassLoader(ClassLoader parent)
1.1	●◆	Class	defineClass(String name, byte[] b, int off, int len) *throws* ClassFormatError
	●◆	Class	defineClass(String name, byte[] b, int off, int len, java.security.ProtectionDomain protectionDomain) *throws* ClassFormatError
1.2	◆	Package	definePackage(String name, String specTitle, String specVersion, String specVendor, String implTitle, String implVersion, String implVendor, java.net.URL sealBase) *throws* IllegalArgumentException
1.2	◆	Class	findClass(String name) *throws* ClassNotFoundException
1.2	◆	String	findLibrary(String libname)
1.1	●◆	Class	findLoadedClass(String name)
1.2	◆	java.net.URL	findResource(String name)
1.2	◆	java.util.Enumeration	findResources(String name) *throws* java.io.IOException
	●◆	Class	findSystemClass(String name) *throws* ClassNotFoundException
1.2	◆	Package	getPackage(String name)
1.2	◆	Package[]	getPackages()
1.2	●	ClassLoader	getParent()
1.1		java.net.URL	getResource(String name)
1.1		java.io.InputStream	getResourceAsStream(String name)
1.2	●	java.util.Enumeration	getResources(String name) *throws* java.io.IOException
1.2	▢	ClassLoader	getSystemClassLoader()
1.1	▢	java.net.URL	getSystemResource(String name)
1.1	▢	java.io.InputStream	getSystemResourceAsStream(String name)
1.2	▢	java.util.Enumeration	getSystemResources(String name) *throws* java.io.IOException
		Class	loadClass(String name) *throws* ClassNotFoundException
	◆	Class	loadClass(String name, boolean resolve) *throws* ClassNotFoundException
	●◆	void	resolveClass(Class c)
1.1	●◆	void	setSigners(Class c, Object[] signers)

ClassNotFoundException   `java.lang`

```
Object
  ➥Throwable                        java.io.Serializable
    ➥Exception
      ➥ClassNotFoundException
```

	✳		ClassNotFoundException()
	✳		ClassNotFoundException(String s)
1.2	✳		ClassNotFoundException(String s, Throwable ex)
1.2		Throwable	getException()
		void	printStackTrace()

	void	**printStackTrace**(java.io.PrintStream ps)
	void	**printStackTrace**(java.io.PrintWriter pw)

Cloneable　　　　　　　　　　　　　　　　　　　　　java.lang

Cloneable

CloneNotSupportedException　　　　　　　　　　　　java.lang

Object
　➡Throwable　　　　　　　　　　java.io.Serializable
　　➡Exception
　　　➡CloneNotSupportedException

✳		**CloneNotSupportedException**()
✳		**CloneNotSupportedException**(String s)

CodeSource　　　　　　　　　　　　　　　　　　　　java.security

Object
　➡CodeSource　　　　　　　　　　java.io.Serializable

✳		**CodeSource**(java.net.URL url,
		cert.Certificate[] certs)
	boolean	**equals**(Object obj)
●	cert.Certificate[]	**getCertificates**()
●	java.net.URL	**getLocation**()
	int	**hashCode**()
	boolean	**implies**(CodeSource codesource)
	String	**toString**()

CollationElementIterator　　　　　　　　　　　　　java.text

Object
　➡CollationElementIterator

	int	**getMaxExpansion**(int order)
	int	**getOffset**()
	int	**next**()
⬛	int	**NULLORDER**
	int	**previous**()
⬛	int	**primaryOrder**(int order)
	void	**reset**()
⬛	short	**secondaryOrder**(int order)
	void	**setOffset**(int newOffset)
	void	**setText**(CharacterIterator source)
	void	**setText**(String source)
⬛	short	**tertiaryOrder**(int order)

CollationKey   java.text

Object
   ➡CollationKey   Comparable

1.2	int	**compareTo**(CollationKey target)
	int	**compareTo**(Object o)
	boolean	**equals**(Object target)
	String	**getSourceString**()
	int	**hashCode**()
	byte[]	**toByteArray**()

Collator   java.text

Object
   ➡Collator   java.util.Comparator, Cloneable

✐■	int	**CANONICAL_DECOMPOSITION**
	Object	**clone**()
✳◆		**Collator**()
1.2	int	**compare**(Object o1, Object o2)
○	int	**compare**(String source, String target)
	boolean	**equals**(Object that)
	boolean	**equals**(String source, String target)
✐■	int	**FULL_DECOMPOSITION**
❑	java.util.Locale[]	**getAvailableLocales**()
○	CollationKey	**getCollationKey**(String source)
	int	**getDecomposition**()
❑	Collator	**getInstance**()
❑	Collator	**getInstance**(java.util.Locale desiredLocale)
	int	**getStrength**()
○	int	**hashCode**()
✐■	int	**IDENTICAL**
✐■	int	**NO_DECOMPOSITION**
✐■	int	**PRIMARY**
✐■	int	**SECONDARY**
	void	**setDecomposition**(int decompositionMode)
	void	**setStrength**(int newStrength)
✐■	int	**TERTIARY**

Collection   java.util

Collection

	boolean	**add**(Object o)
	boolean	**addAll**(Collection c)
	void	**clear**()
	boolean	**contains**(Object o)
	boolean	**containsAll**(Collection c)
	boolean	**equals**(Object o)
	int	**hashCode**()

boolean	**isEmpty**()
Iterator	**iterator**()
boolean	**remove**(Object o)
boolean	**removeAll**(Collection c)
boolean	**retainAll**(Collection c)
int	**size**()
Object[]	**toArray**()
Object[]	**toArray**(Object[] a)

Collections   java.util

Object
➡Collections

		int	**binarySearch**(List list, Object key)
		int	**binarySearch**(List list, Object key, Comparator c)
		void	**copy**(List dest, List src)
		List	**EMPTY_LIST**
1.3		Map	**EMPTY_MAP**
		Set	**EMPTY_SET**
		Enumeration	**enumeration**(Collection c)
		void	**fill**(List list, Object o)
		Object	**max**(Collection coll)
		Object	**max**(Collection coll, Comparator comp)
		Object	**min**(Collection coll)
		Object	**min**(Collection coll, Comparator comp)
		List	**nCopies**(int n, Object o)
		void	**reverse**(List l)
		Comparator	**reverseOrder**()
		void	**shuffle**(List list)
		void	**shuffle**(List list, Random rnd)
		Set	**singleton**(Object o)
1.3		List	**singletonList**(Object o)
1.3		Map	**singletonMap**(Object key, Object value)
		void	**sort**(List list)
		void	**sort**(List list, Comparator c)
		Collection	**synchronizedCollection**(Collection c)
		List	**synchronizedList**(List list)
		Map	**synchronizedMap**(Map m)
		Set	**synchronizedSet**(Set s)
		SortedMap	**synchronizedSortedMap**(SortedMap m)
		SortedSet	**synchronizedSortedSet**(SortedSet s)
		Collection	**unmodifiableCollection**(Collection c)
		List	**unmodifiableList**(List list)
		Map	**unmodifiableMap**(Map m)
		Set	**unmodifiableSet**(Set s)
		SortedMap	**unmodifiableSortedMap**(SortedMap m)
		SortedSet	**unmodifiableSortedSet**(SortedSet s)

Comparable — java.lang

Comparable

	int	**compareTo**(Object o)

Comparator — java.util

Comparator

	int	**compare**(Object o1, Object o2)
	boolean	**equals**(Object obj)

Compiler — java.lang

Object
➥Compiler

❑	Object	**command**(Object any)
❑	boolean	**compileClass**(Class clazz)
❑	boolean	**compileClasses**(String string)
❑	void	**disable**()
❑	void	**enable**()

ConcurrentModificationException — java.util

Object
➥Throwable — java.io.Serializable
➥Exception
➥RuntimeException
➥ConcurrentModificationException

✻		**ConcurrentModificationException**()
✻		**ConcurrentModificationException**(String message)

ConnectException — java.net

Object
➥Throwable — java.io.Serializable
➥Exception
➥java.io.IOException
➥SocketException
➥ConnectException

✻		**ConnectException**()
✻		**ConnectException**(String msg)

Connection   javax.microedition.io

Connection

void **close**() *throws* java.io.IOException

ConnectionNotFoundException   javax.microedition.io

Object
  ➥Throwable   java.io.Serializable
    ➥Exception
      ➥java.io.IOException
        ➥ConnectionNotFoundException

❋	**ConnectionNotFoundException**()
❋	**ConnectionNotFoundException**(String s)

Connector   javax.microedition.io

Object
  ➥Connector

❏	Connection	**open**(String name) *throws* java.io.IOException
❏	Connection	**open**(String name, int mode)
		throws java.io.IOException
❏	Connection	**open**(String name, int mode, boolean timeouts)
		throws java.io.IOException
❏	java.io.DataInput¬	**openDataInputStream**(String name)
	Stream	*throws* java.io.IOException
❏	java.io.DataOutput¬	**openDataOutputStream**(String name)
	Stream	*throws* java.io.IOException
❏	java.io.InputStream	**openInputStream**(String name)
		throws java.io.IOException
❏	java.io.OutputStream	**openOutputStream**(String name)
		throws java.io.IOException
✍▪	int	**READ**
✍▪	int	**READ_WRITE**
✍▪	int	**WRITE**

Constructor   java.lang.reflect

Object
  ➥AccessibleObject
    ➥Constructor   Member

boolean	**equals**(Object obj)
Class	**getDeclaringClass**()
Class[]	**getExceptionTypes**()
int	**getModifiers**()

```
          String  getName()
         Class[]  getParameterTypes()
             int  hashCode()
          Object  newInstance(Object[] initargs)
                    throws InstantiationException,
                           IllegalAccessException,
                           IllegalArgumentException,
                           InvocationTargetException
          String  toString()
```

ContentConnection   javax.microedition.io
ContentConnection   StreamConnection

```
          String  getEncoding()
            long  getLength()
          String  getType()
```

ContentHandler   java.net
Object
  ➥ContentHandler

```
  ✳                   ContentHandler()
  ○        Object  getContent(URLConnection urlc)
                      throws java.io.IOException
           Object  getContent(URLConnection urlc, Class[] classes)
                      throws java.io.IOException
```

ContentHandlerFactory   java.net
ContentHandlerFactory

```
  ContentHandler  createContentHandler(String mimetype)
```

CRC32   java.util.zip
Object
  ➥CRC32   Checksum

```
  ✳                   CRC32()
            long  getValue()
            void  reset()
            void  update(byte[] b)
            void  update(byte[] b, int off, int len)
            void  update(int b)
```

CRL   java.security.cert

```
Object
  ➡CRL
```

✳◆		**CRL**(String type)
●	String	**getType**()
○	boolean	**isRevoked**(Certificate cert)
○	String	**toString**()

CRLException   java.security.cert

```
Object
  ➡Throwable                            java.io.Serializable
    ➡Exception
      ➡java.security.GeneralSecurityException
        ➡CRLException
```

✳		**CRLException**()
✳		**CRLException**(String message)

DataFormatException   java.util.zip

```
Object
  ➡Throwable                            java.io.Serializable
    ➡Exception
      ➡DataFormatException
```

✳		**DataFormatException**()
✳		**DataFormatException**(String s)

Datagram   javax.microedition.io

```
Datagram                               java.io.DataInput, java.io.DataOutput
```

String	**getAddress**()
byte[]	**getData**()
int	**getLength**()
int	**getOffset**()
void	**reset**()
void	**setAddress**(Datagram reference)
void	**setAddress**(String addr) *throws* java.io.IOException
void	**setData**(byte[] buffer, int offset, int len)
void	**setLength**(int len)

DatagramConnection   javax.microedition.io

```
DatagramConnection                     Connection
```

int	**getMaximumLength**() *throws* java.io.IOException
int	**getNominalLength**() *throws* java.io.IOException

Datagram	**newDatagram**(byte[] buf, int size)
	throws java.io.IOException
Datagram	**newDatagram**(byte[] buf, int size, String addr)
	throws java.io.IOException
Datagram	**newDatagram**(int size) *throws* java.io.IOException
Datagram	**newDatagram**(int size, String addr)
	throws java.io.IOException
void	**receive**(Datagram dgram) *throws* java.io.IOException
void	**send**(Datagram dgram) *throws* java.io.IOException

DatagramPacket   java.net

Object
➥DatagramPacket

	❊		**DatagramPacket**(byte[] buf, int length)
	❊		**DatagramPacket**(byte[] buf, int length,
			InetAddress address, int port)
1.2	❊		**DatagramPacket**(byte[] buf, int offset, int length)
1.2	❊		**DatagramPacket**(byte[] buf, int offset, int length,
			InetAddress address, int port)
		InetAddress	**getAddress**()
		byte[]	**getData**()
		int	**getLength**()
1.2		int	**getOffset**()
		int	**getPort**()
1.1		void	**setAddress**(InetAddress iaddr)
1.1		void	**setData**(byte[] buf)
1.2		void	**setData**(byte[] buf, int offset, int length)
1.1		void	**setLength**(int length)
1.1		void	**setPort**(int iport)

DatagramSocket   java.net

Object
➥DatagramSocket

		void	**close**()
		void	**connect**(InetAddress address, int port)
	❊		**DatagramSocket**() *throws* SocketException
	❊		**DatagramSocket**(int port) *throws* SocketException
1.1	❊		**DatagramSocket**(int port, InetAddress laddr)
			throws SocketException
		void	**disconnect**()
		InetAddress	**getInetAddress**()
1.1		InetAddress	**getLocalAddress**()
		int	**getLocalPort**()
		int	**getPort**()
		int	**getReceiveBufferSize**() *throws* SocketException
		int	**getSendBufferSize**() *throws* SocketException
1.1		int	**getSoTimeout**() *throws* SocketException

	void	**receive**(DatagramPacket p)
		throws java.io.IOException
	void	**send**(DatagramPacket p) *throws* java.io.IOException
❑	void	**setDatagramSocketImplFactory**(
		DatagramSocketImplFactory fac)
		throws java.io.IOException
	void	**setReceiveBufferSize**(int size)
		throws SocketException
	void	**setSendBufferSize**(int size) *throws* SocketException
1.1	void	**setSoTimeout**(int timeout) *throws* SocketException

---

DatagramSocketImpl   java.net

Object
   ➡DatagramSocketImpl   SocketOptions

○◆	void	**bind**(int lport, InetAddress laddr)
		throws SocketException
○◆	void	**close**()
○◆	void	**create**() *throws* SocketException
❈		**DatagramSocketImpl**()
✍◆	java.io.FileDescriptor	**fd**
◆	java.io.FileDescriptor	**getFileDescriptor**()
◆	int	**getLocalPort**()
○◆	int	**getTimeToLive**() *throws* java.io.IOException
○◆	void	**join**(InetAddress inetaddr)
		throws java.io.IOException
○◆	void	**leave**(InetAddress inetaddr)
		throws java.io.IOException
✍◆	int	**localPort**
○◆	int	**peek**(InetAddress i) *throws* java.io.IOException
○◆	void	**receive**(DatagramPacket p)
		throws java.io.IOException
○◆	void	**send**(DatagramPacket p) *throws* java.io.IOException
○◆	void	**setTimeToLive**(int ttl) *throws* java.io.IOException

---

DatagramSocketImplFactory   java.net

DatagramSocketImplFactory

	DatagramSocketImpl	**createDatagramSocketImpl**()

DataInput   java.io

DataInput

	boolean	**readBoolean**() *throws* IOException
	byte	**readByte**() *throws* IOException
	char	**readChar**() *throws* IOException
	double	**readDouble**() *throws* IOException

```
       float  readFloat() throws IOException
        void  readFully(byte[] b) throws IOException
        void  readFully(byte[] b, int off, int len)
                   throws IOException
         int  readInt() throws IOException
      String  readLine() throws IOException
        long  readLong() throws IOException
       short  readShort() throws IOException
         int  readUnsignedByte() throws IOException
         int  readUnsignedShort() throws IOException
      String  readUTF() throws IOException
         int  skipBytes(int n) throws IOException
```

DataInputStream   java.io

```
Object
  ➥InputStream
      ➥FilterInputStream
          ➥DataInputStream              DataInput
```

```
  ✳                DataInputStream(InputStream in)
  ●          int  read(byte[] b) throws IOException
  ●          int  read(byte[] b, int off, int len) throws IOException
  ●      boolean  readBoolean() throws IOException
  ●         byte  readByte() throws IOException
  ●         char  readChar() throws IOException
  ●       double  readDouble() throws IOException
  ●        float  readFloat() throws IOException
  ●         void  readFully(byte[] b) throws IOException
  ●         void  readFully(byte[] b, int off, int len)
                      throws IOException
  ●          int  readInt() throws IOException
  ●       String  readLine() throws IOException
  ●         long  readLong() throws IOException
  ●        short  readShort() throws IOException
  ●          int  readUnsignedByte() throws IOException
  ●          int  readUnsignedShort() throws IOException
  ●       String  readUTF() throws IOException
  ■       String  readUTF(DataInput in) throws IOException
  ●          int  skipBytes(int n) throws IOException
```

DataOutput   java.io

```
DataOutput
```

```
        void  write(byte[] b) throws IOException
        void  write(byte[] b, int off, int len)
                  throws IOException
        void  write(int b) throws IOException
        void  writeBoolean(boolean v) throws IOException
        void  writeByte(int v) throws IOException
```

```
                    void  writeBytes(String s) throws IOException
                    void  writeChar(int v) throws IOException
                    void  writeChars(String s) throws IOException
                    void  writeDouble(double v) throws IOException
                    void  writeFloat(float v) throws IOException
                    void  writeInt(int v) throws IOException
                    void  writeLong(long v) throws IOException
                    void  writeShort(int v) throws IOException
                    void  writeUTF(String str) throws IOException
```

DataOutputStream	java.io

```
Object
  ➡OutputStream
      ➡FilterOutputStream
          ➡DataOutputStream              DataOutput
```

✳		**DataOutputStream**(OutputStream out)
	void	**flush**() throws IOException
●	int	**size**()
	void	**write**(byte[] b, int off, int len) throws IOException
	void	**write**(int b) throws IOException
●	void	**writeBoolean**(boolean v) throws IOException
●	void	**writeByte**(int v) throws IOException
●	void	**writeBytes**(String s) throws IOException
●	void	**writeChar**(int v) throws IOException
●	void	**writeChars**(String s) throws IOException
●	void	**writeDouble**(double v) throws IOException
●	void	**writeFloat**(float v) throws IOException
●	void	**writeInt**(int v) throws IOException
●	void	**writeLong**(long v) throws IOException
●	void	**writeShort**(int v) throws IOException
●	void	**writeUTF**(String str) throws IOException
⚐◆	int	**written**

Date	java.util

```
Object
  ➡Date                         java.io.Serializable, Cloneable, Comparable
```

	boolean	**after**(Date when)
	boolean	**before**(Date when)
	Object	**clone**()
1.2	int	**compareTo**(Date anotherDate)
1.2	int	**compareTo**(Object o)
✳		**Date**()
✳		**Date**(long date)
	boolean	**equals**(Object obj)
	long	**getTime**()
	int	**hashCode**()

	void	setTime(long time)
	String	toString()

DateFormat java.text

Object
→Format   java.io.Serializable, Cloneable
  →DateFormat

✍■	int	**AM_PM_FIELD**
✍◆	java.util.Calendar	**calendar**
	Object	**clone**()
✍■	int	**DATE_FIELD**
❋◆		**DateFormat**()
✍■	int	**DAY_OF_WEEK_FIELD**
✍■	int	**DAY_OF_WEEK_IN_MONTH_FIELD**
✍■	int	**DAY_OF_YEAR_FIELD**
✍■	int	**DEFAULT**
	boolean	**equals**(Object obj)
✍■	int	**ERA_FIELD**
●	String	**format**(java.util.Date date)
○	StringBuffer	**format**(java.util.Date date, StringBuffer toAppendTo, FieldPosition fieldPosition)
●	StringBuffer	**format**(Object obj, StringBuffer toAppendTo, FieldPosition fieldPosition)
✍■	int	**FULL**
❑	java.util.Locale[]	**getAvailableLocales**()
	java.util.Calendar	**getCalendar**()
■	DateFormat	**getDateInstance**()
■	DateFormat	**getDateInstance**(int style)
■	DateFormat	**getDateInstance**(int style, java.util.Locale aLocale)
■	DateFormat	**getDateTimeInstance**()
■	DateFormat	**getDateTimeInstance**(int dateStyle, int timeStyle)
■	DateFormat	**getDateTimeInstance**(int dateStyle, int timeStyle, java.util.Locale aLocale)
■	DateFormat	**getInstance**()
	NumberFormat	**getNumberFormat**()
■	DateFormat	**getTimeInstance**()
■	DateFormat	**getTimeInstance**(int style)
■	DateFormat	**getTimeInstance**(int style, java.util.Locale aLocale)
	java.util.TimeZone	**getTimeZone**()
	int	**hashCode**()
✍■	int	**HOUR_OF_DAY0_FIELD**
✍■	int	**HOUR_OF_DAY1_FIELD**
✍■	int	**HOUR0_FIELD**
✍■	int	**HOUR1_FIELD**
	boolean	**isLenient**()
✍■	int	**LONG**
✍■	int	**MEDIUM**
✍■	int	**MILLISECOND_FIELD**

✍■	int	MINUTE_FIELD
✍■	int	MONTH_FIELD
✍◆	NumberFormat	numberFormat
	java.util.Date	parse(String text) *throws* ParseException
○	java.util.Date	parse(String text, ParsePosition pos)
	Object	parseObject(String source, ParsePosition pos)
✍■	int	SECOND_FIELD
	void	setCalendar(java.util.Calendar newCalendar)
	void	setLenient(boolean lenient)
	void	setNumberFormat(NumberFormat newNumberFormat)
	void	setTimeZone(java.util.TimeZone zone)
✍■	int	SHORT
✍■	int	TIMEZONE_FIELD
✍■	int	WEEK_OF_MONTH_FIELD
✍■	int	WEEK_OF_YEAR_FIELD
✍■	int	YEAR_FIELD

DateFormatSymbols   java.text

Object
　→DateFormatSymbols   java.io.Serializable, Cloneable

	Object	clone()
❋		DateFormatSymbols()
❋		DateFormatSymbols(java.util.Locale locale)
	boolean	equals(Object obj)
	String[]	getAmPmStrings()
	String[]	getEras()
	String	getLocalPatternChars()
	String[]	getMonths()
	String[]	getShortMonths()
	String[]	getShortWeekdays()
	String[]	getWeekdays()
	String[][]	getZoneStrings()
	int	hashCode()
	void	setAmPmStrings(String[] newAmpms)
	void	setEras(String[] newEras)
	void	setLocalPatternChars(String newLocalPatternChars)
	void	setMonths(String[] newMonths)
	void	setShortMonths(String[] newShortMonths)
	void	setShortWeekdays(String[] newShortWeekdays)
	void	setWeekdays(String[] newWeekdays)
	void	setZoneStrings(String[][] newZoneStrings)

DecimalFormat   java.text

Object
　→Format   java.io.Serializable, Cloneable
　　→NumberFormat
　　　→DecimalFormat

	void	**applyLocalizedPattern**(String pattern)
	void	**applyPattern**(String pattern)
	Object	**clone**()
✷		**DecimalFormat**()
✷		**DecimalFormat**(String pattern)
✷		**DecimalFormat**(String pattern, DecimalFormatSymbols symbols)
	boolean	**equals**(Object obj)
	StringBuffer	**format**(double number, StringBuffer result, FieldPosition fieldPosition)
	StringBuffer	**format**(long number, StringBuffer result, FieldPosition fieldPosition)
	DecimalFormatSymbols	**getDecimalFormatSymbols**()
	int	**getGroupingSize**()
	int	**getMultiplier**()
	String	**getNegativePrefix**()
	String	**getNegativeSuffix**()
	String	**getPositivePrefix**()
	String	**getPositiveSuffix**()
	int	**hashCode**()
	boolean	**isDecimalSeparatorAlwaysShown**()
	Number	**parse**(String text, ParsePosition parsePosition)
	void	**setDecimalFormatSymbols**(DecimalFormatSymbols newSymbols)
	void	**setDecimalSeparatorAlwaysShown**(boolean newValue)
	void	**setGroupingSize**(int newValue)
	void	**setMaximumFractionDigits**(int newValue)
	void	**setMaximumIntegerDigits**(int newValue)
	void	**setMinimumFractionDigits**(int newValue)
	void	**setMinimumIntegerDigits**(int newValue)
	void	**setMultiplier**(int newValue)
	void	**setNegativePrefix**(String newValue)
	void	**setNegativeSuffix**(String newValue)
	void	**setPositivePrefix**(String newValue)
	void	**setPositiveSuffix**(String newValue)
	String	**toLocalizedPattern**()
	String	**toPattern**()

DecimalFormatSymbols   `java.text`

Object
  ➡DecimalFormatSymbols   Cloneable, java.io.Serializable

	Object	**clone**()
✷		**DecimalFormatSymbols**()
✷		**DecimalFormatSymbols**(java.util.Locale locale)
	boolean	**equals**(Object obj)
	String	**getCurrencySymbol**()
	char	**getDecimalSeparator**()
	char	**getDigit**()
	char	**getGroupingSeparator**()
	String	**getInfinity**()

	String	getInternationalCurrencySymbol()
	char	getMinusSign()
	char	getMonetaryDecimalSeparator()
	String	getNaN()
	char	getPatternSeparator()
	char	getPercent()
	char	getPerMill()
	char	getZeroDigit()
	int	hashCode()
	void	setCurrencySymbol(String currency)
	void	setDecimalSeparator(char decimalSeparator)
	void	setDigit(char digit)
	void	setGroupingSeparator(char groupingSeparator)
	void	setInfinity(String infinity)
	void	setInternationalCurrencySymbol(String currency)
	void	setMinusSign(char minusSign)
	void	setMonetaryDecimalSeparator(char sep)
	void	setNaN(String NaN)
	void	setPatternSeparator(char patternSeparator)
	void	setPercent(char percent)
	void	setPerMill(char perMill)
	void	setZeroDigit(char zeroDigit)

Deflater   java.util.zip

Object
→ Deflater

⚁■		int	BEST_COMPRESSION
⚁■		int	BEST_SPEED
⚁■		int	DEFAULT_COMPRESSION
⚁■		int	DEFAULT_STRATEGY
		int	deflate(byte[] b)
		int	deflate(byte[] b, int off, int len)
⚁■		int	DEFLATED
✳			Deflater()
✳			Deflater(int level)
✳			Deflater(int level, boolean nowrap)
		void	end()
⚁■		int	FILTERED
◆		void	finalize()
		void	finish()
	boolean		finished()
		int	getAdler()
		int	getTotalIn()
		int	getTotalOut()
⚁■		int	HUFFMAN_ONLY
	boolean		needsInput()
⚁■		int	NO_COMPRESSION
		void	reset()
		void	setDictionary(byte[] b)
		void	setDictionary(byte[] b, int off, int len)

void	**setInput**(byte[] b)	
void	**setInput**(byte[] b, int off, int len)	
void	**setLevel**(int level)	
void	**setStrategy**(int strategy)	

DeflaterOutputStream   `java.util.zip`

Object
    ↳java.io.OutputStream
        ↳java.io.FilterOutputStream
            ↳DeflaterOutputStream

✍◆	byte[]	**buf**
	void	**close**() *throws* java.io.IOException
✍◆	Deflater	**def**
◆	void	**deflate**() *throws* java.io.IOException
✳		**DeflaterOutputStream**(java.io.OutputStream out)
✳		**DeflaterOutputStream**(java.io.OutputStream out, Deflater def)
✳		**DeflaterOutputStream**(java.io.OutputStream out, Deflater def, int size)
	void	**finish**() *throws* java.io.IOException
	void	**write**(byte[] b, int off, int len) *throws* java.io.IOException
	void	**write**(int b) *throws* java.io.IOException

Dictionary   `java.util`

Object
    ↳Dictionary

✳		**Dictionary**()
○	Enumeration	**elements**()
○	Object	**get**(Object key)
○	boolean	**isEmpty**()
○	Enumeration	**keys**()
○	Object	**put**(Object key, Object value)
○	Object	**remove**(Object key)
○	int	**size**()

DigestException   `java.security`

Object
    ↳Throwable   java.io.Serializable
        ↳Exception
            ↳GeneralSecurityException
                ↳DigestException

✳		**DigestException**()
✳		**DigestException**(String msg)

DigestInputStream			java.security

```
Object
    ➥java.io.InputStream
        ➥java.io.FilterInputStream
            ➥DigestInputStream
```

✍◆ ❊	MessageDigest	**digest**	
		DigestInputStream(java.io.InputStream stream, MessageDigest digest)	
	MessageDigest	**getMessageDigest**()	
	void	**on**(boolean on)	
	int	**read**() *throws* java.io.IOException	
	int	**read**(byte[] b, int off, int len) *throws* java.io.IOException	
	void	**setMessageDigest**(MessageDigest digest)	
	String	**toString**()	

DigestOutputStream			java.security

```
Object
    ➥java.io.OutputStream
        ➥java.io.FilterOutputStream
            ➥DigestOutputStream
```

✍◆ ❊	MessageDigest	**digest**	
		DigestOutputStream(java.io.OutputStream stream, MessageDigest digest)	
	MessageDigest	**getMessageDigest**()	
	void	**on**(boolean on)	
	void	**setMessageDigest**(MessageDigest digest)	
	String	**toString**()	
	void	**write**(byte[] b, int off, int len) *throws* java.io.IOException	
	void	**write**(int b) *throws* java.io.IOException	

DomainCombiner		java.security

```
DomainCombiner
```

	ProtectionDomain[]	**combine**(ProtectionDomain[] currentDomains, ProtectionDomain[] assignedDomains)

Double		java.lang

```
Object
    ➥Number                          java.io.Serializable
        ➥Double                      Comparable
```

1.1		byte	**byteValue**()
1.2		int	**compareTo**(Double anotherDouble)

1.2		int	**compareTo**(Object o)
	❊		**Double**(double value)
	❊		**Double**(String s) *throws* NumberFormatException
	❏	long	**doubleToLongBits**(double value)
	❏	long	**doubleToRawLongBits**(double value)
		double	**doubleValue**()
		boolean	**equals**(Object obj)
1.0		float	**floatValue**()
		int	**hashCode**()
		int	**intValue**()
		boolean	**isInfinite**()
	❏	boolean	**isInfinite**(double v)
		boolean	**isNaN**()
	❏	boolean	**isNaN**(double v)
	❏	double	**longBitsToDouble**(long bits)
		long	**longValue**()
	◢■	double	**MAX_VALUE**
	◢■	double	**MIN_VALUE**
	◢■	double	**NaN**
	◢■	double	**NEGATIVE_INFINITY**
1.2	❏	double	**parseDouble**(String s) *throws* NumberFormatException
	◢■	double	**POSITIVE_INFINITY**
1.1		short	**shortValue**()
		String	**toString**()
	❏	String	**toString**(double d)
1.1	◢■	Class	**TYPE**
	❏	Double	**valueOf**(String s) *throws* NumberFormatException

---

EmptyStackException	**java.util**

Object
→Throwable   java.io.Serializable
  →Exception
    →RuntimeException
      →EmptyStackException

❊	**EmptyStackException**()

Enumeration	**java.util**

Enumeration

boolean	**hasMoreElements**()
Object	**nextElement**()

EOFException	**java.io**

Object
→Throwable   Serializable
  →Exception

➡IOException
   ➡EOFException

✳	**EOFException**()
✳	**EOFException**(String s)

Error   **java.lang**

Object
  ➡Throwable   java.io.Serializable
    ➡Error

✳	**Error**()
✳	**Error**(String s)

EventListener   **java.util**

EventListener

EventObject   **java.util**

Object
  ➡EventObject   java.io.Serializable

✳		**EventObject**(Object source)
	Object	**getSource**()
✎◆	Object	**source**
	String	**toString**()

Exception   **java.lang**

Object
  ➡Throwable   java.io.Serializable
    ➡Exception

✳	**Exception**()
✳	**Exception**(String s)

ExceptionInInitializerError   **java.lang**

Object
  ➡Throwable   java.io.Serializable
    ➡Error
      ➡LinkageError
        ➡ExceptionInInitializerError

✳		**ExceptionInInitializerError**()
✳		**ExceptionInInitializerError**(String s)
✳		**ExceptionInInitializerError**(Throwable thrown)
	Throwable	**getException**()

void	**printStackTrace**()
void	**printStackTrace**(java.io.PrintStream ps)
void	**printStackTrace**(java.io.PrintWriter pw)

Externalizable   java.io

Externalizable   Serializable

void	**readExternal**(ObjectInput in) *throws* IOException, ClassNotFoundException
void	**writeExternal**(ObjectOutput out) *throws* IOException

Field   java.lang.reflect

Object
➥AccessibleObject
    ➥Field   Member

boolean	**equals**(Object obj)
Object	**get**(Object obj) *throws* IllegalArgumentException, IllegalAccessException
boolean	**getBoolean**(Object obj) *throws* IllegalArgumentException, IllegalAccessException
byte	**getByte**(Object obj) *throws* IllegalArgumentException, IllegalAccessException
char	**getChar**(Object obj) *throws* IllegalArgumentException, IllegalAccessException
Class	**getDeclaringClass**()
double	**getDouble**(Object obj) *throws* IllegalArgumentException, IllegalAccessException
float	**getFloat**(Object obj) *throws* IllegalArgumentException, IllegalAccessException
int	**getInt**(Object obj) *throws* IllegalArgumentException, IllegalAccessException
long	**getLong**(Object obj) *throws* IllegalArgumentException, IllegalAccessException
int	**getModifiers**()
String	**getName**()
short	**getShort**(Object obj) *throws* IllegalArgumentException, IllegalAccessException
Class	**getType**()
int	**hashCode**()
void	**set**(Object obj, Object value) *throws* IllegalArgumentException, IllegalAccessException

	void	setBoolean(Object obj, boolean z)
		throws IllegalArgumentException,
		IllegalAccessException
	void	setByte(Object obj, byte b)
		throws IllegalArgumentException,
		IllegalAccessException
	void	setChar(Object obj, char c)
		throws IllegalArgumentException,
		IllegalAccessException
	void	setDouble(Object obj, double d)
		throws IllegalArgumentException,
		IllegalAccessException
	void	setFloat(Object obj, float f)
		throws IllegalArgumentException,
		IllegalAccessException
	void	setInt(Object obj, int i)
		throws IllegalArgumentException,
		IllegalAccessException
	void	setLong(Object obj, long l)
		throws IllegalArgumentException,
		IllegalAccessException
	void	setShort(Object obj, short s)
		throws IllegalArgumentException,
		IllegalAccessException
	String	toString()

FieldPosition   java.text

Object
    ➥FieldPosition

	boolean	equals(Object obj)
✳		FieldPosition(int field)
	int	getBeginIndex()
	int	getEndIndex()
	int	getField()
	int	hashCode()
	void	setBeginIndex(int bi)
	void	setEndIndex(int ei)
	String	toString()

File   java.io

Object
    ➥File   Serializable, Comparable

	boolean	canRead()
	boolean	canWrite()
1.2	int	compareTo(File pathname)
1.2	int	compareTo(Object o)
1.2	boolean	createNewFile() *throws* IOException

1.2	❑	File	**createTempFile**(String prefix, String suffix) *throws* IOException
1.2	❑	File	**createTempFile**(String prefix, String suffix, File directory) *throws* IOException
		boolean	**delete**()
1.2		void	**deleteOnExit**()
		boolean	**equals**(Object obj)
		boolean	**exists**()
	❊		**File**(File parent, String child)
	❊		**File**(String pathname)
	❊		**File**(String parent, String child)
1.2		File	**getAbsoluteFile**()
		String	**getAbsolutePath**()
1.2		File	**getCanonicalFile**() *throws* IOException
1.1		String	**getCanonicalPath**() *throws* IOException
		String	**getName**()
		String	**getParent**()
1.2		File	**getParentFile**()
		String	**getPath**()
		int	**hashCode**()
		boolean	**isAbsolute**()
		boolean	**isDirectory**()
		boolean	**isFile**()
1.2		boolean	**isHidden**()
		long	**lastModified**()
		long	**length**()
		String[]	**list**()
		String[]	**list**(FilenameFilter filter)
1.2		File[]	**listFiles**()
1.2		File[]	**listFiles**(FileFilter filter)
1.2		File[]	**listFiles**(FilenameFilter filter)
1.2	❑	File[]	**listRoots**()
		boolean	**mkdir**()
		boolean	**mkdirs**()
	✍■	String	**pathSeparator**
	✍■	char	**pathSeparatorChar**
		boolean	**renameTo**(File dest)
	✍■	String	**separator**
	✍■	char	**separatorChar**
1.2		boolean	**setLastModified**(long time)
1.2		boolean	**setReadOnly**()
		String	**toString**()
1.2		java.net.URL	**toURL**() *throws* java.net.MalformedURLException

---

FileDescriptor	**java.io**

Object
   ➡FileDescriptor

	✍■	FileDescriptor	**err**
	❊		**FileDescriptor**()

✍▪	FileDescriptor	**in**	
✍▪	FileDescriptor	**out**	
1.1	void	**sync()** *throws* SyncFailedException	
	boolean	**valid()**	

FileFilter   java.io

FileFilter

boolean	**accept**(File pathname)

FileInputStream   java.io

Object
   ➡InputStream
      ➡FileInputStream

	int	**available**() *throws* IOException
	void	**close**() *throws* IOException
❋		**FileInputStream**(File file)
		throws FileNotFoundException
❋		**FileInputStream**(FileDescriptor fdObj)
❋		**FileInputStream**(String name)
		throws FileNotFoundException
♦	void	**finalize**() *throws* IOException
●	FileDescriptor	**getFD**() *throws* IOException
	int	**read**() *throws* IOException
	int	**read**(byte[] b) *throws* IOException
	int	**read**(byte[] b, int off, int len) *throws* IOException
	long	**skip**(long n) *throws* IOException

FilenameFilter   java.io

FilenameFilter

boolean	**accept**(File dir, String name)

FileNameMap   java.net

FileNameMap

String	**getContentTypeFor**(String fileName)

FileNotFoundException   java.io

Object
   ➡Throwable   Serializable
      ➡Exception
         ➡IOException
            ➡FileNotFoundException

✳		FileNotFoundException()
✳		FileNotFoundException(String s)

FileOutputStream java.io

```
Object
   ➥OutputStream
      ➥FileOutputStream
```

		void	close() throws IOException
✳			FileOutputStream(File file)
			throws FileNotFoundException
✳			FileOutputStream(FileDescriptor fdObj)
✳			FileOutputStream(String name)
			throws FileNotFoundException
1.1	✳		FileOutputStream(String name, boolean append)
			throws FileNotFoundException
♦		void	finalize() throws IOException
●		FileDescriptor	getFD() throws IOException
		void	write(byte[] b) throws IOException
		void	write(byte[] b, int off, int len)
			throws IOException
		void	write(int b) throws IOException

FilePermission java.io

```
Object
   ➥java.security.Permission          java.security.Guard, Serializable
      ➥FilePermission                 Serializable
```

	boolean	equals(Object obj)
✳		FilePermission(String path, String actions)
	String	getActions()
	int	hashCode()
	boolean	implies(java.security.Permission p)
	java.security.¬	newPermissionCollection()
	PermissionCollection	

FileReader java.io

```
Object
   ➥Reader
      ➥InputStreamReader
         ➥FileReader
```

✳		FileReader(File file) throws FileNotFoundException
✳		FileReader(FileDescriptor fd)
✳		FileReader(String fileName)
		throws FileNotFoundException

FileWriter   java.io

```
Object
    ➡Writer
        ➡OutputStreamWriter
            ➡FileWriter
```

❋		**FileWriter**(File file) *throws* IOException
❋		**FileWriter**(FileDescriptor fd)
❋		**FileWriter**(String fileName) *throws* IOException
❋		**FileWriter**(String fileName, boolean append)
		throws IOException

FilterInputStream   java.io

```
Object
    ➡InputStream
        ➡FilterInputStream
```

	int	**available**() *throws* IOException
	void	**close**() *throws* IOException
❋◆		**FilterInputStream**(InputStream in)
✍◆	InputStream	**in**
	void	**mark**(int readlimit)
	boolean	**markSupported**()
	int	**read**() *throws* IOException
	int	**read**(byte[] b) *throws* IOException
	int	**read**(byte[] b, int off, int len) *throws* IOException
	void	**reset**() *throws* IOException
	long	**skip**(long n) *throws* IOException

FilterOutputStream   java.io

```
Object
    ➡OutputStream
        ➡FilterOutputStream
```

	void	**close**() *throws* IOException
❋		**FilterOutputStream**(OutputStream out)
	void	**flush**() *throws* IOException
✍◆	OutputStream	**out**
	void	**write**(byte[] b) *throws* IOException
	void	**write**(byte[] b, int off, int len) *throws* IOException
	void	**write**(int b) *throws* IOException

FilterReader   java.io

```
Object
    ➡Reader
        ➡FilterReader
```

```
          void  close() throws IOException
                FilterReader(Reader in)
        Reader  in
          void  mark(int readAheadLimit) throws IOException
       boolean  markSupported()
           int  read() throws IOException
           int  read(char[] cbuf, int off, int len)
                    throws IOException
       boolean  ready() throws IOException
          void  reset() throws IOException
          long  skip(long n) throws IOException
```

FilterWriter   java.io

```
Object
   ➡Writer
       ➡FilterWriter
```

```
          void  close() throws IOException
                FilterWriter(Writer out)
          void  flush() throws IOException
        Writer  out
          void  write(char[] cbuf, int off, int len)
                    throws IOException
          void  write(int c) throws IOException
          void  write(String str, int off, int len)
                    throws IOException
```

Float   java.lang

```
Object
   ➡Number                          java.io.Serializable
       ➡Float                       Comparable
```

```
1.1        byte  byteValue()
1.2         int  compareTo(Float anotherFloat)
1.2         int  compareTo(Object o)
         double  doubleValue()
        boolean  equals(Object obj)
                 Float(double value)
                 Float(float value)
                 Float(String s) throws NumberFormatException
            int  floatToIntBits(float value)
            int  floatToRawIntBits(float value)
          float  floatValue()
            int  hashCode()
          float  intBitsToFloat(int bits)
            int  intValue()
        boolean  isInfinite()
        boolean  isInfinite(float v)
        boolean  isNaN()
```

	□	boolean	**isNaN**(float v)
		long	**longValue**()
	⌂■	float	**MAX_VALUE**
	⌂■	float	**MIN_VALUE**
	⌂■	float	**NaN**
	⌂■	float	**NEGATIVE_INFINITY**
1.2	□	float	**parseFloat**(String s) *throws* NumberFormatException
	⌂■	float	**POSITIVE_INFINITY**
1.1		short	**shortValue**()
		String	**toString**()
		String	**toString**(float f)
1.1	⌂■	Class	**TYPE**
	□	Float	**valueOf**(String s) *throws* NumberFormatException

---

Format   java.text

Object
　➡Format   java.io.Serializable, Cloneable

		Object	**clone**()
	✳		**Format**()
	●	String	**format**(Object obj)
	○	StringBuffer	**format**(Object obj, StringBuffer toAppendTo, FieldPosition pos)
		Object	**parseObject**(String source) *throws* ParseException
	○	Object	**parseObject**(String source, ParsePosition status)

GeneralSecurityException   java.security

Object
　➡Throwable   java.io.Serializable
　　➡Exception
　　　➡GeneralSecurityException

	✳		**GeneralSecurityException**()
	✳		**GeneralSecurityException**(String msg)

GregorianCalendar   java.util

Object
　➡Calendar   java.io.Serializable, Cloneable
　　➡GregorianCalendar

	⌂■	int	**AD**
		void	**add**(int field, int amount)
	⌂■	int	**BC**
	◆	void	**computeFields**()
	◆	void	**computeTime**()
		boolean	**equals**(Object obj)
1.2		int	**getActualMaximum**(int field)
1.2		int	**getActualMinimum**(int field)

	int	getGreatestMinimum(int field)
●	Date	getGregorianChange()
	int	getLeastMaximum(int field)
	int	getMaximum(int field)
	int	getMinimum(int field)
❊		GregorianCalendar()
❊		GregorianCalendar(int year, int month, int date)
❊		GregorianCalendar(int year, int month, int date, int hour, int minute)
❊		GregorianCalendar(int year, int month, int date, int hour, int minute, int second)
❊		GregorianCalendar(Locale aLocale)
❊		GregorianCalendar(TimeZone zone)
❊		GregorianCalendar(TimeZone zone, Locale aLocale)
	int	hashCode()
	boolean	isLeapYear(int year)
1.2	void	roll(int field, boolean up)
	void	roll(int field, int amount)
	void	setGregorianChange(Date date)

Guard   java.security

Guard

	void	checkGuard(Object object) *throws* SecurityException

GuardedObject   java.security

Object
　➡GuardedObject   java.io.Serializable

	Object	getObject() *throws* SecurityException
❊		GuardedObject(Object object, Guard guard)

GZIPInputStream   java.util.zip

Object
　➡java.io.InputStream
　　➡java.io.FilterInputStream
　　　➡InflaterInputStream
　　　　➡GZIPInputStream

	void	close() *throws* java.io.IOException
✎◆	CRC32	crc
✎◆	boolean	eos
✎■	int	GZIP_MAGIC
❊		GZIPInputStream(java.io.InputStream in) *throws* java.io.IOException
❊		GZIPInputStream(java.io.InputStream in, int size) *throws* java.io.IOException

	int	**read**(byte[] buf, int off, int len)
		throws java.io.IOException

GZIPOutputStream   `java.util.zip`

```
Object
  ➡java.io.OutputStream
      ➡java.io.FilterOutputStream
          ➡DeflaterOutputStream
              ➡GZIPOutputStream
```

	void	**close**() *throws* java.io.IOException
⚏◆	CRC32	**crc**
	void	**finish**() *throws* java.io.IOException
✳		**GZIPOutputStream**(java.io.OutputStream out)
		throws java.io.IOException
✳		**GZIPOutputStream**(java.io.OutputStream out,
		int size) *throws* java.io.IOException
	void	**write**(byte[] buf, int off, int len)
		throws java.io.IOException

HashMap   `java.util`

```
Object
  ➡AbstractMap                     Map
      ➡HashMap                      Map, Cloneable, java.io.Serializable
```

	void	**clear**()
	Object	**clone**()
	boolean	**containsKey**(Object key)
	boolean	**containsValue**(Object value)
	Set	**entrySet**()
	Object	**get**(Object key)
✳		**HashMap**()
✳		**HashMap**(int initialCapacity)
✳		**HashMap**(int initialCapacity, float loadFactor)
✳		**HashMap**(Map t)
	boolean	**isEmpty**()
	Set	**keySet**()
	Object	**put**(Object key, Object value)
	void	**putAll**(Map t)
	Object	**remove**(Object key)
	int	**size**()
	Collection	**values**()

HashSet   `java.util`

```
Object
  ➡AbstractCollection              Collection
      ➡AbstractSet                 Set
          ➡HashSet                 Set, Cloneable, java.io.Serializable
```

	boolean	**add**(Object o)	
	void	**clear**()	
	Object	**clone**()	
	boolean	**contains**(Object o)	
✳		**HashSet**()	
✳		**HashSet**(Collection c)	
✳		**HashSet**(int initialCapacity)	
✳		**HashSet**(int initialCapacity, float loadFactor)	
	boolean	**isEmpty**()	
	Iterator	**iterator**()	
	boolean	**remove**(Object o)	
	int	**size**()	

Hashtable   java.util

Object
➡Dictionary
　➡Hashtable   Map, Cloneable, java.io.Serializable

		void	**clear**()
		Object	**clone**()
		boolean	**contains**(Object value)
		boolean	**containsKey**(Object key)
1.2		boolean	**containsValue**(Object value)
		Enumeration	**elements**()
1.2		Set	**entrySet**()
1.2		boolean	**equals**(Object o)
		Object	**get**(Object key)
1.2		int	**hashCode**()
	✳		**Hashtable**()
	✳		**Hashtable**(int initialCapacity)
	✳		**Hashtable**(int initialCapacity, float loadFactor)
1.2	✳		**Hashtable**(Map t)
		boolean	**isEmpty**()
		Enumeration	**keys**()
1.2		Set	**keySet**()
		Object	**put**(Object key, Object value)
1.2		void	**putAll**(Map t)
	◆	void	**rehash**()
		Object	**remove**(Object key)
		int	**size**()
		String	**toString**()
1.2		Collection	**values**()

HttpConnection   javax.microedition.io

HttpConnection   ContentConnection

⬛	String	**GET**	
	long	**getDate**() *throws* java.io.IOException	
	long	**getExpiration**() *throws* java.io.IOException	

	String	**getFile**()
	String	**getHeaderField**(int n) *throws* java.io.IOException
	String	**getHeaderField**(String name)
		throws java.io.IOException
	long	**getHeaderFieldDate**(String name, long def)
		throws java.io.IOException
	int	**getHeaderFieldInt**(String name, int def)
		throws java.io.IOException
	String	**getHeaderFieldKey**(int n) *throws* java.io.IOException
	String	**getHost**()
	long	**getLastModified**() *throws* java.io.IOException
	int	**getPort**()
	String	**getProtocol**()
	String	**getQuery**()
	String	**getRef**()
	String	**getRequestMethod**()
	String	**getRequestProperty**(String key)
	int	**getResponseCode**() *throws* java.io.IOException
	String	**getResponseMessage**() *throws* java.io.IOException
	String	**getURL**()
⚿■	String	**HEAD**
⚿■	int	**HTTP_ACCEPTED**
⚿■	int	**HTTP_BAD_GATEWAY**
⚿■	int	**HTTP_BAD_METHOD**
⚿■	int	**HTTP_BAD_REQUEST**
⚿■	int	**HTTP_CLIENT_TIMEOUT**
⚿■	int	**HTTP_CONFLICT**
⚿■	int	**HTTP_CREATED**
⚿■	int	**HTTP_ENTITY_TOO_LARGE**
⚿■	int	**HTTP_EXPECT_FAILED**
⚿■	int	**HTTP_FORBIDDEN**
⚿■	int	**HTTP_GATEWAY_TIMEOUT**
⚿■	int	**HTTP_GONE**
⚿■	int	**HTTP_INTERNAL_ERROR**
⚿■	int	**HTTP_LENGTH_REQUIRED**
⚿■	int	**HTTP_MOVED_PERM**
⚿■	int	**HTTP_MOVED_TEMP**
⚿■	int	**HTTP_MULT_CHOICE**
⚿■	int	**HTTP_NO_CONTENT**
⚿■	int	**HTTP_NOT_ACCEPTABLE**
⚿■	int	**HTTP_NOT_AUTHORITATIVE**
⚿■	int	**HTTP_NOT_FOUND**
⚿■	int	**HTTP_NOT_IMPLEMENTED**
⚿■	int	**HTTP_NOT_MODIFIED**
⚿■	int	**HTTP_OK**
⚿■	int	**HTTP_PARTIAL**
⚿■	int	**HTTP_PAYMENT_REQUIRED**
⚿■	int	**HTTP_PRECON_FAILED**
⚿■	int	**HTTP_PROXY_AUTH**
⚿■	int	**HTTP_REQ_TOO_LONG**
⚿■	int	**HTTP_RESET**
⚿■	int	**HTTP_SEE_OTHER**

	int	**HTTP_TEMP_REDIRECT**
	int	**HTTP_UNAUTHORIZED**
	int	**HTTP_UNAVAILABLE**
	int	**HTTP_UNSUPPORTED_RANGE**
	int	**HTTP_UNSUPPORTED_TYPE**
	int	**HTTP_USE_PROXY**
	int	**HTTP_VERSION**
	String	**POST**
	void	**setRequestMethod**(String method) *throws* java.io.IOException
	void	**setRequestProperty**(String key, String value) *throws* java.io.IOException

HttpURLConnection   `java.net`

Object
  ➥URLConnection
    ➥HttpURLConnection

○	void	**disconnect**()
	java.io.InputStream	**getErrorStream**()
□	boolean	**getFollowRedirects**()
	long	**getHeaderFieldDate**(String name, long Default)
	boolean	**getInstanceFollowRedirects**()
	java.security.¬Permission	**getPermission**() *throws* java.io.IOException
	String	**getRequestMethod**()
	int	**getResponseCode**() *throws* java.io.IOException
	String	**getResponseMessage**() *throws* java.io.IOException
	int	**HTTP_ACCEPTED**
	int	**HTTP_BAD_GATEWAY**
	int	**HTTP_BAD_METHOD**
	int	**HTTP_BAD_REQUEST**
	int	**HTTP_CLIENT_TIMEOUT**
	int	**HTTP_CONFLICT**
	int	**HTTP_CREATED**
	int	**HTTP_ENTITY_TOO_LARGE**
	int	**HTTP_FORBIDDEN**
	int	**HTTP_GATEWAY_TIMEOUT**
	int	**HTTP_GONE**
	int	**HTTP_INTERNAL_ERROR**
	int	**HTTP_LENGTH_REQUIRED**
	int	**HTTP_MOVED_PERM**
	int	**HTTP_MOVED_TEMP**
	int	**HTTP_MULT_CHOICE**
	int	**HTTP_NO_CONTENT**
	int	**HTTP_NOT_ACCEPTABLE**
	int	**HTTP_NOT_AUTHORITATIVE**
	int	**HTTP_NOT_FOUND**
	int	**HTTP_NOT_IMPLEMENTED**
	int	**HTTP_NOT_MODIFIED**
	int	**HTTP_OK**

✍️⬛	int	`HTTP_PARTIAL`	
✍️⬛	int	`HTTP_PAYMENT_REQUIRED`	
✍️⬛	int	`HTTP_PRECON_FAILED`	
✍️⬛	int	`HTTP_PROXY_AUTH`	
✍️⬛	int	`HTTP_REQ_TOO_LONG`	
✍️⬛	int	`HTTP_RESET`	
✍️⬛	int	`HTTP_SEE_OTHER`	
✍️⬛	int	`HTTP_UNAUTHORIZED`	
✍️⬛	int	`HTTP_UNAVAILABLE`	
✍️⬛	int	`HTTP_UNSUPPORTED_TYPE`	
✍️⬛	int	`HTTP_USE_PROXY`	
✍️⬛	int	`HTTP_VERSION`	
✳️◆		`HttpURLConnection(URL u)`	
✍️◆	boolean	`instanceFollowRedirects`	
✍️◆	String	`method`	
✍️◆	int	`responseCode`	
✍️◆	String	`responseMessage`	
❑	void	`setFollowRedirects(boolean set)`	
	void	`setInstanceFollowRedirects(boolean followRedirects)`	
	void	`setRequestMethod(String method)`	
		throws ProtocolException	
○	boolean	`usingProxy()`	

Identity	**java.security**

```
Object
   ➥Identity                              Principal, java.io.Serializable
```

	void	`addCertificate(Certificate certificate)`
		throws KeyManagementException
	Certificate[]	`certificates()`
●	boolean	`equals(Object identity)`
	String	`getInfo()`
●	String	`getName()`
	PublicKey	`getPublicKey()`
●	IdentityScope	`getScope()`
	int	`hashCode()`
✳️◆		`Identity()`
✳️		`Identity(String name)`
✳️		`Identity(String name, IdentityScope scope)`
		throws KeyManagementException
◆	boolean	`identityEquals(Identity identity)`
	void	`removeCertificate(Certificate certificate)`
		throws KeyManagementException
	void	`setInfo(String info)`
	void	`setPublicKey(PublicKey key)`
		throws KeyManagementException
	String	`toString()`
	String	`toString(boolean detailed)`

IllegalScope   `java.security`

```
IdentityScope                                                java.security
```

```
Object
    ➡Identity                            Principal, java.io.Serializable
        ➡IdentityScope
```

○	void	**addIdentity**(Identity identity)
		throws KeyManagementException
	Identity	**getIdentity**(Principal principal)
○	Identity	**getIdentity**(PublicKey key)
○	Identity	**getIdentity**(String name)
❑	IdentityScope	**getSystemScope**()
○	java.util.Enumeration	**identities**()
✳◆		**IdentityScope**()
✳		**IdentityScope**(String name)
✳		**IdentityScope**(String name, IdentityScope scope)
		throws KeyManagementException
○	void	**removeIdentity**(Identity identity)
		throws KeyManagementException
❑◆	void	**setSystemScope**(IdentityScope scope)
○	int	**size**()
	String	**toString**()

```
IllegalAccessError                                                java.lang
```

```
Object
    ➡Throwable                              java.io.Serializable
        ➡Error
            ➡LinkageError
                ➡IncompatibleClassChangeError
                    ➡IllegalAccessError
```

✳	**IllegalAccessError**()
✳	**IllegalAccessError**(String s)

```
IllegalAccessException                                            java.lang
```

```
Object
    ➡Throwable                              java.io.Serializable
        ➡Exception
            ➡IllegalAccessException
```

✳	**IllegalAccessException**()
✳	**IllegalAccessException**(String s)

```
IllegalArgumentException                                          java.lang
```

```
Object
    ➡Throwable                              java.io.Serializable
        ➡Exception
```

➡️RuntimeException
  ➡️IllegalArgumentException

✳	IllegalArgumentException()
✳	IllegalArgumentException(String s)

IllegalMonitorStateException   java.lang

Object
  ➡️Throwable   java.io.Serializable
    ➡️Exception
      ➡️RuntimeException
        ➡️IllegalMonitorStateException

✳	IllegalMonitorStateException()
✳	IllegalMonitorStateException(String s)

IllegalStateException   java.lang

Object
  ➡️Throwable   java.io.Serializable
    ➡️Exception
      ➡️RuntimeException
        ➡️IllegalStateException

✳	IllegalStateException()
✳	IllegalStateException(String s)

IllegalThreadStateException   java.lang

Object
  ➡️Throwable   java.io.Serializable
    ➡️Exception
      ➡️RuntimeException
        ➡️IllegalArgumentException
          ➡️IllegalThreadStateException

✳	IllegalThreadStateException()
✳	IllegalThreadStateException(String s)

IncompatibleClassChangeError   java.lang

Object
  ➡️Throwable   java.io.Serializable
    ➡️Error
      ➡️LinkageError
        ➡️IncompatibleClassChangeError

✳	IncompatibleClassChangeError()
✳	IncompatibleClassChangeError(String s)

IndexOutOfBoundsException — java.lang

```
Object
  ➥Throwable                                    java.io.Serializable
      ➥Exception
          ➥RuntimeException
              ➥IndexOutOfBoundsException
```

✳	**IndexOutOfBoundsException**()
✳	**IndexOutOfBoundsException**(String s)

InetAddress — java.net

```
Object
  ➥InetAddress                                  java.io.Serializable
```

	boolean	**equals**(Object obj)
	byte[]	**getAddress**()
❑	InetAddress[]	**getAllByName**(String host)
		throws UnknownHostException
❑	InetAddress	**getByName**(String host) *throws* UnknownHostException
1.0.2	String	**getHostAddress**()
	String	**getHostName**()
❑	InetAddress	**getLocalHost**() *throws* UnknownHostException
	int	**hashCode**()
1.1	boolean	**isMulticastAddress**()
	String	**toString**()

Inflater — java.util.zip

```
Object
  ➥Inflater
```

	void	**end**()
◆	void	**finalize**()
	boolean	**finished**()
	int	**getAdler**()
	int	**getRemaining**()
	int	**getTotalIn**()
	int	**getTotalOut**()
	int	**inflate**(byte[] b) *throws* DataFormatException
	int	**inflate**(byte[] b, int off, int len)
		throws DataFormatException
✳		**Inflater**()
✳		**Inflater**(boolean nowrap)
	boolean	**needsDictionary**()
	boolean	**needsInput**()
	void	**reset**()
	void	**setDictionary**(byte[] b)
	void	**setDictionary**(byte[] b, int off, int len)
	void	**setInput**(byte[] b)
	void	**setInput**(byte[] b, int off, int len)

InflaterInputStream   java.util.zip

```
Object
    ➡java.io.InputStream
        ➡java.io.FilterInputStream
            ➡InflaterInputStream
```

	int	**available**() *throws* java.io.IOException
⚹♦	byte[]	**buf**
	void	**close**() *throws* java.io.IOException
♦	void	**fill**() *throws* java.io.IOException
⚹♦	Inflater	**inf**
✳		**InflaterInputStream**(java.io.InputStream in)
✳		**InflaterInputStream**(java.io.InputStream in, Inflater inf)
✳		**InflaterInputStream**(java.io.InputStream in, Inflater inf, int size)
⚹♦	int	**len**
	int	**read**() *throws* java.io.IOException
	int	**read**(byte[] b, int off, int len) *throws* java.io.IOException
	long	**skip**(long n) *throws* java.io.IOException

InheritableThreadLocal   java.lang

```
Object
    ➡ThreadLocal
        ➡InheritableThreadLocal
```

♦	Object	**childValue**(Object parentValue)
	Object	**get**()
✳		**InheritableThreadLocal**()
	void	**set**(Object value)

InputConnection   javax.microedition.io

InputConnection   Connection

java.io.DataInputStream	**openDataInputStream**() *throws* java.io.IOException
java.io.InputStream	**openInputStream**() *throws* java.io.IOException

InputStream   java.io

```
Object
    ➡InputStream
```

	int	**available**() *throws* IOException
	void	**close**() *throws* IOException
✳		**InputStream**()
	void	**mark**(int readlimit)

```
          boolean   markSupported()
  ○           int   read() throws IOException
              int   read(byte[] b) throws IOException
              int   read(byte[] b, int off, int len) throws IOException
             void   reset() throws IOException
             long   skip(long n) throws IOException
```

InputStreamReader	java.io

```
Object
  ➥Reader
     ➥InputStreamReader
```

```
             void   close() throws IOException
           String   getEncoding()
  ✳                 InputStreamReader(InputStream in)
  ✳                 InputStreamReader(InputStream in, String enc)
                        throws UnsupportedEncodingException
              int   read() throws IOException
              int   read(char[] cbuf, int off, int len)
                        throws IOException
          boolean   ready() throws IOException
```

InstantiationError	java.lang

```
Object
  ➥Throwable                        java.io.Serializable
     ➥Error
        ➥LinkageError
           ➥IncompatibleClassChangeError
              ➥InstantiationError
```

```
  ✳                 InstantiationError()
  ✳                 InstantiationError(String s)
```

InstantiationException	java.lang

```
Object
  ➥Throwable                        java.io.Serializable
     ➥Exception
        ➥InstantiationException
```

```
  ✳                 InstantiationException()
  ✳                 InstantiationException(String s)
```

Integer	java.lang

```
Object
  ➥Number                           java.io.Serializable
     ➥Integer                       Comparable
```

1.1		byte	**byteValue**()
1.2		int	**compareTo**(Integer anotherInteger)
1.2		int	**compareTo**(Object o)
	❏	Integer	**decode**(String nm) *throws* NumberFormatException
		double	**doubleValue**()
		boolean	**equals**(Object obj)
		float	**floatValue**()
	❏	Integer	**getInteger**(String nm)
	❏	Integer	**getInteger**(String nm, int val)
	❏	Integer	**getInteger**(String nm, Integer val)
		int	**hashCode**()
	✳		**Integer**(int value)
	✳		**Integer**(String s) *throws* NumberFormatException
		int	**intValue**()
		long	**longValue**()
	△■	int	**MAX_VALUE**
	△■	int	**MIN_VALUE**
	❏	int	**parseInt**(String s) *throws* NumberFormatException
	❏	int	**parseInt**(String s, int radix)
			throws NumberFormatException
1.1		short	**shortValue**()
1.0.2	❏	String	**toBinaryString**(int i)
1.0.2	❏	String	**toHexString**(int i)
1.0.2	❏	String	**toOctalString**(int i)
		String	**toString**()
	❏	String	**toString**(int i)
	❏	String	**toString**(int i, int radix)
1.1	△■	Class	**TYPE**
	❏	Integer	**valueOf**(String s) *throws* NumberFormatException
	❏	Integer	**valueOf**(String s, int radix)
			throws NumberFormatException

InternalError			**java.lang**

```
Object
  ➡Throwable                        java.io.Serializable
     ➡Error
        ➡VirtualMachineError
           ➡InternalError
```

✳		**InternalError**()
✳		**InternalError**(String s)

InterruptedException			**java.lang**

```
Object
  ➡Throwable                        java.io.Serializable
     ➡Exception
        ➡InterruptedException
```

✱		InterruptedException()
✱		InterruptedException(String s)

InterruptedIOException   java.io

```
Object
    ➥Throwable                        Serializable
        ➥Exception
            ➥IOException
                ➥InterruptedIOException
```

✍	int	bytesTransferred
✱		InterruptedIOException()
✱		InterruptedIOException(String s)

InvalidAlgorithmParameterException   java.security

```
Object
    ➥Throwable                        java.io.Serializable
        ➥Exception
            ➥GeneralSecurityException
                ➥InvalidAlgorithmParameterException
```

✱	InvalidAlgorithmParameterException()
✱	InvalidAlgorithmParameterException(String msg)

InvalidClassException   java.io

```
Object
    ➥Throwable                        Serializable
        ➥Exception
            ➥IOException
                ➥ObjectStreamException
                    ➥InvalidClassException
```

✍	String	classname
	String	getMessage()
✱		InvalidClassException(String reason)
✱		InvalidClassException(String cname, String reason)

InvalidKeyException   java.security

```
Object
    ➥Throwable                        java.io.Serializable
        ➥Exception
            ➥GeneralSecurityException
                ➥KeyException
                    ➥InvalidKeyException
```

❋	InvalidKeyException()
❋	InvalidKeyException(String msg)

InvalidObjectException   java.io

```
Object
  ➥Throwable                    Serializable
     ➥Exception
        ➥IOException
           ➥ObjectStreamException
              ➥InvalidObjectException
```

❋	InvalidObjectException(String reason)

InvalidParameterException   java.security

```
Object
  ➥Throwable                    java.io.Serializable
     ➥Exception
        ➥RuntimeException
           ➥IllegalArgumentException
              ➥InvalidParameterException
```

❋	InvalidParameterException()
❋	InvalidParameterException(String msg)

InvocationHandler   java.lang.reflect

InvocationHandler

Object	invoke(Object proxy, Method method, Object[] args) *throws* Throwable

InvocationTargetException   java.lang.reflect

```
Object
  ➥Throwable                    java.io.Serializable
     ➥Exception
        ➥InvocationTargetException
```

Throwable	getTargetException()
❋◆	InvocationTargetException()
❋	InvocationTargetException(Throwable target)
❋	InvocationTargetException(Throwable target, String s)
void	printStackTrace()
void	printStackTrace(java.io.PrintStream ps)
void	printStackTrace(java.io.PrintWriter pw)

IOException

java.io

```
Object
  ➡Throwable                        Serializable
    ➡Exception
      ➡IOException
```

✳	**IOException**()
✳	**IOException**(String s)

Iterator

java.util

```
Iterator
```

boolean	**hasNext**()
Object	**next**()
void	**remove**()

JarEntry

java.util.jar

```
Object
  ➡java.util.zip.ZipEntry            java.util.zip.ZipConstants, Cloneable
    ➡JarEntry
```

Attributes	**getAttributes**() *throws* java.io.IOException
java.security.cert.¬ Certificate[]	**getCertificates**()
✳	**JarEntry**(JarEntry je)
✳	**JarEntry**(String name)
✳	**JarEntry**(java.util.zip.ZipEntry ze)

JarException

java.util.jar

```
Object
  ➡Throwable                        java.io.Serializable
    ➡Exception
      ➡java.io.IOException
        ➡java.util.zip.ZipException
          ➡JarException
```

✳	**JarException**()
✳	**JarException**(String s)

JarFile

java.util.jar

```
Object
  ➡java.util.zip.ZipFile            java.util.zip.ZipConstants
    ➡JarFile
```

java.util.Enumeration	**entries**()
java.util.zip.ZipEntry	**getEntry**(String name)

	java.io.InputStream	**getInputStream**(java.util.zip.ZipEntry ze)
		throws java.io.IOException
	JarEntry	**getJarEntry**(String name)
	Manifest	**getManifest**() *throws* java.io.IOException
✳		**JarFile**(java.io.File file)
		throws java.io.IOException
✳		**JarFile**(java.io.File file, boolean verify)
		throws java.io.IOException
✳		**JarFile**(java.io.File file, boolean verify,
		int mode) *throws* java.io.IOException
✳		**JarFile**(String name) *throws* java.io.IOException
✳		**JarFile**(String name, boolean verify)
		throws java.io.IOException
◿▪	String	**MANIFEST_NAME**

JarInputStream   java.util.jar

```
Object
   ➡java.io.InputStream
      ➡java.io.FilterInputStream
         ➡java.util.zip.InflaterInputStream
            ➡java.util.zip.ZipInputStreamjava.util.zip.ZipConstants
               ➡JarInputStream
```

◆	java.util.zip.ZipEntry	**createZipEntry**(String name)
	Manifest	**getManifest**()
	java.util.zip.ZipEntry	**getNextEntry**() *throws* java.io.IOException
	JarEntry	**getNextJarEntry**() *throws* java.io.IOException
✳		**JarInputStream**(java.io.InputStream in)
		throws java.io.IOException
✳		**JarInputStream**(java.io.InputStream in,
		boolean verify) *throws* java.io.IOException
	int	**read**(byte[] b, int off, int len)
		throws java.io.IOException

JarOutputStream   java.util.jar

```
Object
   ➡java.io.OutputStream
      ➡java.io.FilterOutputStream
         ➡java.util.zip.DeflaterOutputStream
            ➡java.util.zip.ZipOutputStreamjava.util.zip.ZipConstants
               ➡JarOutputStream
```

✳		**JarOutputStream**(java.io.OutputStream out)
		throws java.io.IOException
✳		**JarOutputStream**(java.io.OutputStream out,
		Manifest man) *throws* java.io.IOException
	void	**putNextEntry**(java.util.zip.ZipEntry ze)
		throws java.io.IOException

JarURLConnection   java.net

```
Object
    ➡URLConnection
        ➡JarURLConnection
```

	java.util.jar.¬ Attributes	**getAttributes**() *throws* java.io.IOException
	java.security.cert.¬ Certificate[]	**getCertificates**() *throws* java.io.IOException
	String	**getEntryName**()
	java.util.jar.JarEntry	**getJarEntry**() *throws* java.io.IOException
○	java.util.jar.JarFile	**getJarFile**() *throws* java.io.IOException
	URL	**getJarFileURL**()
	java.util.jar.¬ Attributes	**getMainAttributes**() *throws* java.io.IOException
	java.util.jar.Manifest	**getManifest**() *throws* java.io.IOException
⚠◆	URLConnection	**jarFileURLConnection**
✳◆		**JarURLConnection**(URL url) *throws* MalformedURLException

Key   java.security

Key   java.io.Serializable

	String	**getAlgorithm**()
	byte[]	**getEncoded**()
	String	**getFormat**()
⚠■	long	**serialVersionUID**

KeyException   java.security

```
Object
    ➡Throwable                          java.io.Serializable
        ➡Exception
            ➡GeneralSecurityException
                ➡KeyException
```

✳		**KeyException**()
✳		**KeyException**(String msg)

KeyFactory   java.security

```
Object
    ➡KeyFactory
```

●	PrivateKey	**generatePrivate**(spec.KeySpec keySpec) *throws* spec.InvalidKeySpecException
●	PublicKey	**generatePublic**(spec.KeySpec keySpec) *throws* spec.InvalidKeySpecException

●	String	**getAlgorithm**()
❑	KeyFactory	**getInstance**(String algorithm)
		throws NoSuchAlgorithmException
❑	KeyFactory	**getInstance**(String algorithm, String provider)
		throws NoSuchAlgorithmException,
		NoSuchProviderException
●	spec.KeySpec	**getKeySpec**(Key key, Class keySpec)
		throws spec.InvalidKeySpecException
●	Provider	**getProvider**()
❋◆		**KeyFactory**(KeyFactorySpi keyFacSpi,
		Provider provider, String algorithm)
●	Key	**translateKey**(Key key) *throws* InvalidKeyException

KeyFactorySpi `java.security`

Object
　➥KeyFactorySpi

○◆	PrivateKey	**engineGeneratePrivate**(spec.KeySpec keySpec)
		throws spec.InvalidKeySpecException
○◆	PublicKey	**engineGeneratePublic**(spec.KeySpec keySpec)
		throws spec.InvalidKeySpecException
○◆	spec.KeySpec	**engineGetKeySpec**(Key key, Class keySpec)
		throws spec.InvalidKeySpecException
○◆	Key	**engineTranslateKey**(Key key)
		throws InvalidKeyException
❋		**KeyFactorySpi**()

KeyManagementException `java.security`

Object
　➥Throwable　　　　　　　　　java.io.Serializable
　　➥Exception
　　　➥GeneralSecurityException
　　　　➥KeyException
　　　　　➥KeyManagementException

❋		**KeyManagementException**()
❋		**KeyManagementException**(String msg)

KeyPair `java.security`

Object
　➥KeyPair　　　　　　　　　　java.io.Serializable

	PrivateKey	**getPrivate**()
	PublicKey	**getPublic**()
❋		**KeyPair**(PublicKey publicKey, PrivateKey privateKey)

KeyPairGenerator   java.security

```
Object
    ➥KeyPairGeneratorSpi
        ➥KeyPairGenerator
```

1.2	●	KeyPair	**generateKeyPair**()
	●	KeyPair	**genKeyPair**()
		String	**getAlgorithm**()
	❑	KeyPairGenerator	**getInstance**(String algorithm)
			throws NoSuchAlgorithmException
	❑	KeyPairGenerator	**getInstance**(String algorithm, String provider)
			throws NoSuchAlgorithmException,
			NoSuchProviderException
	●	Provider	**getProvider**()
1.2		void	**initialize**(spec.AlgorithmParameterSpec params)
			throws InvalidAlgorithmParameterException
1.2		void	**initialize**(spec.AlgorithmParameterSpec params,
			SecureRandom random)
			throws InvalidAlgorithmParameterException
		void	**initialize**(int keysize)
1.2		void	**initialize**(int keysize, SecureRandom random)
	❋◆		**KeyPairGenerator**(String algorithm)

KeyPairGeneratorSpi   java.security

```
Object
    ➥KeyPairGeneratorSpi
```

	○	KeyPair	**generateKeyPair**()
1.2		void	**initialize**(spec.AlgorithmParameterSpec params,
			SecureRandom random)
			throws InvalidAlgorithmParameterException
	○	void	**initialize**(int keysize, SecureRandom random)
	❋		**KeyPairGeneratorSpi**()

KeyStore   java.security

```
Object
    ➥KeyStore
```

	●	java.util.Enumeration	**aliases**() *throws* KeyStoreException
	●	boolean	**containsAlias**(String alias) *throws* KeyStoreException
	●	void	**deleteEntry**(String alias) *throws* KeyStoreException
	●	cert.Certificate	**getCertificate**(String alias)
			throws KeyStoreException
	●	String	**getCertificateAlias**(cert.Certificate cert)
			throws KeyStoreException
	●	cert.Certificate[]	**getCertificateChain**(String alias)
			throws KeyStoreException
	●	java.util.Date	**getCreationDate**(String alias)
			throws KeyStoreException

■	String	**getDefaultType**()
❏	KeyStore	**getInstance**(String type) *throws* KeyStoreException
❏	KeyStore	**getInstance**(String type, String provider)
		throws KeyStoreException,
		NoSuchProviderException
●	Key	**getKey**(String alias, char[] password)
		throws KeyStoreException,
		NoSuchAlgorithmException,
		UnrecoverableKeyException
●	Provider	**getProvider**()
●	String	**getType**()
●	boolean	**isCertificateEntry**(String alias)
		throws KeyStoreException
●	boolean	**isKeyEntry**(String alias) *throws* KeyStoreException
✳◆		**KeyStore**(KeyStoreSpi keyStoreSpi,
		Provider provider, String type)
●	void	**load**(java.io.InputStream stream, char[] password)
		throws java.io.IOException,
		NoSuchAlgorithmException,
		cert.CertificateException
●	void	**setCertificateEntry**(String alias,
		cert.Certificate cert) *throws* KeyStoreException
●	void	**setKeyEntry**(String alias, byte[] key,
		cert.Certificate[] chain)
		throws KeyStoreException
●	void	**setKeyEntry**(String alias, Key key, char[] password,
		cert.Certificate[] chain)
		throws KeyStoreException
●	int	**size**() *throws* KeyStoreException
●	void	**store**(java.io.OutputStream stream, char[] password)
		throws KeyStoreException, java.io.IOException,
		NoSuchAlgorithmException,
		cert.CertificateException

KeyStoreException   java.security

```
Object
  ➡Throwable                          java.io.Serializable
    ➡Exception
      ➡GeneralSecurityException
        ➡KeyStoreException
```

✳	**KeyStoreException**()
✳	**KeyStoreException**(String msg)

KeyStoreSpi   java.security

```
Object
  ➡KeyStoreSpi
```

○	java.util.Enumeration	**engineAliases**()
○	boolean	**engineContainsAlias**(String alias)
○	void	**engineDeleteEntry**(String alias)
		throws KeyStoreException
○	cert.Certificate	**engineGetCertificate**(String alias)
○	String	**engineGetCertificateAlias**(cert.Certificate cert)
○	cert.Certificate[]	**engineGetCertificateChain**(String alias)
○	java.util.Date	**engineGetCreationDate**(String alias)
○	Key	**engineGetKey**(String alias, char[] password)
		throws NoSuchAlgorithmException,
		UnrecoverableKeyException
○	boolean	**engineIsCertificateEntry**(String alias)
○	boolean	**engineIsKeyEntry**(String alias)
○	void	**engineLoad**(java.io.InputStream stream,
		char[] password) _throws_ java.io.IOException,
		NoSuchAlgorithmException,
		cert.CertificateException
○	void	**engineSetCertificateEntry**(String alias,
		cert.Certificate cert) _throws_ KeyStoreException
○	void	**engineSetKeyEntry**(String alias, byte[] key,
		cert.Certificate[] chain)
		throws KeyStoreException
○	void	**engineSetKeyEntry**(String alias, Key key,
		char[] password, cert.Certificate[] chain)
		throws KeyStoreException
○	int	**engineSize**()
○	void	**engineStore**(java.io.OutputStream stream,
		char[] password) _throws_ java.io.IOException,
		NoSuchAlgorithmException,
		cert.CertificateException
✳		**KeyStoreSpi**()

LineNumberReader   `java.io`

```
Object
  ➥Reader
    ➥BufferedReader
      ➥LineNumberReader
```

	int	**getLineNumber**()
✳		**LineNumberReader**(Reader in)
✳		**LineNumberReader**(Reader in, int sz)
	void	**mark**(int readAheadLimit) _throws_ IOException
	int	**read**() _throws_ IOException
	int	**read**(char[] cbuf, int off, int len)
		throws IOException
	String	**readLine**() _throws_ IOException
	void	**reset**() _throws_ IOException
	void	**setLineNumber**(int lineNumber)
	long	**skip**(long n) _throws_ IOException

LinkageError   java.lang

```
Object
  ➥Throwable                        java.io.Serializable
      ➥Error
          ➥LinkageError
```

✽	**LinkageError**()
✽	**LinkageError**(String s)

LinkedList   java.util

```
Object
  ➥AbstractCollection              Collection
      ➥AbstractList                List
          ➥AbstractSequentialList
              ➥LinkedList          List, Cloneable, java.io.Serializable
```

	void	**add**(int index, Object element)
	boolean	**add**(Object o)
	boolean	**addAll**(Collection c)
	boolean	**addAll**(int index, Collection c)
	void	**addFirst**(Object o)
	void	**addLast**(Object o)
	void	**clear**()
	Object	**clone**()
	boolean	**contains**(Object o)
	Object	**get**(int index)
	Object	**getFirst**()
	Object	**getLast**()
	int	**indexOf**(Object o)
	int	**lastIndexOf**(Object o)
✽		**LinkedList**()
✽		**LinkedList**(Collection c)
	ListIterator	**listIterator**(int index)
	Object	**remove**(int index)
	boolean	**remove**(Object o)
	Object	**removeFirst**()
	Object	**removeLast**()
	Object	**set**(int index, Object element)
	int	**size**()
	Object[]	**toArray**()
	Object[]	**toArray**(Object[] a)

List   java.util

```
List                               Collection
```

void	**add**(int index, Object element)
boolean	**add**(Object o)
boolean	**addAll**(Collection c)
boolean	**addAll**(int index, Collection c)

void	**clear**()
boolean	**contains**(Object o)
boolean	**containsAll**(Collection c)
boolean	**equals**(Object o)
Object	**get**(int index)
int	**hashCode**()
int	**indexOf**(Object o)
boolean	**isEmpty**()
Iterator	**iterator**()
int	**lastIndexOf**(Object o)
ListIterator	**listIterator**()
ListIterator	**listIterator**(int index)
Object	**remove**(int index)
boolean	**remove**(Object o)
boolean	**removeAll**(Collection c)
boolean	**retainAll**(Collection c)
Object	**set**(int index, Object element)
int	**size**()
List	**subList**(int fromIndex, int toIndex)
Object[]	**toArray**()
Object[]	**toArray**(Object[] a)

ListIterator   java.util
ListIterator   Iterator

void	**add**(Object o)
boolean	**hasNext**()
boolean	**hasPrevious**()
Object	**next**()
int	**nextIndex**()
Object	**previous**()
int	**previousIndex**()
void	**remove**()
void	**set**(Object o)

ListResourceBundle   java.util
Object
→ResourceBundle
 →ListResourceBundle

○♦	Object[][]	**getContents**()
	Enumeration	**getKeys**()
●	Object	**handleGetObject**(String key)
✳		**ListResourceBundle**()

Locale   java.util
Object
→Locale   Cloneable, java.io.Serializable

✍■	Locale	**CANADA**
✍■	Locale	**CANADA_FRENCH**
✍■	Locale	**CHINA**
✍■	Locale	**CHINESE**
	Object	**clone**()
✍■	Locale	**ENGLISH**
	boolean	**equals**(Object obj)
✍■	Locale	**FRANCE**
✍■	Locale	**FRENCH**
✍■	Locale	**GERMAN**
✍■	Locale	**GERMANY**
❑	Locale[]	**getAvailableLocales**()
	String	**getCountry**()
❑	Locale	**getDefault**()
●	String	**getDisplayCountry**()
	String	**getDisplayCountry**(Locale inLocale)
●	String	**getDisplayLanguage**()
	String	**getDisplayLanguage**(Locale inLocale)
●	String	**getDisplayName**()
	String	**getDisplayName**(Locale inLocale)
●	String	**getDisplayVariant**()
	String	**getDisplayVariant**(Locale inLocale)
	String	**getISO3Country**() *throws* MissingResourceException
	String	**getISO3Language**() *throws* MissingResourceException
❑	String[]	**getISOCountries**()
❑	String[]	**getISOLanguages**()
	String	**getLanguage**()
	String	**getVariant**()
	int	**hashCode**()
✍■	Locale	**ITALIAN**
✍■	Locale	**ITALY**
✍■	Locale	**JAPAN**
✍■	Locale	**JAPANESE**
✍■	Locale	**KOREA**
✍■	Locale	**KOREAN**
✳		**Locale**(String language, String country)
✳		**Locale**(String language, String country, String variant)
✍■	Locale	**PRC**
❑	void	**setDefault**(Locale newLocale)
✍■	Locale	**SIMPLIFIED_CHINESE**
✍■	Locale	**TAIWAN**
●	String	**toString**()
✍■	Locale	**TRADITIONAL_CHINESE**
✍■	Locale	**UK**
✍■	Locale	**US**

Long	java.lang

Object
➥Number
  ➥Long

java.io.Serializable
Comparable

1.1		byte	**byteValue**()
1.2		int	**compareTo**(Long anotherLong)
1.2		int	**compareTo**(Object o)
	❑	Long	**decode**(String nm) *throws* NumberFormatException
		double	**doubleValue**()
		boolean	**equals**(Object obj)
		float	**floatValue**()
	❑	Long	**getLong**(String nm)
	❑	Long	**getLong**(String nm, long val)
	❑	Long	**getLong**(String nm, Long val)
		int	**hashCode**()
		int	**intValue**()
	✳		**Long**(long value)
	✳		**Long**(String s) *throws* NumberFormatException
		long	**longValue**()
	⚠■	long	**MAX_VALUE**
	⚠■	long	**MIN_VALUE**
	❑	long	**parseLong**(String s) *throws* NumberFormatException
	❑	long	**parseLong**(String s, int radix)
			throws NumberFormatException
1.1		short	**shortValue**()
1.0.2	❑	String	**toBinaryString**(long i)
1.0.2	❑	String	**toHexString**(long i)
1.0.2	❑	String	**toOctalString**(long i)
		String	**toString**()
	❑	String	**toString**(long i)
	❑	String	**toString**(long i, int radix)
1.1	⚠■	Class	**TYPE**
	❑	Long	**valueOf**(String s) *throws* NumberFormatException
	❑	Long	**valueOf**(String s, int radix)
			throws NumberFormatException

MalformedURLException   java.net

```
Object
  ➡Throwable                        java.io.Serializable
    ➡Exception
      ➡java.io.IOException
        ➡MalformedURLException
```

✳		**MalformedURLException**()
✳		**MalformedURLException**(String msg)

Manifest   java.util.jar

```
Object
  ➡Manifest                         Cloneable
```

	void	**clear**()
	Object	**clone**()
	boolean	**equals**(Object o)

	Attributes	**getAttributes**(String name)
	java.util.Map	**getEntries**()
	Attributes	**getMainAttributes**()
	int	**hashCode**()
❋		**Manifest**()
❋		**Manifest**(java.io.InputStream is)
		throws java.io.IOException
❋		**Manifest**(Manifest man)
	void	**read**(java.io.InputStream is)
		throws java.io.IOException
	void	**write**(java.io.OutputStream out)
		throws java.io.IOException

Map   java.util
Map

	void	**clear**()
	boolean	**containsKey**(Object key)
	boolean	**containsValue**(Object value)
	Set	**entrySet**()
	boolean	**equals**(Object o)
	Object	**get**(Object key)
	int	**hashCode**()
	boolean	**isEmpty**()
	Set	**keySet**()
	Object	**put**(Object key, Object value)
	void	**putAll**(Map t)
	Object	**remove**(Object key)
	int	**size**()
	Collection	**values**()

Map.Entry   java.util
Map.Entry

	boolean	**equals**(Object o)
	Object	**getKey**()
	Object	**getValue**()
	int	**hashCode**()
	Object	**setValue**(Object value)

Math   java.lang
Object
  ➡Math

	double	**abs**(double a)
❏	float	**abs**(float a)
❏	int	**abs**(int a)

❏	long	**abs**(long a)
❏	double	**acos**(double a)
❏	double	**asin**(double a)
❏	double	**atan**(double a)
❏	double	**atan2**(double a, double b)
❏	double	**ceil**(double a)
❏	double	**cos**(double a)
✍■	double	**E**
❏	double	**exp**(double a)
❏	double	**floor**(double a)
❏	double	**IEEEremainder**(double f1, double f2)
❏	double	**log**(double a)
❏	double	**max**(double a, double b)
❏	float	**max**(float a, float b)
❏	int	**max**(int a, int b)
❏	long	**max**(long a, long b)
❏	double	**min**(double a, double b)
❏	float	**min**(float a, float b)
❏	int	**min**(int a, int b)
❏	long	**min**(long a, long b)
✍■	double	**PI**
❏	double	**pow**(double a, double b)
❏	double	**random**()
❏	double	**rint**(double a)
❏	long	**round**(double a)
❏	int	**round**(float a)
❏	double	**sin**(double a)
❏	double	**sqrt**(double a)
❏	double	**tan**(double a)
1.2 ❏	double	**toDegrees**(double angrad)
1.2 ❏	double	**toRadians**(double angdeg)

Member   `java.lang.reflect`

Member

✍■	int	**DECLARED**
	Class	**getDeclaringClass**()
	int	**getModifiers**()
	String	**getName**()
✍■	int	**PUBLIC**

MessageDigest   `java.security`

Object
    ➥MessageDigestSpi
        ➥MessageDigest

	Object	**clone**() *throws* CloneNotSupportedException
	byte[]	**digest**()

	byte[]	**digest**(byte[] input)
	int	**digest**(byte[] buf, int offset, int len)
		throws DigestException
●	String	**getAlgorithm**()
1.2 ●	int	**getDigestLength**()
❑	MessageDigest	**getInstance**(String algorithm)
		throws NoSuchAlgorithmException
❑	MessageDigest	**getInstance**(String algorithm, String provider)
		throws NoSuchAlgorithmException,
		NoSuchProviderException
●	Provider	**getProvider**()
❑	boolean	**isEqual**(byte[] digesta, byte[] digestb)
✳◆		**MessageDigest**(String algorithm)
	void	**reset**()
	String	**toString**()
	void	**update**(byte input)
	void	**update**(byte[] input)
	void	**update**(byte[] input, int offset, int len)

MessageDigestSpi   java.security

Object
　➡MessageDigestSpi

	Object	**clone**() *throws* CloneNotSupportedException
○◆	byte[]	**engineDigest**()
1.2 ◆	int	**engineDigest**(byte[] buf, int offset, int len)
		throws DigestException
1.2 ◆	int	**engineGetDigestLength**()
○◆	void	**engineReset**()
○◆	void	**engineUpdate**(byte input)
○◆	void	**engineUpdate**(byte[] input, int offset, int len)
✳		**MessageDigestSpi**()

MessageFormat   java.text

Object
　➡Format   java.io.Serializable, Cloneable
　　➡MessageFormat

	void	**applyPattern**(String newPattern)
	Object	**clone**()
	boolean	**equals**(Object obj)
●	StringBuffer	**format**(Object[] source, StringBuffer result,
		FieldPosition ignore)
●	StringBuffer	**format**(Object source, StringBuffer result,
		FieldPosition ignore)
❑	String	**format**(String pattern, Object[] arguments)
	Format[]	**getFormats**()
	java.util.Locale	**getLocale**()
	int	**hashCode**()

✳		**MessageFormat**(String pattern)
	Object[]	**parse**(String source) *throws* ParseException
	Object[]	**parse**(String source, ParsePosition status)
	Object	**parseObject**(String text, ParsePosition status)
	void	**setFormat**(int variable, Format newFormat)
	void	**setFormats**(Format[] newFormats)
	void	**setLocale**(java.util.Locale theLocale)
	String	**toPattern**()

Method   java.lang.reflect

Object
➡AccessibleObject
➡Method   Member

	boolean	**equals**(Object obj)
	Class	**getDeclaringClass**()
	Class[]	**getExceptionTypes**()
	int	**getModifiers**()
	String	**getName**()
	Class[]	**getParameterTypes**()
	Class	**getReturnType**()
	int	**hashCode**()
	Object	**invoke**(Object obj, Object[] args)
		throws IllegalAccessException,
		IllegalArgumentException,
		InvocationTargetException
	String	**toString**()

MissingResourceException   java.util

Object
➡Throwable   java.io.Serializable
➡Exception
➡RuntimeException
➡MissingResourceException

	String	**getClassName**()
	String	**getKey**()
✳		**MissingResourceException**(String s,
		String className, String key)

Modifier   java.lang.reflect

Object
➡Modifier

◿■	int	**ABSTRACT**
◿■	int	**FINAL**
◿■	int	**INTERFACE**

❏		boolean	**isAbstract**(int mod)
❏		boolean	**isFinal**(int mod)
❏		boolean	**isInterface**(int mod)
❏		boolean	**isNative**(int mod)
❏		boolean	**isPrivate**(int mod)
❏		boolean	**isProtected**(int mod)
❏		boolean	**isPublic**(int mod)
❏		boolean	**isStatic**(int mod)
❏		boolean	**isStrict**(int mod)
❏		boolean	**isSynchronized**(int mod)
❏		boolean	**isTransient**(int mod)
❏		boolean	**isVolatile**(int mod)
❋			**Modifier**()
⚠■		int	**NATIVE**
⚠■		int	**PRIVATE**
⚠■		int	**PROTECTED**
⚠■		int	**PUBLIC**
⚠■		int	**STATIC**
⚠■		int	**STRICT**
⚠■		int	**SYNCHRONIZED**
❏		String	**toString**(int mod)
⚠■		int	**TRANSIENT**
⚠■		int	**VOLATILE**

MulticastSocket   java.net

Object
➥DatagramSocket
  ➥MulticastSocket

	InetAddress	**getInterface**() *throws* SocketException
	int	**getTimeToLive**() *throws* java.io.IOException
	void	**joinGroup**(InetAddress mcastaddr) *throws* java.io.IOException
	void	**leaveGroup**(InetAddress mcastaddr) *throws* java.io.IOException
❋		**MulticastSocket**() *throws* java.io.IOException
❋		**MulticastSocket**(int port) *throws* java.io.IOException
	void	**send**(DatagramPacket p, byte ttl) *throws* java.io.IOException
	void	**setInterface**(InetAddress inf) *throws* SocketException
	void	**setTimeToLive**(int ttl) *throws* java.io.IOException

NegativeArraySizeException   java.lang

Object
➥Throwable   java.io.Serializable
  ➥Exception

➡RuntimeException
    ➡NegativeArraySizeException

❊	NegativeArraySizeException()
❊	NegativeArraySizeException(String s)

NetPermission   **java.net**

Object
  ➡java.security.Permission   java.security.Guard, java.io.Serializable
    ➡java.security.BasicPermission   java.io.Serializable
      ➡NetPermission

❊	NetPermission(String name)
❊	NetPermission(String name, String actions)

NoClassDefFoundError   **java.lang**

Object
  ➡Throwable   java.io.Serializable
    ➡Error
      ➡LinkageError
        ➡NoClassDefFoundError

❊	NoClassDefFoundError()
❊	NoClassDefFoundError(String s)

NoRouteToHostException   **java.net**

Object
  ➡Throwable   java.io.Serializable
    ➡Exception
      ➡java.io.IOException
        ➡SocketException
          ➡NoRouteToHostException

❊	NoRouteToHostException()
❊	NoRouteToHostException(String msg)

NoSuchAlgorithmException   **java.security**

Object
  ➡Throwable   java.io.Serializable
    ➡Exception
      ➡GeneralSecurityException
        ➡NoSuchAlgorithmException

❊	NoSuchAlgorithmException()
❊	NoSuchAlgorithmException(String msg)

NoSuchElementException   java.util

```
Object
  ➡Throwable                        java.io.Serializable
      ➡Exception
          ➡RuntimeException
              ➡NoSuchElementException
```

| ❋ | **NoSuchElementException()** |
| ❋ | **NoSuchElementException**(String s) |

NoSuchFieldError   java.lang

```
Object
  ➡Throwable                        java.io.Serializable
      ➡Error
          ➡LinkageError
              ➡IncompatibleClassChangeError
                  ➡NoSuchFieldError
```

| ❋ | **NoSuchFieldError()** |
| ❋ | **NoSuchFieldError**(String s) |

NoSuchFieldException   java.lang

```
Object
  ➡Throwable                        java.io.Serializable
      ➡Exception
          ➡NoSuchFieldException
```

| ❋ | **NoSuchFieldException()** |
| ❋ | **NoSuchFieldException**(String s) |

NoSuchMethodError   java.lang

```
Object
  ➡Throwable                        java.io.Serializable
      ➡Error
          ➡LinkageError
              ➡IncompatibleClassChangeError
                  ➡NoSuchMethodError
```

| ❋ | **NoSuchMethodError()** |
| ❋ | **NoSuchMethodError**(String s) |

NoSuchMethodException   java.lang

```
Object
  ➡Throwable                        java.io.Serializable
      ➡Exception
          ➡NoSuchMethodException
```

✳	NoSuchMethodException()
✳	NoSuchMethodException(String s)

NoSuchProviderException   java.security

```
Object
  ➥Throwable                        java.io.Serializable
     ➥Exception
        ➥GeneralSecurityException
           ➥NoSuchProviderException
```

✳	NoSuchProviderException()
✳	NoSuchProviderException(String msg)

NotActiveException   java.io

```
Object
  ➥Throwable                        Serializable
     ➥Exception
        ➥IOException
           ➥ObjectStreamException
              ➥NotActiveException
```

✳	NotActiveException()
✳	NotActiveException(String reason)

NotSerializableException   java.io

```
Object
  ➥Throwable                        Serializable
     ➥Exception
        ➥IOException
           ➥ObjectStreamException
              ➥NotSerializableException
```

✳	NotSerializableException()
✳	NotSerializableException(String classname)

NullPointerException   java.lang

```
Object
  ➥Throwable                        java.io.Serializable
     ➥Exception
        ➥RuntimeException
           ➥NullPointerException
```

✳	NullPointerException()
✳	NullPointerException(String s)

Number			**java.lang**

Object
→Number   java.io.Serializable

1.1		byte	**byteValue**()
	○	double	**doubleValue**()
	○	float	**floatValue**()
	○	int	**intValue**()
	○	long	**longValue**()
	✳		**Number**()
1.1		short	**shortValue**()

NumberFormat			**java.text**

Object
→Format   java.io.Serializable, Cloneable
  →NumberFormat

		Object	**clone**()
		boolean	**equals**(Object obj)
	●	String	**format**(double number)
	○	StringBuffer	**format**(double number, StringBuffer toAppendTo, FieldPosition pos)
	●	String	**format**(long number)
	○	StringBuffer	**format**(long number, StringBuffer toAppendTo, FieldPosition pos)
	●	StringBuffer	**format**(Object number, StringBuffer toAppendTo, FieldPosition pos)
	⚠■	int	**FRACTION_FIELD**
	□	java.util.Locale[]	**getAvailableLocales**()
	■	NumberFormat	**getCurrencyInstance**()
	□	NumberFormat	**getCurrencyInstance**(java.util.Locale inLocale)
	■	NumberFormat	**getInstance**()
	□	NumberFormat	**getInstance**(java.util.Locale inLocale)
		int	**getMaximumFractionDigits**()
		int	**getMaximumIntegerDigits**()
		int	**getMinimumFractionDigits**()
		int	**getMinimumIntegerDigits**()
	■	NumberFormat	**getNumberInstance**()
	□	NumberFormat	**getNumberInstance**(java.util.Locale inLocale)
	■	NumberFormat	**getPercentInstance**()
	□	NumberFormat	**getPercentInstance**(java.util.Locale inLocale)
		int	**hashCode**()
	⚠■	int	**INTEGER_FIELD**
		boolean	**isGroupingUsed**()
		boolean	**isParseIntegerOnly**()
	✳		**NumberFormat**()
		Number	**parse**(String text) *throws* ParseException
	○	Number	**parse**(String text, ParsePosition parsePosition)
	●	Object	**parseObject**(String source, ParsePosition parsePosition)

```
             void  setGroupingUsed(boolean newValue)
             void  setMaximumFractionDigits(int newValue)
             void  setMaximumIntegerDigits(int newValue)
             void  setMinimumFractionDigits(int newValue)
             void  setMinimumIntegerDigits(int newValue)
             void  setParseIntegerOnly(boolean value)
```

NumberFormatException   java.lang

```
Object
  ➥Throwable                        java.io.Serializable
     ➥Exception
        ➥RuntimeException
           ➥IllegalArgumentException
              ➥NumberFormatException
```

```
   ※                    NumberFormatException()
   ※                    NumberFormatException(String s)
```

Object   java.lang

```
Object
```

```
   ◆      Object  clone() throws CloneNotSupportedException
         boolean  equals(Object obj)
   ◆        void  finalize() throws Throwable
   ●       Class  getClass()
             int  hashCode()
   ●        void  notify()
   ●        void  notifyAll()
   ※                Object()
          String  toString()
   ●        void  wait() throws InterruptedException
   ●        void  wait(long timeout) throws InterruptedException
   ●        void  wait(long timeout, int nanos)
                     throws InterruptedException
```

ObjectInput   java.io

```
ObjectInput                      DataInput
```

```
             int  available() throws IOException
            void  close() throws IOException
             int  read() throws IOException
             int  read(byte[] b) throws IOException
             int  read(byte[] b, int off, int len) throws IOException
          Object  readObject() throws ClassNotFoundException,
                     IOException
            long  skip(long n) throws IOException
```

ObjectInputStream			**java.io**

```
Object
    ➥InputStream
        ➥ObjectInputStream                    ObjectInput, ObjectStreamConstants
```

		int	**available**() *throws* IOException
		void	**close**() *throws* IOException
		void	**defaultReadObject**() *throws* IOException, ClassNotFoundException, NotActiveException
	◆	boolean	**enableResolveObject**(boolean enable) *throws* SecurityException
	✳◆		**ObjectInputStream**() *throws* IOException, SecurityException
	✳		**ObjectInputStream**(InputStream in) *throws* IOException, StreamCorruptedException
		int	**read**() *throws* IOException
		int	**read**(byte[] b, int off, int len) *throws* IOException
		boolean	**readBoolean**() *throws* IOException
		byte	**readByte**() *throws* IOException
		char	**readChar**() *throws* IOException
1.3	◆	ObjectStreamClass	**readClassDescriptor**() *throws* IOException, ClassNotFoundException
		double	**readDouble**() *throws* IOException
1.2		ObjectInputStream.¬ GetField	**readFields**() *throws* IOException, ClassNotFoundException, NotActiveException
		float	**readFloat**() *throws* IOException
		void	**readFully**(byte[] data) *throws* IOException
		void	**readFully**(byte[] data, int offset, int size) *throws* IOException
		int	**readInt**() *throws* IOException
		String	**readLine**() *throws* IOException
		long	**readLong**() *throws* IOException
	●	Object	**readObject**() *throws* OptionalDataException, ClassNotFoundException, IOException
1.2	◆	Object	**readObjectOverride**() *throws* OptionalDataException, ClassNotFoundException, IOException
		short	**readShort**() *throws* IOException
	◆	void	**readStreamHeader**() *throws* IOException, StreamCorruptedException
		int	**readUnsignedByte**() *throws* IOException
		int	**readUnsignedShort**() *throws* IOException
		String	**readUTF**() *throws* IOException
		void	**registerValidation**(ObjectInputValidation obj, int prio) *throws* NotActiveException, InvalidObjectException
	◆	Class	**resolveClass**(ObjectStreamClass v) *throws* IOException, ClassNotFoundException
	◆	Object	**resolveObject**(Object obj) *throws* IOException
1.3	◆	Class	**resolveProxyClass**(String[] interfaces) *throws* IOException, ClassNotFoundException
		int	**skipBytes**(int len) *throws* IOException

ObjectInputStream.GetField			**java.io**

Object
➥ObjectInputStream.GetField

○	boolean	**defaulted**(String name) *throws* IOException, IllegalArgumentException
○	boolean	**get**(String name, boolean defvalue) *throws* IOException, IllegalArgumentException
○	byte	**get**(String name, byte defvalue) *throws* IOException, IllegalArgumentException
○	char	**get**(String name, char defvalue) *throws* IOException, IllegalArgumentException
○	double	**get**(String name, double defvalue) *throws* IOException, IllegalArgumentException
○	float	**get**(String name, float defvalue) *throws* IOException, IllegalArgumentException
○	int	**get**(String name, int defvalue) *throws* IOException, IllegalArgumentException
○	long	**get**(String name, long defvalue) *throws* IOException, IllegalArgumentException
○	Object	**get**(String name, Object defvalue) *throws* IOException, IllegalArgumentException
○	short	**get**(String name, short defvalue) *throws* IOException, IllegalArgumentException
○	ObjectStreamClass	**getObjectStreamClass**()
✳		**ObjectInputStream.GetField**()

ObjectInputValidation		**java.io**

ObjectInputValidation

	void	**validateObject**() *throws* InvalidObjectException

ObjectOutput		**java.io**

ObjectOutput   DataOutput

void	**close**() *throws* IOException
void	**flush**() *throws* IOException
void	**write**(byte[] b) *throws* IOException
void	**write**(byte[] b, int off, int len) *throws* IOException
void	**write**(int b) *throws* IOException
void	**writeObject**(Object obj) *throws* IOException

ObjectOutputStream		**java.io**

Object
➥OutputStream
　➥ObjectOutputStream   ObjectOutput, ObjectStreamConstants

	♦	void	**annotateClass**(Class cl) *throws* IOException
1.3	♦	void	**annotateProxyClass**(Class cl) *throws* IOException
		void	**close**() *throws* IOException
		void	**defaultWriteObject**() *throws* IOException
	♦	void	**drain**() *throws* IOException
	♦	boolean	**enableReplaceObject**(boolean enable)
			throws SecurityException
		void	**flush**() *throws* IOException
	✲♦		**ObjectOutputStream**() *throws* IOException,
			SecurityException
	✲		**ObjectOutputStream**(OutputStream out)
			throws IOException
1.2		ObjectOutputStream.¬	**putFields**() *throws* IOException
		PutField	
	♦	Object	**replaceObject**(Object obj) *throws* IOException
		void	**reset**() *throws* IOException
1.2		void	**useProtocolVersion**(int version) *throws* IOException
		void	**write**(byte[] b) *throws* IOException
		void	**write**(byte[] b, int off, int len)
			throws IOException
		void	**write**(int data) *throws* IOException
		void	**writeBoolean**(boolean data) *throws* IOException
		void	**writeByte**(int data) *throws* IOException
		void	**writeBytes**(String data) *throws* IOException
		void	**writeChar**(int data) *throws* IOException
		void	**writeChars**(String data) *throws* IOException
1.3	♦	void	**writeClassDescriptor**(ObjectStreamClass classdesc)
			throws IOException
		void	**writeDouble**(double data) *throws* IOException
1.2		void	**writeFields**() *throws* IOException
		void	**writeFloat**(float data) *throws* IOException
		void	**writeInt**(int data) *throws* IOException
		void	**writeLong**(long data) *throws* IOException
	●	void	**writeObject**(Object obj) *throws* IOException
1.2	♦	void	**writeObjectOverride**(Object obj) *throws* IOException
		void	**writeShort**(int data) *throws* IOException
	♦	void	**writeStreamHeader**() *throws* IOException
		void	**writeUTF**(String s) *throws* IOException

ObjectOutputStream.PutField java.io

Object
→ObjectOutputStream.PutField

	✲		**ObjectOutputStream.PutField**()
	○	void	**put**(String name, boolean value)
	○	void	**put**(String name, byte value)
	○	void	**put**(String name, char value)
	○	void	**put**(String name, double value)
	○	void	**put**(String name, float value)
	○	void	**put**(String name, int value)

○	void	**put**(String name, long value)	
○	void	**put**(String name, Object value)	
○	void	**put**(String name, short value)	
○	void	**write**(ObjectOutput out) *throws* IOException	

ObjectStreamClass — java.io

Object
→ObjectStreamClass   Serializable

	Class	**forClass**()
	ObjectStreamField	**getField**(String name)
1.2	ObjectStreamField[]	**getFields**()
	String	**getName**()
	long	**getSerialVersionUID**()
❑	ObjectStreamClass	**lookup**(Class cl)
	ObjectStreamField[]	**NO_FIELDS**
	String	**toString**()

ObjectStreamConstants — java.io

ObjectStreamConstants

	int	**baseWireHandle**
1.2	int	**PROTOCOL_VERSION_1**
1.2	int	**PROTOCOL_VERSION_2**
1.2	byte	**SC_BLOCK_DATA**
	byte	**SC_EXTERNALIZABLE**
	byte	**SC_SERIALIZABLE**
	byte	**SC_WRITE_METHOD**
	short	**STREAM_MAGIC**
	short	**STREAM_VERSION**
1.2	SerializablePermission	**SUBCLASS_IMPLEMENTATION_PERMISSION**
1.2	SerializablePermission	**SUBSTITUTION_PERMISSION**
	byte	**TC_ARRAY**
	byte	**TC_BASE**
	byte	**TC_BLOCKDATA**
	byte	**TC_BLOCKDATALONG**
	byte	**TC_CLASS**
	byte	**TC_CLASSDESC**
	byte	**TC_ENDBLOCKDATA**
	byte	**TC_EXCEPTION**
	byte	**TC_LONGSTRING**
	byte	**TC_MAX**
	byte	**TC_NULL**
	byte	**TC_OBJECT**
	byte	**TC_PROXYCLASSDESC**
	byte	**TC_REFERENCE**
	byte	**TC_RESET**
	byte	**TC_STRING**

ObjectStreamException   java.io

```
Object
  ➥Throwable                            Serializable
      ➥Exception
          ➥IOException
              ➥ObjectStreamException
```

✳◆	**ObjectStreamException**()
✳◆	**ObjectStreamException**(String classname)

ObjectStreamField   java.io

```
Object
  ➥ObjectStreamField                    Comparable
```

int	**compareTo**(Object o)
String	**getName**()
int	**getOffset**()
Class	**getType**()
char	**getTypeCode**()
String	**getTypeString**()
boolean	**isPrimitive**()
✳	**ObjectStreamField**(String n, Class clazz)
◆ void	**setOffset**(int offset)
String	**toString**()

Observable   java.util

```
Object
  ➥Observable
```

void	**addObserver**(Observer o)
◆ void	**clearChanged**()
int	**countObservers**()
void	**deleteObserver**(Observer o)
void	**deleteObservers**()
boolean	**hasChanged**()
void	**notifyObservers**()
void	**notifyObservers**(Object arg)
✳	**Observable**()
◆ void	**setChanged**()

Observer   java.util

```
Observer
```

void	**update**(Observable o, Object arg)

OptionalDataException   java.io

```
Object
    ➥Throwable                              Serializable
        ➥Exception
            ➥IOException
                ➥ObjectStreamException
                    ➥OptionalDataException
```

✎	boolean	**eof**
✎	int	**length**

OutOfMemoryError   java.lang

```
Object
    ➥Throwable                        java.io.Serializable
        ➥Error
            ➥VirtualMachineError
                ➥OutOfMemoryError
```

✳	**OutOfMemoryError**()
✳	**OutOfMemoryError**(String s)

OutputConnection   javax.microedition.io

```
OutputConnection                              Connection
```

java.io.DataOutput¬ Stream	**openDataOutputStream**() *throws* java.io.IOException
java.io.OutputStream	**openOutputStream**() *throws* java.io.IOException

OutputStream   java.io

```
Object
    ➥OutputStream
```

	void	**close**() *throws* IOException
	void	**flush**() *throws* IOException
✳		**OutputStream**()
	void	**write**(byte[] b) *throws* IOException
	void	**write**(byte[] b, int off, int len) *throws* IOException
○	void	**write**(int b) *throws* IOException

OutputStreamWriter   java.io

```
Object
    ➥Writer
        ➥OutputStreamWriter
```

	void	**close**() *throws* IOException
	void	**flush**() *throws* IOException
	String	**getEncoding**()
✳		**OutputStreamWriter**(OutputStream out)
✳		**OutputStreamWriter**(OutputStream out, String enc)
		throws UnsupportedEncodingException
	void	**write**(char[] cbuf, int off, int len)
		throws IOException
	void	**write**(int c) *throws* IOException
	void	**write**(String str, int off, int len)
		throws IOException

Package   java.lang

Object
➡Package

	String	**getImplementationTitle**()
	String	**getImplementationVendor**()
	String	**getImplementationVersion**()
	String	**getName**()
❑	Package	**getPackage**(String name)
❑	Package[]	**getPackages**()
	String	**getSpecificationTitle**()
	String	**getSpecificationVendor**()
	String	**getSpecificationVersion**()
	int	**hashCode**()
	boolean	**isCompatibleWith**(String desired)
		throws NumberFormatException
	boolean	**isSealed**()
	boolean	**isSealed**(java.net.URL url)
	String	**toString**()

ParseException   java.text

Object
➡Throwable   java.io.Serializable
    ➡Exception
        ➡ParseException

	int	**getErrorOffset**()
✳		**ParseException**(String s, int errorOffset)

ParsePosition   java.text

Object
➡ParsePosition

	boolean	**equals**(Object obj)
	int	**getErrorIndex**()

	int	**getIndex**()
	int	**hashCode**()
✳		**ParsePosition**(int index)
	void	**setErrorIndex**(int ei)
	void	**setIndex**(int index)
	String	**toString**()

PasswordAuthentication   java.net

Object
➡ PasswordAuthentication

	char[]	**getPassword**()
	String	**getUserName**()
✳		**PasswordAuthentication**(String userName, char[] password)

Permission   java.security

Object
➡ Permission   Guard, java.io.Serializable

	void	**checkGuard**(Object object) *throws* SecurityException
○	boolean	**equals**(Object obj)
○	String	**getActions**()
●	String	**getName**()
○	int	**hashCode**()
○	boolean	**implies**(Permission permission)
	PermissionCollection	**newPermissionCollection**()
✳		**Permission**(String name)
	String	**toString**()

PermissionCollection   java.security

Object
➡ PermissionCollection   java.io.Serializable

○	void	**add**(Permission permission)
○	java.util.Enumeration	**elements**()
○	boolean	**implies**(Permission permission)
	boolean	**isReadOnly**()
✳		**PermissionCollection**()
	void	**setReadOnly**()
	String	**toString**()

Permissions   java.security

Object
➡ PermissionCollection   java.io.Serializable
  ➡ Permissions   java.io.Serializable

	void	add(Permission permission)
	java.util.Enumeration	elements()
	boolean	implies(Permission permission)
❉		Permissions()

PhantomReference   java.lang.ref

Object
→Reference
  →PhantomReference

	Object	get()
❉		PhantomReference(Object referent, ReferenceQueue q)

PipedInputStream   java.io

Object
→InputStream
  →PipedInputStream

1.0.2		int	available() *throws* IOException
1.1	⌱◆	byte[]	buffer
		void	close() *throws* IOException
		void	connect(PipedOutputStream src) *throws* IOException
1.1	⌱◆	int	in
1.1	⌱◆	int	out
1.1	⌱■◆	int	PIPE_SIZE
	❉		PipedInputStream()
	❉		PipedInputStream(PipedOutputStream src)
			throws IOException
		int	read() *throws* IOException
		int	read(byte[] b, int off, int len) *throws* IOException
1.1	◆	void	receive(int b) *throws* IOException

PipedOutputStream   java.io

Object
→OutputStream
  →PipedOutputStream

	void	close() *throws* IOException
	void	connect(PipedInputStream snk) *throws* IOException
	void	flush() *throws* IOException
❉		PipedOutputStream()
❉		PipedOutputStream(PipedInputStream snk)
		throws IOException
	void	write(byte[] b, int off, int len)
		throws IOException
	void	write(int b) *throws* IOException

PipedReader
java.io

```
Object
    Reader
        PipedReader
```

	void	**close**() *throws* IOException
	void	**connect**(PipedWriter src) *throws* IOException
✳		**PipedReader**()
✳		**PipedReader**(PipedWriter src) *throws* IOException
	int	**read**() *throws* IOException
	int	**read**(char[] cbuf, int off, int len) *throws* IOException
	boolean	**ready**() *throws* IOException

PipedWriter
java.io

```
Object
    Writer
        PipedWriter
```

	void	**close**() *throws* IOException
	void	**connect**(PipedReader snk) *throws* IOException
	void	**flush**() *throws* IOException
✳		**PipedWriter**()
✳		**PipedWriter**(PipedReader snk) *throws* IOException
	void	**write**(char[] cbuf, int off, int len) *throws* IOException
	void	**write**(int c) *throws* IOException

Policy
java.security

```
Object
    Policy
```

○	PermissionCollection	**getPermissions**(CodeSource codesource)
❑	Policy	**getPolicy**()
✳		**Policy**()
○	void	**refresh**()
❑	void	**setPolicy**(Policy policy)

Principal
java.security

```
Principal
```

	boolean	**equals**(Object another)
	String	**getName**()
	int	**hashCode**()
	String	**toString**()

PrintStream	java.io

```
Object
  ➡OutputStream
      ➡FilterOutputStream
          ➡PrintStream
```

		boolean	**checkError**()
		void	**close**()
		void	**flush**()
		void	**print**(boolean b)
		void	**print**(char c)
		void	**print**(char[] s)
		void	**print**(double d)
		void	**print**(float f)
		void	**print**(int i)
		void	**print**(long l)
		void	**print**(Object obj)
		void	**print**(String s)
		void	**println**()
		void	**println**(boolean x)
		void	**println**(char x)
		void	**println**(char[] x)
		void	**println**(double x)
		void	**println**(float x)
		void	**println**(int x)
		void	**println**(long x)
		void	**println**(Object x)
		void	**println**(String x)
	✻		**PrintStream**(OutputStream out)
	✻		**PrintStream**(OutputStream out, boolean autoFlush)
1.1	♦	void	**setError**()
		void	**write**(byte[] buf, int off, int len)
		void	**write**(int b)

PrintWriter	java.io

```
Object
  ➡Writer
      ➡PrintWriter
```

		boolean	**checkError**()
		void	**close**()
		void	**flush**()
1.2	✎♦	Writer	**out**
		void	**print**(boolean b)
		void	**print**(char c)
		void	**print**(char[] s)
		void	**print**(double d)
		void	**print**(float f)
		void	**print**(int i)
		void	**print**(long l)

	void	**print**(Object obj)
	void	**print**(String s)
	void	**println**()
	void	**println**(boolean x)
	void	**println**(char x)
	void	**println**(char[] x)
	void	**println**(double x)
	void	**println**(float x)
	void	**println**(int x)
	void	**println**(long x)
	void	**println**(Object x)
	void	**println**(String x)
✳		**PrintWriter**(OutputStream out)
✳		**PrintWriter**(OutputStream out, boolean autoFlush)
✳		**PrintWriter**(Writer out)
✳		**PrintWriter**(Writer out, boolean autoFlush)
◆	void	**setError**()
	void	**write**(char[] buf)
	void	**write**(char[] buf, int off, int len)
	void	**write**(int c)
	void	**write**(String s)
	void	**write**(String s, int off, int len)

PrivateKey   java.security

PrivateKey   Key

	long	**serialVersionUID**

PrivilegedAction   java.security

PrivilegedAction

	Object	**run**()

PrivilegedActionException   java.security

Object
  ➥Throwable   java.io.Serializable
    ➥Exception
      ➥PrivilegedActionException

	Exception	**getException**()
	void	**printStackTrace**()
	void	**printStackTrace**(java.io.PrintStream ps)
	void	**printStackTrace**(java.io.PrintWriter pw)
✳		**PrivilegedActionException**(Exception exception)
	String	**toString**()

PrivilegedExceptionAction   java.security
PrivilegedExceptionAction

Object	**run**() *throws* Exception

Process   java.lang
Object
➡Process

○	void	**destroy**()
○	int	**exitValue**()
○	java.io.InputStream	**getErrorStream**()
○	java.io.InputStream	**getInputStream**()
○	java.io.OutputStream	**getOutputStream**()
✳		**Process**()
○	int	**waitFor**() *throws* InterruptedException

Properties   java.util
Object
➡Dictionary
   ➡Hashtable   Map, Cloneable, java.io.Serializable
      ➡Properties

	♙◆	Properties **defaults**
	String	**getProperty**(String key)
	String	**getProperty**(String key, String defaultValue)
1.1	void	**list**(java.io.PrintStream out)
	void	**list**(java.io.PrintWriter out)
	void	**load**(java.io.InputStream inStream)
		throws java.io.IOException
	✳	**Properties**()
	✳	**Properties**(Properties defaults)
	Enumeration	**propertyNames**()
	void	**save**(java.io.OutputStream out, String header)
1.2	Object	**setProperty**(String key, String value)
	void	**store**(java.io.OutputStream out, String header)
		throws java.io.IOException

PropertyPermission   java.util
Object
➡java.security.Permission   java.security.Guard, java.io.Serializable
   ➡java.security.BasicPermission   java.io.Serializable
      ➡PropertyPermission

boolean	**equals**(Object obj)
String	**getActions**()
int	**hashCode**()
boolean	**implies**(java.security.Permission p)

	java.security.¬ PermissionCollection	**newPermissionCollection**()
✳		**PropertyPermission**(String name, String actions)

PropertyResourceBundle   java.util

```
Object
  ➡ResourceBundle
      ➡PropertyResourceBundle
```

	Enumeration	**getKeys**()
	Object	**handleGetObject**(String key)
✳		**PropertyResourceBundle**(java.io.InputStream stream) *throws* java.io.IOException

ProtectionDomain   java.security

```
Object
  ➡ProtectionDomain
```

●	CodeSource	**getCodeSource**()
●	PermissionCollection	**getPermissions**()
	boolean	**implies**(Permission permission)
✳		**ProtectionDomain**(CodeSource codesource, PermissionCollection permissions)
	String	**toString**()

ProtocolException   java.net

```
Object
  ➡Throwable                              java.io.Serializable
      ➡Exception
          ➡java.io.IOException
              ➡ProtocolException
```

✳		**ProtocolException**()
✳		**ProtocolException**(String host)

Provider   java.security

```
Object
  ➡java.util.Dictionary
      ➡java.util.Hashtable          java.util.Map, Cloneable, java.io.Serializable
          ➡java.util.Properties
              ➡Provider
```

1.2	void	**clear**()
1.2	java.util.Set	**entrySet**()
	String	**getInfo**()
	String	**getName**()

	double	**getVersion**()
1.2	java.util.Set	**keySet**()
	void	**load**(java.io.InputStream inStream)
		throws java.io.IOException
❊◆		**Provider**(String name, double version, String info)
1.2	Object	**put**(Object key, Object value)
1.2	void	**putAll**(java.util.Map t)
1.2	Object	**remove**(Object key)
	String	**toString**()
1.2	java.util.Collection	**values**()

ProviderException   java.security

Object
  ➡Throwable   java.io.Serializable
    ➡Exception
      ➡RuntimeException
        ➡ProviderException

❊	**ProviderException**()
❊◆	**ProviderException**(String s)

Proxy   java.lang.reflect

Object
  ➡Proxy   java.io.Serializable

❑	InvocationHandler	**getInvocationHandler**(Object proxy)
		throws IllegalArgumentException
❑	Class	**getProxyClass**(ClassLoader loader, Class[] interfaces)
		throws IllegalArgumentException
✍◆	InvocationHandler	**h**
❑	boolean	**isProxyClass**(Class cl)
❑	Object	**newProxyInstance**(ClassLoader loader,
		Class[] interfaces, InvocationHandler h)
		throws IllegalArgumentException
❊◆		**Proxy**(InvocationHandler h)

PublicKey   java.security

PublicKey   Key

✍■	long	**serialVersionUID**

PushbackInputStream   java.io

Object
  ➡InputStream
    ➡FilterInputStream
      ➡PushbackInputStream

		int	available() *throws* IOException
1.1	⚖◆	byte[]	buf
		void	close() *throws* IOException
		boolean	markSupported()
1.1	⚖◆	int	pos
	✳		PushbackInputStream(InputStream in)
1.1	✳		PushbackInputStream(InputStream in, int size)
		int	read() *throws* IOException
		int	read(byte[] b, int off, int len) *throws* IOException
1.2		long	skip(long n) *throws* IOException
1.1		void	unread(byte[] b) *throws* IOException
1.1		void	unread(byte[] b, int off, int len) *throws* IOException
		void	unread(int b) *throws* IOException

PushbackReader   java.io

```
Object
  ➡Reader
      ➡FilterReader
          ➡PushbackReader
```

		void	close() *throws* IOException
		void	mark(int readAheadLimit) *throws* IOException
		boolean	markSupported()
	✳		PushbackReader(Reader in)
	✳		PushbackReader(Reader in, int size)
		int	read() *throws* IOException
		int	read(char[] cbuf, int off, int len) *throws* IOException
		boolean	ready() *throws* IOException
		void	reset() *throws* IOException
		void	unread(char[] cbuf) *throws* IOException
		void	unread(char[] cbuf, int off, int len) *throws* IOException
		void	unread(int c) *throws* IOException

Random   java.util

```
Object
  ➡Random                        java.io.Serializable
```

		int	next(int bits)
1.1	◆	int	next(int bits)
1.2		boolean	nextBoolean()
1.1		void	nextBytes(byte[] bytes)
		double	nextDouble()
		float	nextFloat()
		double	nextGaussian()
		int	nextInt()
1.2		int	nextInt(int n)
		long	nextLong()

✳		**Random**()
✳		**Random**(long seed)
	void	**setSeed**(long seed)

RandomAccessFile   java.io

Object
➥RandomAccessFile   DataOutput, DataInput

---

	void	**close**() *throws* IOException
●	FileDescriptor	**getFD**() *throws* IOException
	long	**getFilePointer**() *throws* IOException
	long	**length**() *throws* IOException
✳		**RandomAccessFile**(File file, String mode)
		throws FileNotFoundException
✳		**RandomAccessFile**(String name, String mode)
		throws FileNotFoundException
	int	**read**() *throws* IOException
	int	**read**(byte[] b) *throws* IOException
	int	**read**(byte[] b, int off, int len) *throws* IOException
●	boolean	**readBoolean**() *throws* IOException
●	byte	**readByte**() *throws* IOException
●	char	**readChar**() *throws* IOException
●	double	**readDouble**() *throws* IOException
●	float	**readFloat**() *throws* IOException
●	void	**readFully**(byte[] b) *throws* IOException
●	void	**readFully**(byte[] b, int off, int len)
		throws IOException
●	int	**readInt**() *throws* IOException
●	String	**readLine**() *throws* IOException
●	long	**readLong**() *throws* IOException
●	short	**readShort**() *throws* IOException
●	int	**readUnsignedByte**() *throws* IOException
●	int	**readUnsignedShort**() *throws* IOException
●	String	**readUTF**() *throws* IOException
	void	**seek**(long pos) *throws* IOException
	void	**setLength**(long newLength) *throws* IOException
1.2	int	**skipBytes**(int n) *throws* IOException
	void	**write**(byte[] b) *throws* IOException
	void	**write**(byte[] b, int off, int len)
		throws IOException
	void	**write**(int b) *throws* IOException
●	void	**writeBoolean**(boolean v) *throws* IOException
●	void	**writeByte**(int v) *throws* IOException
●	void	**writeBytes**(String s) *throws* IOException
●	void	**writeChar**(int v) *throws* IOException
●	void	**writeChars**(String s) *throws* IOException
●	void	**writeDouble**(double v) *throws* IOException
●	void	**writeFloat**(float v) *throws* IOException
●	void	**writeInt**(int v) *throws* IOException
●	void	**writeLong**(long v) *throws* IOException

●	void	**writeShort**(int v) *throws* IOException
●	void	**writeUTF**(String str) *throws* IOException

Reader   java.io

Object
  ➡Reader

○	void	**close**() *throws* IOException
⌂♦	Object	**lock**
	void	**mark**(int readAheadLimit) *throws* IOException
	boolean	**markSupported**()
	int	**read**() *throws* IOException
	int	**read**(char[] cbuf) *throws* IOException
○	int	**read**(char[] cbuf, int off, int len)
		throws IOException
❋♦		**Reader**()
❋♦		**Reader**(Object lock)
	boolean	**ready**() *throws* IOException
	void	**reset**() *throws* IOException
	long	**skip**(long n) *throws* IOException

Reference   java.lang.ref

Object
  ➡Reference

	void	**clear**()
	boolean	**enqueue**()
	Object	**get**()
	boolean	**isEnqueued**()

ReferenceQueue   java.lang.ref

Object
  ➡ReferenceQueue

	Reference	**poll**()
❋		**ReferenceQueue**()
	Reference	**remove**() *throws* InterruptedException
	Reference	**remove**(long timeout)
		throws IllegalArgumentException,
		InterruptedException

ReflectPermission   java.lang.reflect

Object
  ➡java.security.Permission   java.security.Guard, java.io.Serializable

➥java.security.BasicPermission   java.io.Serializable
   ➥ReflectPermission

✳	**ReflectPermission**(String name)
✳	**ReflectPermission**(String name, String actions)

ResourceBundle   java.util

Object
  ➥ResourceBundle

■	ResourceBundle	**getBundle**(String baseName)
		throws MissingResourceException
■	ResourceBundle	**getBundle**(String baseName, Locale locale)
❑	ResourceBundle	**getBundle**(String baseName, Locale locale,
		ClassLoader loader)
		throws MissingResourceException
○	Enumeration	**getKeys**()
	Locale	**getLocale**()
●	Object	**getObject**(String key)
		throws MissingResourceException
●	String	**getString**(String key)
		throws MissingResourceException
●	String[]	**getStringArray**(String key)
		throws MissingResourceException
○◆	Object	**handleGetObject**(String key)
		throws MissingResourceException
⚠◆	ResourceBundle	**parent**
✳		**ResourceBundle**()
◆	void	**setParent**(ResourceBundle parent)

RuleBasedCollator   java.text

Object
  ➥Collator   java.util.Comparator, Cloneable
    ➥RuleBasedCollator

	Object	**clone**()
	int	**compare**(String source, String target)
	boolean	**equals**(Object obj)
	CollationElementItera-tor	**getCollationElementIterator**(CharacterIterator source)
	CollationElementItera-tor	**getCollationElementIterator**(String source)
	CollationKey	**getCollationKey**(String source)
	String	**getRules**()
	int	**hashCode**()
✳		**RuleBasedCollator**(String rules)
		throws ParseException

Runnable — java.lang

Runnable

		void	**run**()

Runtime — java.lang

Object
➥Runtime

1.3		void	**addShutdownHook**(Thread hook)
		Process	**exec**(String command) *throws* java.io.IOException
		Process	**exec**(String[] cmdarray) *throws* java.io.IOException
		Process	**exec**(String[] cmdarray, String[] envp) *throws* java.io.IOException
		Process	**exec**(String[] cmdarray, String[] envp, java.io.File dir) *throws* java.io.IOException
		Process	**exec**(String cmd, String[] envp) *throws* java.io.IOException
		Process	**exec**(String command, String[] envp, java.io.File dir) *throws* java.io.IOException
		void	**exit**(int status)
		long	**freeMemory**()
		void	**gc**()
	❑	Runtime	**getRuntime**()
1.3		void	**halt**(int status)
		void	**load**(String filename)
		void	**loadLibrary**(String libname)
1.3		boolean	**removeShutdownHook**(Thread hook)
		void	**runFinalization**()
		long	**totalMemory**()
		void	**traceInstructions**(boolean on)
		void	**traceMethodCalls**(boolean on)

RuntimeException — java.lang

Object
➥Throwable — java.io.Serializable
➥Exception
➥RuntimeException

❇		**RuntimeException**()
❇		**RuntimeException**(String s)

RuntimePermission — java.lang

Object
➥java.security.Permission — java.security.Guard, java.io.Serializable

➥java.security.BasicPermission   java.io.Serializable
   ➥RuntimePermission

✳	**RuntimePermission**(String name)
✳	**RuntimePermission**(String name, String actions)

SecureClassLoader   java.security

Object
➥ClassLoader
   ➥SecureClassLoader

●◆	Class	**defineClass**(String name, byte[] b, int off, int len, CodeSource cs)
◆	PermissionCollection	**getPermissions**(CodeSource codesource)
✳◆		**SecureClassLoader**()
✳◆		**SecureClassLoader**(ClassLoader parent)

SecureRandom   java.security

Object
➥java.util.Random   java.io.Serializable
   ➥SecureRandom

		byte[]	**generateSeed**(int numBytes)
1.2	❑	SecureRandom	**getInstance**(String algorithm) *throws* NoSuchAlgorithmException
1.2	❑	SecureRandom	**getInstance**(String algorithm, String provider) *throws* NoSuchAlgorithmException, NoSuchProviderException
	●	Provider	**getProvider**()
	❑	byte[]	**getSeed**(int numBytes)
	●◆	int	**next**(int numBits)
		void	**nextBytes**(byte[] bytes)
	✳		**SecureRandom**()
	✳		**SecureRandom**(byte[] seed)
	✳◆		**SecureRandom**(SecureRandomSpi secureRandomSpi, Provider provider)
		void	**setSeed**(byte[] seed)
		void	**setSeed**(long seed)

SecureRandomSpi   java.security

Object
➥SecureRandomSpi   java.io.Serializable

○◆	byte[]	**engineGenerateSeed**(int numBytes)
○◆	void	**engineNextBytes**(byte[] bytes)
○◆	void	**engineSetSeed**(byte[] seed)
✳		**SecureRandomSpi**()

Security — java.security

```
Object
  ➥Security
```

❑	int	**addProvider**(Provider provider)
❑	String	**getProperty**(String key)
❑	Provider	**getProvider**(String name)
❑	Provider[]	**getProviders**()
❑	Provider[]	**getProviders**(java.util.Map filter)
❑	Provider[]	**getProviders**(String filter)
❑	int	**insertProviderAt**(Provider provider, int position)
❑	void	**removeProvider**(String name)
❑	void	**setProperty**(String key, String datum)

SecurityException — java.lang

```
Object
  ➥Throwable                          java.io.Serializable
     ➥Exception
        ➥RuntimeException
           ➥SecurityException
```

✻		**SecurityException**()
✻		**SecurityException**(String s)

SecurityManager — java.lang

```
Object
  ➥SecurityManager
```

	void	**checkAccept**(String host, int port)
	void	**checkAccess**(Thread t)
	void	**checkAccess**(ThreadGroup g)
1.1	void	**checkAwtEventQueueAccess**()
	void	**checkConnect**(String host, int port)
	void	**checkConnect**(String host, int port, Object context)
	void	**checkCreateClassLoader**()
	void	**checkDelete**(String file)
	void	**checkExec**(String cmd)
	void	**checkExit**(int status)
	void	**checkLink**(String lib)
	void	**checkListen**(int port)
1.1	void	**checkMemberAccess**(Class clazz, int which)
1.1	void	**checkMulticast**(java.net.InetAddress maddr)
1.1	void	**checkMulticast**(java.net.InetAddress maddr, byte ttl)
	void	**checkPackageAccess**(String pkg)
	void	**checkPackageDefinition**(String pkg)
1.2	void	**checkPermission**(java.security.Permission perm)
1.2	void	**checkPermission**(java.security.Permission perm, Object context)

1.1		void	**checkPrintJobAccess**()
		void	**checkPropertiesAccess**()
		void	**checkPropertyAccess**(String key)
		void	**checkRead**(java.io.FileDescriptor fd)
		void	**checkRead**(String file)
		void	**checkRead**(String file, Object context)
1.1		void	**checkSecurityAccess**(String target)
		void	**checkSetFactory**()
1.1		void	**checkSystemClipboardAccess**()
		boolean	**checkTopLevelWindow**(Object window)
		void	**checkWrite**(java.io.FileDescriptor fd)
		void	**checkWrite**(String file)
	♦	Class[]	**getClassContext**()
		Object	**getSecurityContext**()
1.1		ThreadGroup	**getThreadGroup**()
	✳		**SecurityManager**()

SecurityPermission   java.security

```
Object
   ➡Permission                        Guard, java.io.Serializable
      ➡BasicPermission                java.io.Serializable
         ➡SecurityPermission
```

✳		**SecurityPermission**(String name)
✳		**SecurityPermission**(String name, String actions)

SequenceInputStream   java.io

```
Object
   ➡InputStream
      ➡SequenceInputStream
```

1.1		int	**available**() *throws* IOException
		void	**close**() *throws* IOException
		int	**read**() *throws* IOException
		int	**read**(byte[] b, int off, int len) *throws* IOException
	✳		**SequenceInputStream**(java.util.Enumeration e)
	✳		**SequenceInputStream**(InputStream s1, InputStream s2)

Serializable   java.io

```
Serializable
```

SerializablePermission   java.io

```
Object
   ➡java.security.Permission              java.security.Guard, Serializable
      ➡java.security.BasicPermission      Serializable
         ➡SerializablePermission
```

	✳		**SerializablePermission**(String name)
	✳		**SerializablePermission**(String name, String actions)

ServerSocket   java.net

Object
   ➥ServerSocket

		Socket	**accept**() *throws* java.io.IOException
		void	**close**() *throws* java.io.IOException
		InetAddress	**getInetAddress**()
		int	**getLocalPort**()
1.1		int	**getSoTimeout**() *throws* java.io.IOException
1.1	●◆	void	**implAccept**(Socket s) *throws* java.io.IOException
	✳		**ServerSocket**(int port) *throws* java.io.IOException
	✳		**ServerSocket**(int port, int backlog) *throws* java.io.IOException

1.1	✳		**ServerSocket**(int port, int backlog,
			   InetAddress bindAddr)
			   throws java.io.IOException

	❑	void	**setSocketFactory**(SocketImplFactory fac) *throws* java.io.IOException
1.1		void	**setSoTimeout**(int timeout) *throws* SocketException
		String	**toString**()

Set   java.util

Set   Collection

boolean	**add**(Object o)
boolean	**addAll**(Collection c)
void	**clear**()
boolean	**contains**(Object o)
boolean	**containsAll**(Collection c)
boolean	**equals**(Object o)
int	**hashCode**()
boolean	**isEmpty**()
Iterator	**iterator**()
boolean	**remove**(Object o)
boolean	**removeAll**(Collection c)
boolean	**retainAll**(Collection c)
int	**size**()
Object[]	**toArray**()
Object[]	**toArray**(Object[] a)

Short   java.lang

Object
   ➥Number   java.io.Serializable
      ➥Short   Comparable

	byte	**byteValue**()
1.2	int	**compareTo**(Object o)
1.2	int	**compareTo**(Short anotherShort)
❏	Short	**decode**(String nm) *throws* NumberFormatException
	double	**doubleValue**()
	boolean	**equals**(Object obj)
	float	**floatValue**()
	int	**hashCode**()
	int	**intValue**()
	long	**longValue**()
✍■	short	**MAX_VALUE**
✍■	short	**MIN_VALUE**
❏	short	**parseShort**(String s) *throws* NumberFormatException
❏	short	**parseShort**(String s, int radix) *throws* NumberFormatException
❋		**Short**(short value)
❋		**Short**(String s) *throws* NumberFormatException
	short	**shortValue**()
	String	**toString**()
❏	String	**toString**(short s)
✍■	Class	**TYPE**
❏	Short	**valueOf**(String s) *throws* NumberFormatException
❏	Short	**valueOf**(String s, int radix) *throws* NumberFormatException

Signature   java.security

Object
  ➡SignatureSpi
      ➡Signature

	Object	**clone**() *throws* CloneNotSupportedException
●	String	**getAlgorithm**()
❏	Signature	**getInstance**(String algorithm) *throws* NoSuchAlgorithmException
❏	Signature	**getInstance**(String algorithm, String provider) *throws* NoSuchAlgorithmException, NoSuchProviderException
●	Provider	**getProvider**()
●	void	**initSign**(PrivateKey privateKey) *throws* InvalidKeyException
●	void	**initSign**(PrivateKey privateKey, SecureRandom random) *throws* InvalidKeyException
●	void	**initVerify**(cert.Certificate certificate) *throws* InvalidKeyException
●	void	**initVerify**(PublicKey publicKey) *throws* InvalidKeyException
●	void	**setParameter**(spec.AlgorithmParameterSpec params) *throws* InvalidAlgorithmParameterException
✍■◆	int	**SIGN**
●	byte[]	**sign**() *throws* SignatureException

1.2	●	int	**sign**(byte[] outbuf, int offset, int len) *throws* SignatureException
	✳◆		**Signature**(String algorithm)
	◿◆	int	**state**
		String	**toString**()
	◿■◆	int	**UNINITIALIZED**
	●	void	**update**(byte b) *throws* SignatureException
	●	void	**update**(byte[] data) *throws* SignatureException
	●	void	**update**(byte[] data, int off, int len) *throws* SignatureException
	◿■◆	int	**VERIFY**
	●	boolean	**verify**(byte[] signature) *throws* SignatureException

---

SignatureException   java.security

```
Object
  ➥Throwable                              java.io.Serializable
     ➥Exception
        ➥GeneralSecurityException
           ➥SignatureException
```

✳	**SignatureException**()
✳	**SignatureException**(String msg)

SignatureSpi   java.security

```
Object
  ➥SignatureSpi
```

	◿◆	SecureRandom	**appRandom**
		Object	**clone**() *throws* CloneNotSupportedException
	○◆	void	**engineInitSign**(PrivateKey privateKey) *throws* InvalidKeyException
	◆	void	**engineInitSign**(PrivateKey privateKey, SecureRandom random) *throws* InvalidKeyException
	○◆	void	**engineInitVerify**(PublicKey publicKey) *throws* InvalidKeyException
	◆	void	**engineSetParameter**(spec.AlgorithmParameterSpec params) *throws* InvalidAlgorithmParameterException
	○◆	byte[]	**engineSign**() *throws* SignatureException
1.2	◆	int	**engineSign**(byte[] outbuf, int offset, int len) *throws* SignatureException
	○◆	void	**engineUpdate**(byte b) *throws* SignatureException
	○◆	void	**engineUpdate**(byte[] b, int off, int len) *throws* SignatureException
	○◆	boolean	**engineVerify**(byte[] sigBytes) *throws* SignatureException
	✳		**SignatureSpi**()

SignedObject · java.security

Object
→ SignedObject   java.io.Serializable

	String	**getAlgorithm**()
	Object	**getObject**() *throws* java.io.IOException, ClassNotFoundException
	byte[]	**getSignature**()
✳		**SignedObject**(java.io.Serializable object, PrivateKey signingKey, Signature signingEngine) *throws* java.io.IOException, InvalidKeyException, SignatureException
	boolean	**verify**(PublicKey verificationKey, Signature verificationEngine) *throws* InvalidKeyException, SignatureException

Signer · java.security

Object
→ Identity   Principal, java.io.Serializable
   → Signer

	PrivateKey	**getPrivateKey**()
●	void	**setKeyPair**(KeyPair pair) *throws* InvalidParameterException, KeyException
✳◆		**Signer**()
✳		**Signer**(String name)
✳		**Signer**(String name, IdentityScope scope) *throws* KeyManagementException
	String	**toString**()

SimpleDateFormat · java.text

Object
→ Format   java.io.Serializable, Cloneable
  → DateFormat
    → SimpleDateFormat

	void	**applyLocalizedPattern**(String pattern)
	void	**applyPattern**(String pattern)
	Object	**clone**()
	boolean	**equals**(Object obj)
	StringBuffer	**format**(java.util.Date date, StringBuffer toAppendTo, FieldPosition pos)
	java.util.Date	**get2DigitYearStart**()
	DateFormatSymbols	**getDateFormatSymbols**()
	int	**hashCode**()
	java.util.Date	**parse**(String text, ParsePosition pos)
	void	**set2DigitYearStart**(java.util.Date startDate)
	void	**setDateFormatSymbols**(DateFormatSymbols newFormatSymbols)

❈			SimpleDateFormat()
❈			SimpleDateFormat(String pattern)
❈			SimpleDateFormat(String pattern, DateFormatSymbols formatData)
❈			SimpleDateFormat(String pattern, java.util.Locale loc)
		String	toLocalizedPattern()
		String	toPattern()

SimpleTimeZone   java.util

Object
  ➡TimeZone   java.io.Serializable, Cloneable
     ➡SimpleTimeZone

		Object	clone()
		boolean	equals(Object obj)
1.2		int	getDSTSavings()
		int	getOffset(int era, int year, int month, int day, int dayOfWeek, int millis)
		int	getRawOffset()
		int	hashCode()
1.2		boolean	hasSameRules(TimeZone other)
		boolean	inDaylightTime(Date date)
1.2		void	setDSTSavings(int millisSavedDuringDST)
1.2		void	setEndRule(int month, int dayOfMonth, int time)
		void	setEndRule(int month, int dayOfWeekInMonth, int dayOfWeek, int time)
1.2		void	setEndRule(int month, int dayOfMonth, int dayOfWeek, int time, boolean after)
		void	setRawOffset(int offsetMillis)
1.2		void	setStartRule(int month, int dayOfMonth, int time)
		void	setStartRule(int month, int dayOfWeekInMonth, int dayOfWeek, int time)
1.2		void	setStartRule(int month, int dayOfMonth, int dayOfWeek, int time, boolean after)
		void	setStartYear(int year)
	❈		SimpleTimeZone(int rawOffset, String ID)
1.1	❈		SimpleTimeZone(int rawOffset, String ID, int startMonth, int startDay, int startDayOfWeek, int startTime, int endMonth, int endDay, int endDayOfWeek, int endTime)
1.2	❈		SimpleTimeZone(int rawOffset, String ID, int startMonth, int startDay, int startDayOfWeek, int startTime, int endMonth, int endDay, int endDayOfWeek, int endTime, int dstSavings)
		String	toString()
		boolean	useDaylightTime()

Socket   **java.net**

```
Object
    ➡Socket
```

		void	**close**() *throws* java.io.IOException
		InetAddress	**getInetAddress**()
		java.io.InputStream	**getInputStream**() *throws* java.io.IOException
1.3		boolean	**getKeepAlive**() *throws* SocketException
1.1		InetAddress	**getLocalAddress**()
		int	**getLocalPort**()
		java.io.OutputStream	**getOutputStream**() *throws* java.io.IOException
		int	**getPort**()
		int	**getReceiveBufferSize**() *throws* SocketException
		int	**getSendBufferSize**() *throws* SocketException
1.1		int	**getSoLinger**() *throws* SocketException
1.1		int	**getSoTimeout**() *throws* SocketException
1.1		boolean	**getTcpNoDelay**() *throws* SocketException
1.3		void	**setKeepAlive**(boolean on) *throws* SocketException
		void	**setReceiveBufferSize**(int size)
			throws SocketException
		void	**setSendBufferSize**(int size) *throws* SocketException
	❑	void	**setSocketImplFactory**(SocketImplFactory fac)
			throws java.io.IOException
1.1		void	**setSoLinger**(boolean on, int linger)
			throws SocketException
1.1		void	**setSoTimeout**(int timeout) *throws* SocketException
1.1		void	**setTcpNoDelay**(boolean on) *throws* SocketException
		void	**shutdownInput**() *throws* java.io.IOException
		void	**shutdownOutput**() *throws* java.io.IOException
1.1	✳◆		**Socket**()
	✳		**Socket**(InetAddress address, int port)
			throws java.io.IOException
1.1	✳		**Socket**(InetAddress address, int port,
			InetAddress localAddr, int localPort)
			throws java.io.IOException
1.1	✳◆		**Socket**(SocketImpl impl) *throws* SocketException
	✳		**Socket**(String host, int port)
			throws UnknownHostException,
			java.io.IOException
1.1	✳		**Socket**(String host, int port,
			InetAddress localAddr, int localPort)
			throws java.io.IOException
		String	**toString**()

SocketException   **java.net**

```
Object
    ➡Throwable                                    java.io.Serializable
        ➡Exception
            ➡java.io.IOException
                ➡SocketException
```

✳		SocketException()
✳		SocketException(String msg)

SocketImpl   java.net

Object
  ➥SocketImpl   SocketOptions

○♦	void	**accept**(SocketImpl s) *throws* java.io.IOException
◿♦	InetAddress	**address**
○♦	int	**available**() *throws* java.io.IOException
○♦	void	**bind**(InetAddress host, int port)
		throws java.io.IOException
○♦	void	**close**() *throws* java.io.IOException
○♦	void	**connect**(InetAddress address, int port)
		throws java.io.IOException
○♦	void	**connect**(String host, int port)
		throws java.io.IOException
○♦	void	**create**(boolean stream) *throws* java.io.IOException
◿♦	java.io.FileDescriptor	**fd**
♦	java.io.FileDescriptor	**getFileDescriptor**()
♦	InetAddress	**getInetAddress**()
○♦	java.io.InputStream	**getInputStream**() *throws* java.io.IOException
♦	int	**getLocalPort**()
○♦	java.io.OutputStream	**getOutputStream**() *throws* java.io.IOException
♦	int	**getPort**()
○♦	void	**listen**(int backlog) *throws* java.io.IOException
◿♦	int	**localport**
◿♦	int	**port**
♦	void	**shutdownInput**() *throws* java.io.IOException
♦	void	**shutdownOutput**() *throws* java.io.IOException
✳		**SocketImpl**()
	String	**toString**()

SocketImplFactory   java.net

SocketImplFactory

	SocketImpl	**createSocketImpl**()

SocketOptions   java.net

SocketOptions

	Object	**getOption**(int optID) *throws* SocketException
◿■	int	**IP_MULTICAST_IF**
	void	**setOption**(int optID, Object value)
		throws SocketException
◿■	int	**SO_BINDADDR**

✍■	int	**SO_KEEPALIVE**
✍■	int	**SO_LINGER**
✍■	int	**SO_RCVBUF**
✍■	int	**SO_REUSEADDR**
✍■	int	**SO_SNDBUF**
✍■	int	**SO_TIMEOUT**
✍■	int	**TCP_NODELAY**

SocketPermission   java.net

```
Object
   ➥java.security.Permission              java.security.Guard, java.io.Serializable
      ➥SocketPermission                   java.io.Serializable
```

boolean	**equals**(Object obj)
String	**getActions**()
int	**hashCode**()
boolean	**implies**(java.security.Permission p)
java.security.¬ PermissionCollection	**newPermissionCollection**()
✳	**SocketPermission**(String host, String action)

SoftReference   java.lang.ref

```
Object
   ➥Reference
      ➥SoftReference
```

Object	**get**()
✳	**SoftReference**(Object referent)
✳	**SoftReference**(Object referent, ReferenceQueue q)

SortedMap   java.util

```
SortedMap                              Map
```

Comparator	**comparator**()
Object	**firstKey**()
SortedMap	**headMap**(Object toKey)
Object	**lastKey**()
SortedMap	**subMap**(Object fromKey, Object toKey)
SortedMap	**tailMap**(Object fromKey)

SortedSet   java.util

```
SortedSet                              Set
```

Comparator	**comparator**()
Object	**first**()

SortedSet	**headSet**(Object toElement)
Object	**last**()
SortedSet	**subSet**(Object fromElement, Object toElement)
SortedSet	**tailSet**(Object fromElement)

Stack `java.util`

```
Object
  ➥AbstractCollection              Collection
     ➥AbstractList                 List
        ➥Vector                    List, Cloneable, java.io.Serializable
           ➥Stack
```

boolean	**empty**()
Object	**peek**()
Object	**pop**()
Object	**push**(Object item)
int	**search**(Object o)
✳	**Stack**()

StackOverflowError `java.lang`

```
Object
  ➥Throwable                    java.io.Serializable
     ➥Error
        ➥VirtualMachineError
           ➥StackOverflowError
```

✳	**StackOverflowError**()
✳	**StackOverflowError**(String s)

StreamConnection `javax.microedition.io`

```
StreamConnection                  InputConnection, OutputConnection
```

StreamConnectionNotifier `javax.microedition.io`

```
StreamConnectionNotifier          Connection
```

StreamConnection	**acceptAndOpen**() *throws* java.io.IOException

StreamCorruptedException `java.io`

```
Object
  ➥Throwable                    Serializable
     ➥Exception
        ➥IOException
           ➥ObjectStreamException
              ➥StreamCorruptedException
```

	✳		`StreamCorruptedException()`
	✳		`StreamCorruptedException(String reason)`

StreamTokenizer   java.io

Object
 ➥StreamTokenizer

		void	`commentChar(int ch)`
		void	`eolIsSignificant(boolean flag)`
		int	`lineno()`
		void	`lowerCaseMode(boolean fl)`
		int	`nextToken()` *throws* IOException
	🖉	double	`nval`
		void	`ordinaryChar(int ch)`
		void	`ordinaryChars(int low, int hi)`
		void	`parseNumbers()`
		void	`pushBack()`
		void	`quoteChar(int ch)`
		void	`resetSyntax()`
		void	`slashSlashComments(boolean flag)`
		void	`slashStarComments(boolean flag)`
1.1	✳		`StreamTokenizer(Reader r)`
	🖉	String	`sval`
		String	`toString()`
	🖉■	int	`TT_EOF`
	🖉■	int	`TT_EOL`
	🖉■	int	`TT_NUMBER`
	🖉■	int	`TT_WORD`
	🖉	int	`ttype`
		void	`whitespaceChars(int low, int hi)`
		void	`wordChars(int low, int hi)`

StrictMath   java.lang

Object
 ➥StrictMath

	❑	double	`abs(double a)`
	❑	float	`abs(float a)`
	❑	int	`abs(int a)`
	❑	long	`abs(long a)`
	❑	double	`acos(double a)`
	❑	double	`asin(double a)`
	❑	double	`atan(double a)`
	❑	double	`atan2(double a, double b)`
	❑	double	`ceil(double a)`
	❑	double	`cos(double a)`
	🖉■	double	`E`
	❑	double	`exp(double a)`
	❑	double	`floor(double a)`

❏		double	**IEEEremainder**(double f1, double f2)
❏		double	**log**(double a)
❏		double	**max**(double a, double b)
❏		float	**max**(float a, float b)
❏		int	**max**(int a, int b)
❏		long	**max**(long a, long b)
❏		double	**min**(double a, double b)
❏		float	**min**(float a, float b)
❏		int	**min**(int a, int b)
❏		long	**min**(long a, long b)
⬛		double	**PI**
❏		double	**pow**(double a, double b)
❏		double	**random**()
❏		double	**rint**(double a)
❏		long	**round**(double a)
❏		int	**round**(float a)
❏		double	**sin**(double a)
❏		double	**sqrt**(double a)
❏		double	**tan**(double a)
❏		double	**toDegrees**(double angrad)
❏		double	**toRadians**(double angdeg)

String   java.lang

Object
  ➡String   java.io.Serializable, Comparable

1.2	⬛	java.util.Comparator	**CASE_INSENSITIVE_ORDER**
		char	**charAt**(int index)
1.2		int	**compareTo**(Object o)
		int	**compareTo**(String anotherString)
1.2		int	**compareToIgnoreCase**(String str)
		String	**concat**(String str)
	❏	String	**copyValueOf**(char[] data)
	❏	String	**copyValueOf**(char[] data, int offset, int count)
		boolean	**endsWith**(String suffix)
		boolean	**equals**(Object anObject)
		boolean	**equalsIgnoreCase**(String anotherString)
1.1		byte[]	**getBytes**()
1.1		byte[]	**getBytes**(String enc)
			throws java.io.UnsupportedEncodingException
		void	**getChars**(int srcBegin, int srcEnd, char[] dst, int dstBegin)
		int	**hashCode**()
		int	**indexOf**(int ch)
		int	**indexOf**(int ch, int fromIndex)
		int	**indexOf**(String str)
		int	**indexOf**(String str, int fromIndex)
		String	**intern**()
		int	**lastIndexOf**(int ch)
		int	**lastIndexOf**(int ch, int fromIndex)

		int	**lastIndexOf**(String str)
		int	**lastIndexOf**(String str, int fromIndex)
		int	**length**()
		boolean	**regionMatches**(boolean ignoreCase, int toffset, String other, int ooffset, int len)
		boolean	**regionMatches**(int toffset, String other, int ooffset, int len)
		String	**replace**(char oldChar, char newChar)
1.0		boolean	**startsWith**(String prefix)
		boolean	**startsWith**(String prefix, int toffset)
	✳		**String**()
1.1	✳		**String**(byte[] bytes)
1.1	✳		**String**(byte[] bytes, int offset, int length)
1.1	✳		**String**(byte[] bytes, int offset, int length, String enc) *throws* java.io.UnsupportedEncodingException
1.1	✳		**String**(byte[] bytes, String enc) *throws* java.io.UnsupportedEncodingException
	✳		**String**(char[] value)
	✳		**String**(char[] value, int offset, int count)
	✳		**String**(String value)
	✳		**String**(StringBuffer buffer)
		String	**substring**(int beginIndex)
		String	**substring**(int beginIndex, int endIndex)
		char[]	**toCharArray**()
		String	**toLowerCase**()
1.1		String	**toLowerCase**(java.util.Locale locale)
		String	**toString**()
		String	**toUpperCase**()
1.1		String	**toUpperCase**(java.util.Locale locale)
		String	**trim**()
	❑	String	**valueOf**(boolean b)
	❑	String	**valueOf**(char c)
	❑	String	**valueOf**(char[] data)
	❑	String	**valueOf**(char[] data, int offset, int count)
	❑	String	**valueOf**(double d)
	❑	String	**valueOf**(float f)
	❑	String	**valueOf**(int i)
	❑	String	**valueOf**(long l)
	❑	String	**valueOf**(Object obj)

StringBuffer   java.lang

Object
➡ StringBuffer   java.io.Serializable

StringBuffer	**append**(boolean b)
StringBuffer	**append**(char c)
StringBuffer	**append**(char[] str)
StringBuffer	**append**(char[] str, int offset, int len)
StringBuffer	**append**(double d)

		StringBuffer	**append**(float f)
		StringBuffer	**append**(int i)
		StringBuffer	**append**(long l)
		StringBuffer	**append**(Object obj)
		StringBuffer	**append**(String str)
		int	**capacity**()
		char	**charAt**(int index)
1.2		StringBuffer	**delete**(int start, int end)
1.2		StringBuffer	**deleteCharAt**(int index)
		void	**ensureCapacity**(int minimumCapacity)
		void	**getChars**(int srcBegin, int srcEnd, char[] dst, int dstBegin)
		StringBuffer	**insert**(int offset, boolean b)
		StringBuffer	**insert**(int offset, char c)
		StringBuffer	**insert**(int offset, char[] str)
1.2		StringBuffer	**insert**(int index, char[] str, int offset, int len)
		StringBuffer	**insert**(int offset, double d)
		StringBuffer	**insert**(int offset, float f)
		StringBuffer	**insert**(int offset, int i)
		StringBuffer	**insert**(int offset, long l)
		StringBuffer	**insert**(int offset, Object obj)
		StringBuffer	**insert**(int offset, String str)
		int	**length**()
1.2		StringBuffer	**replace**(int start, int end, String str)
1.0.2		StringBuffer	**reverse**()
		void	**setCharAt**(int index, char ch)
		void	**setLength**(int newLength)
	❊		**StringBuffer**()
	❊		**StringBuffer**(int length)
	❊		**StringBuffer**(String str)
1.2		String	**substring**(int start)
1.2		String	**substring**(int start, int end)
		String	**toString**()

StringCharacterIterator   java.text

Object
   ➡StringCharacterIterator   CharacterIterator

Object	**clone**()
char	**current**()
boolean	**equals**(Object obj)
char	**first**()
int	**getBeginIndex**()
int	**getEndIndex**()
int	**getIndex**()
int	**hashCode**()
char	**last**()
char	**next**()
char	**previous**()
char	**setIndex**(int p)
void	**setText**(String text)

✳	`StringCharacterIterator`(String text)
✳	`StringCharacterIterator`(String text, int pos)
✳	`StringCharacterIterator`(String text, int begin, int end, int pos)

StringIndexOutOfBoundsException `java.lang`

```
Object
  ➡Throwable                        java.io.Serializable
    ➡Exception
      ➡RuntimeException
        ➡IndexOutOfBoundsException
          ➡StringIndexOutOfBoundsException
```

1.0.	✳	`StringIndexOutOfBoundsException`()
	✳	`StringIndexOutOfBoundsException`(int index)
	✳	`StringIndexOutOfBoundsException`(String s)

StringReader `java.io`

```
Object
  ➡Reader
    ➡StringReader
```

	void	`close`()
	void	`mark`(int readAheadLimit) *throws* IOException
	boolean	`markSupported`()
	int	`read`() *throws* IOException
	int	`read`(char[] cbuf, int off, int len) *throws* IOException
	boolean	`ready`() *throws* IOException
	void	`reset`() *throws* IOException
	long	`skip`(long ns) *throws* IOException
✳		`StringReader`(String s)

StringTokenizer `java.util`

```
Object
  ➡StringTokenizer                       Enumeration
```

	int	`countTokens`()
	boolean	`hasMoreElements`()
	boolean	`hasMoreTokens`()
	Object	`nextElement`()
	String	`nextToken`()
	String	`nextToken`(String delim)
✳		`StringTokenizer`(String str)
✳		`StringTokenizer`(String str, String delim)
✳		`StringTokenizer`(String str, String delim, boolean returnDelims)

StringWriter   java.io

```
Object
    ➥Writer
        ➥StringWriter
```

	void	**close**() *throws* IOException
	void	**flush**()
	StringBuffer	**getBuffer**()
✳		**StringWriter**()
✳		**StringWriter**(int initialSize)
	String	**toString**()
	void	**write**(char[] cbuf, int off, int len)
	void	**write**(int c)
	void	**write**(String str)
	void	**write**(String str, int off, int len)

SyncFailedException   java.io

```
Object
    ➥Throwable                              Serializable
        ➥Exception
            ➥IOException
                ➥SyncFailedException
```

✳	**SyncFailedException**(String desc)

System   java.lang

```
Object
    ➥System
```

	❑	void	**arraycopy**(Object src, int src_position, Object dst, int dst_position, int length)
	❑	long	**currentTimeMillis**()
	⚠■	java.io.PrintStream	**err**
	❑	void	**exit**(int status)
	❑	void	**gc**()
	❑	java.util.Properties	**getProperties**()
	❑	String	**getProperty**(String key)
	❑	String	**getProperty**(String key, String def)
	❑	SecurityManager	**getSecurityManager**()
1.1	❑	int	**identityHashCode**(Object x)
	⚠■	java.io.InputStream	**in**
	❑	void	**load**(String filename)
	❑	void	**loadLibrary**(String libname)
1.2	❑	String	**mapLibraryName**(String libname)
	⚠■	java.io.PrintStream	**out**
	❑	void	**runFinalization**()
1.1	❑	void	**setErr**(java.io.PrintStream err)
1.1	❑	void	**setIn**(java.io.InputStream in)

1.1	❑	void	**setOut**(java.io.PrintStream out)
	❑	void	**setProperties**(java.util.Properties props)
1.2	❑	String	**setProperty**(String key, String value)
	❑	void	**setSecurityManager**(SecurityManager s)

Thread		java.lang

Object
  ➡Thread   Runnable

	❑	int	**activeCount**()
	●	void	**checkAccess**()
	❑	Thread	**currentThread**()
		void	**destroy**()
	❑	void	**dumpStack**()
	❑	int	**enumerate**(Thread[] tarray)
1.2		ClassLoader	**getContextClassLoader**()
	●	String	**getName**()
	●	int	**getPriority**()
	●	ThreadGroup	**getThreadGroup**()
		void	**interrupt**()
	❑	boolean	**interrupted**()
	●	boolean	**isAlive**()
	●	boolean	**isDaemon**()
	●	boolean	**isInterrupted**()
	●	void	**join**() *throws* InterruptedException
	●	void	**join**(long millis) *throws* InterruptedException
	●	void	**join**(long millis, int nanos)
			throws InterruptedException
	⚐■	int	**MAX_PRIORITY**
	⚐■	int	**MIN_PRIORITY**
	⚐■	int	**NORM_PRIORITY**
		void	**run**()
1.2		void	**setContextClassLoader**(ClassLoader cl)
	●	void	**setDaemon**(boolean on)
	●	void	**setName**(String name)
	●	void	**setPriority**(int newPriority)
	❑	void	**sleep**(long millis) *throws* InterruptedException
	❑	void	**sleep**(long millis, int nanos)
			throws InterruptedException
		void	**start**()
	✻		**Thread**()
	✻		**Thread**(Runnable target)
	✻		**Thread**(Runnable target, String name)
	✻		**Thread**(String name)
	✻		**Thread**(ThreadGroup group, Runnable target)
	✻		**Thread**(ThreadGroup group, Runnable target,
			String name)
	✻		**Thread**(ThreadGroup group, String name)
		String	**toString**()
	❑	void	**yield**()

ThreadDeath		java.lang

```
Object
  ➥Throwable                        java.io.Serializable
      ➥Error
          ➥ThreadDeath
```

	❋	ThreadDeath()

ThreadGroup		java.lang

```
Object
  ➥ThreadGroup
```

1.0		int	activeCount()
1.0		int	activeGroupCount()
1.0	●	void	checkAccess()
1.0	●	void	destroy()
1.0		int	enumerate(Thread[] list)
1.0		int	enumerate(Thread[] list, boolean recurse)
1.0		int	enumerate(ThreadGroup[] list)
1.0		int	enumerate(ThreadGroup[] list, boolean recurse)
1.0	●	int	getMaxPriority()
1.0	●	String	getName()
1.0	●	ThreadGroup	getParent()
1.2	●	void	interrupt()
1.0	●	boolean	isDaemon()
1.1		boolean	isDestroyed()
1.0		void	list()
1.0	●	boolean	parentOf(ThreadGroup g)
1.0	●	void	setDaemon(boolean daemon)
1.0	●	void	setMaxPriority(int pri)
1.0	❋		ThreadGroup(String name)
1.0	❋		ThreadGroup(ThreadGroup parent, String name)
1.0		String	toString()
1.0		void	uncaughtException(Thread t, Throwable e)

ThreadLocal		java.lang

```
Object
  ➥ThreadLocal
```

		Object	get()
	♦	Object	initialValue()
		void	set(Object value)
	❋		ThreadLocal()

Throwable		java.lang

```
Object
  ➥Throwable                        java.io.Serializable
```

1.1		Throwable	**fillInStackTrace**()
		String	**getLocalizedMessage**()
		String	**getMessage**()
		void	**printStackTrace**()
		void	**printStackTrace**(java.io.PrintStream s)
1.1		void	**printStackTrace**(java.io.PrintWriter s)
	✳		**Throwable**()
	✳		**Throwable**(String message)
		String	**toString**()

Timer   java.util

Object
   ➡Timer

		void	**cancel**()
		void	**schedule**(TimerTask task, Date time)
		void	**schedule**(TimerTask task, Date firstTime, long period)
		void	**schedule**(TimerTask task, long delay)
		void	**schedule**(TimerTask task, long delay, long period)
		void	**scheduleAtFixedRate**(TimerTask task, Date firstTime, long period)
		void	**scheduleAtFixedRate**(TimerTask task, long delay, long period)
	✳		**Timer**()
	✳		**Timer**(boolean isDaemon)

TimerTask   java.util

Object
   ➡TimerTask   Runnable

		boolean	**cancel**()
	○	void	**run**()
		long	**scheduledExecutionTime**()
	✳◆		**TimerTask**()

TimeZone   java.util

Object
   ➡TimeZone   java.io.Serializable, Cloneable

		Object	**clone**()
	❏	String[]	**getAvailableIDs**()
	❏	String[]	**getAvailableIDs**(int rawOffset)
	❏	TimeZone	**getDefault**()
1.2	●	String	**getDisplayName**()
1.2	●	String	**getDisplayName**(boolean daylight, int style)

1.2		String	**getDisplayName**(boolean daylight, int style, Locale locale)
1.2	●	String	**getDisplayName**(Locale locale)
		String	**getID**()
	○	int	**getOffset**(int era, int year, int month, int day, int dayOfWeek, int milliseconds)
	○	int	**getRawOffset**()
	❑	TimeZone	**getTimeZone**(String ID)
1.2		boolean	**hasSameRules**(TimeZone other)
	○	boolean	**inDaylightTime**(Date date)
1.2	⬜■	int	**LONG**
	❑	void	**setDefault**(TimeZone zone)
		void	**setID**(String ID)
	○	void	**setRawOffset**(int offsetMillis)
1.2	⬜■	int	**SHORT**
	❊		**TimeZone**()
	○	boolean	**useDaylightTime**()

TooManyListenersException   java.util

```
Object
  ➥Throwable                          java.io.Serializable
     ➥Exception
        ➥TooManyListenersException
```

❊		**TooManyListenersException**()
❊		**TooManyListenersException**(String s)

TreeMap   java.util

```
Object
  ➥AbstractMap                    Map
     ➥TreeMap                     SortedMap, Cloneable, java.io.Serializable
```

	void	**clear**()
	Object	**clone**()
	Comparator	**comparator**()
	boolean	**containsKey**(Object key)
1.2	boolean	**containsValue**(Object value)
	Set	**entrySet**()
	Object	**firstKey**()
	Object	**get**(Object key)
	SortedMap	**headMap**(Object toKey)
	Set	**keySet**()
	Object	**lastKey**()
	Object	**put**(Object key, Object value)
	void	**putAll**(Map map)
	Object	**remove**(Object key)
	int	**size**()
	SortedMap	**subMap**(Object fromKey, Object toKey)

SortedMap	**tailMap**(Object fromKey)
✳	**TreeMap**()
✳	**TreeMap**(Comparator c)
✳	**TreeMap**(Map m)
✳	**TreeMap**(SortedMap m)
Collection	**values**()

TreeSet — java.util

```
Object
   ➥AbstractCollection            Collection
      ➥AbstractSet                Set
         ➥TreeSet                 SortedSet, Cloneable, java.io.Serializable
```

boolean	**add**(Object o)
boolean	**addAll**(Collection c)
void	**clear**()
Object	**clone**()
Comparator	**comparator**()
boolean	**contains**(Object o)
Object	**first**()
SortedSet	**headSet**(Object toElement)
boolean	**isEmpty**()
Iterator	**iterator**()
Object	**last**()
boolean	**remove**(Object o)
int	**size**()
SortedSet	**subSet**(Object fromElement, Object toElement)
SortedSet	**tailSet**(Object fromElement)
✳	**TreeSet**()
✳	**TreeSet**(Collection c)
✳	**TreeSet**(Comparator c)
✳	**TreeSet**(SortedSet s)

UndeclaredThrowableException — java.lang.reflect

```
Object
   ➥Throwable                     java.io.Serializable
      ➥Exception
         ➥RuntimeException
            ➥UndeclaredThrowableException
```

Throwable	**getUndeclaredThrowable**()
void	**printStackTrace**()
void	**printStackTrace**(java.io.PrintStream ps)
void	**printStackTrace**(java.io.PrintWriter pw)
✳	**UndeclaredThrowableException**(Throwable undeclaredThrowable)
✳	**UndeclaredThrowableException**(Throwable undeclaredThrowable, String s)

UnknownError   `java.lang`

```
Object
   ➡Throwable                    java.io.Serializable
      ➡Error
         ➡VirtualMachineError
            ➡UnknownError
```

✳	**UnknownError**()
✳	**UnknownError**(String s)

UnknownHostException   `java.net`

```
Object
   ➡Throwable                    java.io.Serializable
      ➡Exception
         ➡java.io.IOException
            ➡UnknownHostException
```

✳	**UnknownHostException**()
✳	**UnknownHostException**(String host)

UnknownServiceException   `java.net`

```
Object
   ➡Throwable                    java.io.Serializable
      ➡Exception
         ➡java.io.IOException
            ➡UnknownServiceException
```

✳	**UnknownServiceException**()
✳	**UnknownServiceException**(String msg)

UnrecoverableKeyException   `java.security`

```
Object
   ➡Throwable                    java.io.Serializable
      ➡Exception
         ➡GeneralSecurityException
            ➡UnrecoverableKeyException
```

✳	**UnrecoverableKeyException**()
✳	**UnrecoverableKeyException**(String msg)

UnresolvedPermission   `java.security`

```
Object
   ➡Permission                   Guard, java.io.Serializable
      ➡UnresolvedPermission      java.io.Serializable
```

	boolean	**equals**(Object obj)
	String	**getActions**()

	int	hashCode()
	boolean	implies(Permission p)
	PermissionCollection	newPermissionCollection()
	String	toString()
✲		UnresolvedPermission(String type, String name, String actions, cert.Certificate[] certs)

UnsatisfiedLinkError   `java.lang`

```
Object
  ➥Throwable                        java.io.Serializable
    ➥Error
      ➥LinkageError
        ➥UnsatisfiedLinkError
```

✲	UnsatisfiedLinkError()
✲	UnsatisfiedLinkError(String s)

UnsupportedClassVersionError   `java.lang`

```
Object
  ➥Throwable                        java.io.Serializable
    ➥Error
      ➥LinkageError
        ➥ClassFormatError
          ➥UnsupportedClassVersionError
```

✲	UnsupportedClassVersionError()
✲	UnsupportedClassVersionError(String s)

UnsupportedEncodingException   `java.io`

```
Object
  ➥Throwable                        Serializable
    ➥Exception
      ➥IOException
        ➥UnsupportedEncodingException
```

✲	UnsupportedEncodingException()
✲	UnsupportedEncodingException(String s)

UnsupportedOperationException   `java.lang`

```
Object
  ➥Throwable                        java.io.Serializable
    ➥Exception
      ➥RuntimeException
        ➥UnsupportedOperationException
```

✲	UnsupportedOperationException()
✲	UnsupportedOperationException(String message)

URL		**java.net**

Object
   ➡URL   java.io.Serializable

	boolean	**equals**(Object obj)	
	String	**getAuthority**()	
●	Object	**getContent**() *throws* java.io.IOException	
●	Object	**getContent**(Class[] classes) *throws* java.io.IOException	
	String	**getFile**()	
	String	**getHost**()	
	String	**getPath**()	
	int	**getPort**()	
	String	**getProtocol**()	
	String	**getQuery**()	
	String	**getRef**()	
	String	**getUserInfo**()	
	int	**hashCode**()	
	URLConnection	**openConnection**() *throws* java.io.IOException	
●	java.io.InputStream	**openStream**() *throws* java.io.IOException	
	boolean	**sameFile**(URL other)	
◆	void	**set**(String protocol, String host, int port, String file, String ref)	
◆	void	**set**(String protocol, String host, int port, String authority, String userInfo, String path, String query, String ref)	
❑	void	**setURLStreamHandlerFactory**(URLStreamHandlerFactory fac)	
	String	**toExternalForm**()	
	String	**toString**()	
✳		**URL**(String spec) *throws* MalformedURLException	
✳		**URL**(String protocol, String host, int port, String file) *throws* MalformedURLException	
		URL(String protocol, String host, int port, String file, URLStreamHandler handler) *throws* MalformedURLException	
✳		**URL**(String protocol, String host, String file) *throws* MalformedURLException	
✳		**URL**(URL context, String spec) *throws* MalformedURLException	
✳		**URL**(URL context, String spec, URLStreamHandler handler) *throws* MalformedURLException	

URLClassLoader		**java.net**

Object
   ➡ClassLoader
      ➡java.security.SecureClassLoader
         ➡URLClassLoader

♦	void	**addURL**(URL url)	
♦	Package	**definePackage**(String name,	
		java.util.jar.Manifest man, URL url)	
		throws IllegalArgumentException	
♦	Class	**findClass**(String name)	
		throws ClassNotFoundException	
	URL	**findResource**(String name)	
	java.util.Enumeration	**findResources**(String name)	
		throws java.io.IOException	
♦	java.security.¬	**getPermissions**(java.security.CodeSource codesource)	
	PermissionCollection		
	URL[]	**getURLs**()	
❑	URLClassLoader	**newInstance**(URL[] urls)	
❑	URLClassLoader	**newInstance**(URL[] urls, ClassLoader parent)	
✳		**URLClassLoader**(URL[] urls)	
✳		**URLClassLoader**(URL[] urls, ClassLoader parent)	
✳		**URLClassLoader**(URL[] urls, ClassLoader parent,	
		URLStreamHandlerFactory factory)	

URLConnection   java.net

Object
➡URLConnection

✍♦	boolean	**allowUserInteraction**	
○	void	**connect**() *throws* java.io.IOException	
✍♦	boolean	**connected**	
✍♦	boolean	**doInput**	
✍♦	boolean	**doOutput**	
	boolean	**getAllowUserInteraction**()	
	Object	**getContent**() *throws* java.io.IOException	
	Object	**getContent**(Class[] classes)	
		throws java.io.IOException	
	String	**getContentEncoding**()	
	int	**getContentLength**()	
	String	**getContentType**()	
	long	**getDate**()	
❑	boolean	**getDefaultAllowUserInteraction**()	
	boolean	**getDefaultUseCaches**()	
	boolean	**getDoInput**()	
	boolean	**getDoOutput**()	
	long	**getExpiration**()	
1.2 ❑	FileNameMap	**getFileNameMap**()	
	String	**getHeaderField**(int n)	
	String	**getHeaderField**(String name)	
	long	**getHeaderFieldDate**(String name, long Default)	
	int	**getHeaderFieldInt**(String name, int Default)	
	String	**getHeaderFieldKey**(int n)	
	long	**getIfModifiedSince**()	
	java.io.InputStream	**getInputStream**() *throws* java.io.IOException	
	long	**getLastModified**()	
	java.io.OutputStream	**getOutputStream**() *throws* java.io.IOException	

		java.security.¬ Permission	**getPermission**() *throws* java.io.IOException
		String	**getRequestProperty**(String key)
		URL	**getURL**()
		boolean	**getUseCaches**()
	□♦	String	**guessContentTypeFromName**(String fname)
	□	String	**guessContentTypeFromStream**(java.io.InputStream is) *throws* java.io.IOException
	⚞♦	long	**ifModifiedSince**
		void	**setAllowUserInteraction**(boolean allowuserinteraction)
	□	void	**setContentHandlerFactory**(ContentHandlerFactory fac)
	□	void	**setDefaultAllowUserInteraction**(boolean defaultallowuserinteraction)
		void	**setDefaultUseCaches**(boolean defaultusecaches)
		void	**setDoInput**(boolean doinput)
		void	**setDoOutput**(boolean dooutput)
1.2	□	void	**setFileNameMap**(FileNameMap map)
		void	**setIfModifiedSince**(long ifmodifiedsince)
		void	**setRequestProperty**(String key, String value)
		void	**setUseCaches**(boolean usecaches)
		String	**toString**()
	⚞♦	URL	**url**
	✳♦		**URLConnection**(URL url)
	⚞♦	boolean	**useCaches**

URLDecoder   **java.net**

Object
➥URLDecoder

	□	String	**decode**(String s)
	✳		**URLDecoder**()

URLEncoder   **java.net**

Object
➥URLEncoder

	□	String	**encode**(String s)

URLStreamHandler   **java.net**

Object
➥URLStreamHandler

	♦	boolean	**equals**(URL u1, URL u2)
	♦	int	**getDefaultPort**()
	♦	InetAddress	**getHostAddress**(URL u)
	♦	int	**hashCode**(URL u)

◆	boolean	**hostsEqual**(URL u1, URL u2)	
○◆	URLConnection	**openConnection**(URL u) *throws* java.io.IOException	
◆	void	**parseURL**(URL u, String spec, int start, int limit)	
◆	boolean	**sameFile**(URL u1, URL u2)	
◆	void	**setURL**(URL u, String protocol, String host, int port, String authority, String userInfo, String path, String query, String ref)	
◆	String	**toExternalForm**(URL u)	
✳		**URLStreamHandler**()	

URLStreamHandlerFactory   `java.net`

URLStreamHandlerFactory

URLStreamHandler	**createURLStreamHandler**(String protocol)

UTFDataFormatException   `java.io`

Object
  ➡Throwable   Serializable
    ➡Exception
      ➡IOException
        ➡UTFDataFormatException

✳		**UTFDataFormatException**()
✳		**UTFDataFormatException**(String s)

Vector   `java.util`

Object
  ➡AbstractCollection   Collection
    ➡AbstractList   List
      ➡Vector   List, Cloneable, java.io.Serializable

1.2		void	**add**(int index, Object element)
1.2		boolean	**add**(Object o)
1.2		boolean	**addAll**(Collection c)
1.2		boolean	**addAll**(int index, Collection c)
		void	**addElement**(Object obj)
		int	**capacity**()
	✍◆	int	**capacityIncrement**
1.2		void	**clear**()
		Object	**clone**()
		boolean	**contains**(Object elem)
		boolean	**containsAll**(Collection c)
		void	**copyInto**(Object[] anArray)
		Object	**elementAt**(int index)
	✍◆	int	**elementCount**
	✍◆	Object[]	**elementData**
		Enumeration	**elements**()

		void	ensureCapacity(int minCapacity)
		boolean	equals(Object o)
		Object	firstElement()
1.2		Object	get(int index)
		int	hashCode()
		int	indexOf(Object elem)
		int	indexOf(Object elem, int index)
		void	insertElementAt(Object obj, int index)
		boolean	isEmpty()
		Object	lastElement()
		int	lastIndexOf(Object elem)
		int	lastIndexOf(Object elem, int index)
1.2		Object	remove(int index)
1.2		boolean	remove(Object o)
1.2		boolean	removeAll(Collection c)
		void	removeAllElements()
		boolean	removeElement(Object obj)
		void	removeElementAt(int index)
	♦	void	removeRange(int fromIndex, int toIndex)
1.2		boolean	retainAll(Collection c)
1.2		Object	set(int index, Object element)
		void	setElementAt(Object obj, int index)
		void	setSize(int newSize)
		int	size()
		List	subList(int fromIndex, int toIndex)
1.2		Object[]	toArray()
		Object[]	toArray(Object[] a)
		String	toString()
		void	trimToSize()
	✻		Vector()
1.2	✻		Vector(Collection c)
	✻		Vector(int initialCapacity)
	✻		Vector(int initialCapacity, int capacityIncrement)

VerifyError   **java.lang**

Object
  ➥Throwable   java.io.Serializable
    ➥Error
      ➥LinkageError
        ➥VerifyError

✻		VerifyError()
✻		VerifyError(String s)

VirtualMachineError   **java.lang**

Object
  ➥Throwable   java.io.Serializable
    ➥Error
      ➥VirtualMachineError

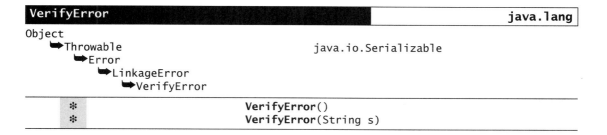

✳	`VirtualMachineError()`
✳	`VirtualMachineError(String s)`

Void — java.lang

```
Object
  ➡Void
```

🔳	Class	**TYPE**

WeakHashMap — java.util

```
Object
  ➡AbstractMap                          Map
      ➡WeakHashMap                      Map
```

	void	**clear**()
	boolean	**containsKey**(Object key)
	Set	**entrySet**()
	Object	**get**(Object key)
	boolean	**isEmpty**()
	Object	**put**(Object key, Object value)
	Object	**remove**(Object key)
	int	**size**()
✳		**WeakHashMap**()
✳		**WeakHashMap**(int initialCapacity)
✳		**WeakHashMap**(int initialCapacity, float loadFactor)
1.3 ✳		**WeakHashMap**(Map t)

WeakReference — java.lang.ref

```
Object
  ➡Reference
      ➡WeakReference
```

✳	**WeakReference**(Object referent)
✳	**WeakReference**(Object referent, ReferenceQueue q)

WriteAbortedException — java.io

```
Object
  ➡Throwable                          Serializable
      ➡Exception
          ➡IOException
              ➡ObjectStreamException
                  ➡WriteAbortedException
```

✎	Exception	**detail**
	String	**getMessage**()
✳		**WriteAbortedException**(String s, Exception ex)

Writer   java.io

Object
➥Writer

○	void	**close**() *throws* IOException
○	void	**flush**() *throws* IOException
🔒♦	Object	**lock**
	void	**write**(char[] cbuf) *throws* IOException
○	void	**write**(char[] cbuf, int off, int len) *throws* IOException
	void	**write**(int c) *throws* IOException
	void	**write**(String str) *throws* IOException
	void	**write**(String str, int off, int len) *throws* IOException
✳♦		**Writer**()
✳♦		**Writer**(Object lock)

X509Certificate   java.security.cert

Object
➥Certificate   java.io.Serializable
  ➥X509Certificate   X509Extension

○	void	**checkValidity**() *throws* CertificateExpiredException, CertificateNotYetValidException
○	void	**checkValidity**(java.util.Date date) *throws* CertificateExpiredException, CertificateNotYetValidException
○	int	**getBasicConstraints**()
○	java.security.¬ Principal	**getIssuerDN**()
○	boolean[]	**getIssuerUniqueID**()
○	boolean[]	**getKeyUsage**()
○	java.util.Date	**getNotAfter**()
○	java.util.Date	**getNotBefore**()
○	java.math.BigInteger	**getSerialNumber**()
○	String	**getSigAlgName**()
○	String	**getSigAlgOID**()
○	byte[]	**getSigAlgParams**()
○	byte[]	**getSignature**()
○	java.security.¬ Principal	**getSubjectDN**()
○	boolean[]	**getSubjectUniqueID**()
○	byte[]	**getTBSCertificate**() *throws* CertificateEncodingException
○	int	**getVersion**()
✳♦		**X509Certificate**()

X509CRL   java.security.cert

```
Object
  ➡CRL
       ➡X509CRL                          X509Extension
```

	boolean	**equals**(Object other)
○	byte[]	**getEncoded**() *throws* CRLException
○	java.security.¬ Principal	**getIssuerDN**()
○	java.util.Date	**getNextUpdate**()
○	X509CRLEntry	**getRevokedCertificate**(java.math.BigInteger serialNumber)
○	java.util.Set	**getRevokedCertificates**()
○	String	**getSigAlgName**()
○	String	**getSigAlgOID**()
○	byte[]	**getSigAlgParams**()
○	byte[]	**getSignature**()
○	byte[]	**getTBSCertList**() *throws* CRLException
○	java.util.Date	**getThisUpdate**()
○	int	**getVersion**()
	int	**hashCode**()
○	void	**verify**(java.security.PublicKey key) *throws* CRLException, java.security.NoSuchAlgorithmException, java.security.InvalidKeyException, java.security.NoSuchProviderException, java.security.SignatureException
○	void	**verify**(java.security.PublicKey key, String sigProvider) *throws* CRLException, java.security.NoSuchAlgorithmException, java.security.InvalidKeyException, java.security.NoSuchProviderException, java.security.SignatureException
❊◆		**X509CRL**()

X509CRLEntry   java.security.cert

```
Object
  ➡X509CRLEntry                          X509Extension
```

	boolean	**equals**(Object other)
○	byte[]	**getEncoded**() *throws* CRLException
○	java.util.Date	**getRevocationDate**()
○	java.math.BigInteger	**getSerialNumber**()
○	boolean	**hasExtensions**()
	int	**hashCode**()
○	String	**toString**()
❊		**X509CRLEntry**()

X509Extension   `java.security.cert`
X509Extension

java.util.Set	**getCriticalExtensionOIDs**()
byte[]	**getExtensionValue**(String oid)
java.util.Set	**getNonCriticalExtensionOIDs**()
boolean	**hasUnsupportedCriticalExtension**()

ZipEntry   `java.util.zip`
Object
➥ZipEntry   ZipConstants, Cloneable

	Object	**clone**()
✍■	int	**DEFLATED**
	String	**getComment**()
	long	**getCompressedSize**()
	long	**getCrc**()
	byte[]	**getExtra**()
	int	**getMethod**()
	String	**getName**()
	long	**getSize**()
	long	**getTime**()
	int	**hashCode**()
	boolean	**isDirectory**()
	void	**setComment**(String comment)
	void	**setCompressedSize**(long csize)
	void	**setCrc**(long crc)
	void	**setExtra**(byte[] extra)
	void	**setMethod**(int method)
	void	**setSize**(long size)
	void	**setTime**(long time)
✍■	int	**STORED**
	String	**toString**()
✳		**ZipEntry**(String name)
✳		**ZipEntry**(ZipEntry e)

ZipException   `java.util.zip`
Object
➥Throwable   java.io.Serializable
  ➥Exception
    ➥java.io.IOException
      ➥ZipException

✳	**ZipException**()
✳	**ZipException**(String s)

ZipFile		java.util.zip

```
Object
   ➤ZipFile                                    ZipConstants
```

	void	**close**() *throws* java.io.IOException
	java.util.Enumeration	**entries**()
◆	void	**finalize**() *throws* java.io.IOException
	ZipEntry	**getEntry**(String name)
	java.io.InputStream	**getInputStream**(ZipEntry entry)
		throws java.io.IOException
	String	**getName**()
⚠■	int	**OPEN_DELETE**
⚠■	int	**OPEN_READ**
	int	**size**()
✳		**ZipFile**(java.io.File file) *throws* ZipException,
		java.io.IOException
✳		**ZipFile**(java.io.File file, int mode)
		throws java.io.IOException
✳		**ZipFile**(String name) *throws* java.io.IOException

ZipInputStream		java.util.zip

```
Object
   ➤java.io.InputStream
      ➤java.io.FilterInputStream
         ➤InflaterInputStream
            ➤ZipInputStream                    ZipConstants
```

	int	**available**() *throws* java.io.IOException
	void	**close**() *throws* java.io.IOException
	void	**closeEntry**() *throws* java.io.IOException
◆	ZipEntry	**createZipEntry**(String name)
	ZipEntry	**getNextEntry**() *throws* java.io.IOException
	int	**read**(byte[] b, int off, int len)
		throws java.io.IOException
	long	**skip**(long n) *throws* java.io.IOException
✳		**ZipInputStream**(java.io.InputStream in)

ZipOutputStream		java.util.zip

```
Object
   ➤java.io.OutputStream
      ➤java.io.FilterOutputStream
         ➤DeflaterOutputStream
            ➤ZipOutputStream                   ZipConstants
```

	void	**close**() *throws* java.io.IOException
	void	**closeEntry**() *throws* java.io.IOException
⚠■	int	**DEFLATED**
	void	**finish**() *throws* java.io.IOException

void	**putNextEntry**(ZipEntry e) *throws* java.io.IOException
void	**setComment**(String comment)
void	**setLevel**(int level)
void	**setMethod**(int method)
int	**STORED**
void	**write**(byte[] b, int off, int len)
	throws java.io.IOException
	ZipOutputStream(java.io.OutputStream out)

J2ME CDC/RMI Optional Package 1.0 Almanac

AccessException   `java.rmi`

```
Object
   ➡Throwable                        java.io.Serializable
      ➡Exception
         ➡java.io.IOException
            ➡RemoteException
               ➡AccessException
```

| 1.1 | ✲ | AccessException(String s) |
| 1.1 | ✲ | AccessException(String s, Exception ex) |

AlreadyBoundException   `java.rmi`

```
Object
   ➡Throwable                        java.io.Serializable
      ➡Exception
         ➡AlreadyBoundException
```

| 1.1 | ✲ | AlreadyBoundException() |
| 1.1 | ✲ | AlreadyBoundException(String s) |

ConnectException   `java.rmi`

```
Object
   ➡Throwable                        java.io.Serializable
      ➡Exception
```

```
➡java.io.IOException
     ➡RemoteException
          ➡ConnectException
```

1.1	✳	**ConnectException**(String s)
1.1	✳	**ConnectException**(String s, Exception ex)

ConnectIOException	**java.rmi**

```
Object
    ➡Throwable                    java.io.Serializable
        ➡Exception
            ➡java.io.IOException
                ➡RemoteException
                    ➡ConnectIOException
```

1.1	✳	**ConnectIOException**(String s)
1.1	✳	**ConnectIOException**(String s, Exception ex)

MarshalException	**java.rmi**

```
Object
    ➡Throwable                    java.io.Serializable
        ➡Exception
            ➡java.io.IOException
                ➡RemoteException
                    ➡MarshalException
```

1.1	✳	**MarshalException**(String s)
1.1	✳	**MarshalException**(String s, Exception ex)

MarshalledObject	**java.rmi**

```
Object
    ➡MarshalledObject                java.io.Serializable
```

1.2		boolean	**equals**(Object obj)
1.2		Object	**get**() *throws* java.io.IOException, ClassNotFoundException
		int	**hashCode**()
1.2	✳		**MarshalledObject**(Object obj) *throws* java.io.IOException

---

Naming	**java.rmi**

```
Object
    ➡Naming
```

1.1	☐	void	**bind**(String name, Remote obj) *throws* AlreadyBoundException, java.net.MalformedURLException, RemoteException

1.1	❏	String[]	**list**(String name) *throws* RemoteException, java.net.MalformedURLException
1.1	❏	Remote	**lookup**(String name) *throws* NotBoundException, java.net.MalformedURLException, RemoteException
1.1	❏	void	**rebind**(String name, Remote obj) *throws* RemoteException, java.net.MalformedURLException
1.1	❏	void	**unbind**(String name) *throws* RemoteException, NotBoundException, java.net.MalformedURLException

---

NoSuchObjectException   java.rmi

```
Object
    ➡Throwable                        java.io.Serializable
        ➡Exception
            ➡java.io.IOException
                ➡RemoteException
                    ➡NoSuchObjectException
```

1.1	✳	**NoSuchObjectException**(String s)

NotBoundException   java.rmi

```
Object
    ➡Throwable                        java.io.Serializable
        ➡Exception
            ➡NotBoundException
```

1.1	✳	**NotBoundException**()
1.1	✳	**NotBoundException**(String s)

Remote   java.rmi

```
Remote
```

RemoteException   java.rmi

```
Object
    ➡Throwable                        java.io.Serializable
        ➡Exception
            ➡java.io.IOException
                ➡RemoteException
```

1.1	⟁	Throwable	**detail**
1.1		String	**getMessage**()
1.2		void	**printStackTrace**()
1.2		void	**printStackTrace**(java.io.PrintStream ps)
1.2		void	**printStackTrace**(java.io.PrintWriter pw)

1.1	❋	**RemoteException**()
1.1	❋	**RemoteException**(String s)
1.1	❋	**RemoteException**(String s, Throwable ex)

RMISecurityManager   java.rmi

Object
➥SecurityManager
   ➥RMISecurityManager

1.1	❋	**RMISecurityManager**()

ServerError   java.rmi

Object
➥Throwable   java.io.Serializable
  ➥Exception
    ➥java.io.IOException
      ➥RemoteException
        ➥ServerError

1.1	❋	**ServerError**(String s, Error err)

ServerException   java.rmi

Object
➥Throwable   java.io.Serializable
➥Exception
  ➥java.io.IOException
    ➥RemoteException
      ➥ServerException

1.1	❋	**ServerException**(String s)
1.1	❋	**ServerException**(String s, Exception ex)

StubNotFoundException   java.rmi

Object
➥Throwable   java.io.Serializable
  ➥Exception
    ➥java.io.IOException
      ➥RemoteException
        ➥StubNotFoundException

1.1	❋	**StubNotFoundException**(String s)
1.1	❋	**StubNotFoundException**(String s, Exception ex)

UnexpectedException   `java.rmi`

```
Object
    ➥Throwable                          java.io.Serializable
        ➥Exception
            ➥java.io.IOException
                ➥RemoteException
                    ➥UnexpectedException
```

| 1.1 | ✳ | | UnexpectedException(String s) |
| 1.1 | ✳ | | UnexpectedException(String s, Exception ex) |

UnknownHostException   `java.rmi`

```
Object
    ➥Throwable                          java.io.Serializable
        ➥Exception
            ➥java.io.IOException
                ➥RemoteException
                    ➥UnknownHostException
```

| 1.1 | ✳ | | UnknownHostException(String s) |
| 1.1 | ✳ | | UnknownHostException(String s, Exception ex) |

UnmarshalException   `java.rmi`

```
Object
    ➥Throwable                          java.io.Serializable
        ➥Exception
            ➥java.io.IOException
                ➥RemoteException
                    ➥UnmarshalException
```

| 1.1 | ✳ | | UnmarshalException(String s) |
| 1.1 | ✳ | | UnmarshalException(String s, Exception ex) |

J2ME CDC Personal Profile (java.applet, java.awt, and java.beans) 1.0 Almanac

ActionEvent		java.awt.event

```
Object
   ➥java.util.EventObject               java.io.Serializable
      ➥java.awt.AWTEvent
         ➥ActionEvent
```

🖉■	int	**ACTION_FIRST**
🖉■	int	**ACTION_LAST**
🖉■	int	**ACTION_PERFORMED**
✳		**ActionEvent**(Object source, int id, String command)
✳		**ActionEvent**(Object source, int id, String command, int modifiers)
🖉■	int	**ALT_MASK**
🖉■	int	**CTRL_MASK**
	String	**getActionCommand**()
	int	**getModifiers**()
🖉■	int	**META_MASK**
	String	**paramString**()
🖉■	int	**SHIFT_MASK**

ActionListener		java.awt.event

ActionListener	java.util.EventListener

	void	**actionPerformed**(ActionEvent e)

ActiveEvent	java.awt

ActiveEvent

void	**dispatch**()

Adjustable	java.awt

Adjustable

void	**addAdjustmentListener**(event.AdjustmentListener l)
int	**getBlockIncrement**()
int	**getMaximum**()
int	**getMinimum**()
int	**getOrientation**()
int	**getUnitIncrement**()
int	**getValue**()
int	**getVisibleAmount**()
int	**HORIZONTAL**
void	**removeAdjustmentListener**(event.AdjustmentListener l)
void	**setBlockIncrement**(int b)
void	**setMaximum**(int max)
void	**setMinimum**(int min)
void	**setUnitIncrement**(int u)
void	**setValue**(int v)
void	**setVisibleAmount**(int v)
int	**VERTICAL**

AdjustmentEvent	java.awt.event

Object
➡java.util.EventObject   java.io.Serializable
  ➡java.awt.AWTEvent
    ➡AdjustmentEvent

	int	**ADJUSTMENT_FIRST**
	int	**ADJUSTMENT_LAST**
	int	**ADJUSTMENT_VALUE_CHANGED**
		AdjustmentEvent(java.awt.Adjustable source, int id, int type, int value)
	int	**BLOCK_DECREMENT**
	int	**BLOCK_INCREMENT**
java.awt.Adjustable	**getAdjustable**()
	int	**getAdjustmentType**()
	int	**getValue**()
String	**paramString**()
	int	**TRACK**
	int	**UNIT_DECREMENT**
	int	**UNIT_INCREMENT**

	AdjustmentListener		java.awt.event
	AdjustmentListener	java.util.EventListener	
	void	adjustmentValueChanged(AdjustmentEvent e)	

	Applet		java.applet

Object
  ➡java.awt.Component   java.awt.image.ImageObserver, java.awt.¬
                                        MenuContainer, java.io.Serializable
    ➡java.awt.Container
      ➡java.awt.Panel
        ➡Applet

	✳			**Applet**()
			void	**destroy**()
			AppletContext	**getAppletContext**()
			String	**getAppletInfo**()
			AudioClip	**getAudioClip**(java.net.URL url)
			AudioClip	**getAudioClip**(java.net.URL url, String name)
			java.net.URL	**getCodeBase**()
			java.net.URL	**getDocumentBase**()
			java.awt.Image	**getImage**(java.net.URL url)
			java.awt.Image	**getImage**(java.net.URL url, String name)
1.1			java.util.Locale	**getLocale**()
			String	**getParameter**(String name)
			String[][]	**getParameterInfo**()
			void	**init**()
			boolean	**isActive**()
1.2	■		AudioClip	**newAudioClip**(java.net.URL url)
			void	**play**(java.net.URL url)
			void	**play**(java.net.URL url, String name)
			void	**resize**(java.awt.Dimension d)
			void	**resize**(int width, int height)
	●		void	**setStub**(AppletStub stub)
			void	**showStatus**(String msg)
			void	**start**()
			void	**stop**()

	AppletContext		java.applet

AppletContext

Applet	**getApplet**(String name)
java.util.Enumeration	**getApplets**()
AudioClip	**getAudioClip**(java.net.URL url)
java.awt.Image	**getImage**(java.net.URL url)
void	**showDocument**(java.net.URL url)
void	**showDocument**(java.net.URL url, String target)
void	**showStatus**(String status)

AppletInitializer   java.beans

AppletInitializer

void	**activate**(java.applet.Applet newApplet)
void	**initialize**(java.applet.Applet newAppletBean,
	beancontext.BeanContext bCtxt)

AppletStub   java.applet

AppletStub

void	**appletResize**(int width, int height)
AppletContext	**getAppletContext**()
java.net.URL	**getCodeBase**()
java.net.URL	**getDocumentBase**()
String	**getParameter**(String name)
boolean	**isActive**()

AreaAveragingScaleFilter   java.awt.image

Object
➡ImageFilter   ImageConsumer, Cloneable
  ➡ReplicateScaleFilter
    ➡AreaAveragingScaleFilter

✳	**AreaAveragingScaleFilter**(int width, int height)
void	**setHints**(int hints)
void	**setPixels**(int x, int y, int w, int h,
	ColorModel model, byte[] pixels, int off,
	int scansize)
void	**setPixels**(int x, int y, int w, int h,
	ColorModel model, int[] pixels, int off,
	int scansize)

AudioClip   java.applet

AudioClip

void	**loop**()
void	**play**()
void	**stop**()

AWTError   java.awt

Object
➡Throwable   java.io.Serializable
  ➡Error
    ➡AWTError

1.0 ✳	**AWTError**(String msg)

AWTEvent   java.awt

```
Object
    ➥java.util.EventObject              java.io.Serializable
        ➥AWTEvent
```

✍▪	long	**ACTION_EVENT_MASK**
✍▪	long	**ADJUSTMENT_EVENT_MASK**
✳		**AWTEvent**(Event event)
✳		**AWTEvent**(Object source, int id)
✍▪	long	**COMPONENT_EVENT_MASK**
◆	void	**consume**()
✍◆	boolean	**consumed**
✍▪	long	**CONTAINER_EVENT_MASK**
✍▪	long	**FOCUS_EVENT_MASK**
	int	**getID**()
✍◆	int	**id**
◆	boolean	**isConsumed**()
✍▪	long	**ITEM_EVENT_MASK**
✍▪	long	**KEY_EVENT_MASK**
✍▪	long	**MOUSE_EVENT_MASK**
✍▪	long	**MOUSE_MOTION_EVENT_MASK**
	String	**paramString**()
✍▪	int	**RESERVED_ID_MAX**
✍▪	long	**TEXT_EVENT_MASK**
	String	**toString**()
✍▪	long	**WINDOW_EVENT_MASK**

AWTEventMulticaster   java.awt

```
Object
    ➥AWTEventMulticaster        event.ComponentListener, event.ContainerListener,
                                event.FocusListener, event.KeyListener,
                                event.MouseListener, event.MouseMotionListener,
                                event.WindowListener, event.ActionListener,
                                event.ItemListener, event.AdjustmentListener,
                                event.TextListener
```

✍●◆	java.util.EventListener	**a**
	void	**actionPerformed**(event.ActionEvent e)
❏	event.ActionListener	**add**(event.ActionListener a, event.ActionListener b)
❏	event.Adjustment¬ Listener	**add**(event.AdjustmentListener a, event.AdjustmentListener b)
❏	event.ComponentListener	**add**(event.ComponentListener a, event.ComponentListener b)
❏	event.ContainerListener	**add**(event.ContainerListener a, event.ContainerListener b)
❏	event.FocusListener	**add**(event.FocusListener a, event.FocusListener b)
❏	event.ItemListener	**add**(event.ItemListener a, event.ItemListener b)
❏	event.KeyListener	**add**(event.KeyListener a, event.KeyListener b)
❏	event.MouseListener	**add**(event.MouseListener a, event.MouseListener b)
❏	event.MouseMotion¬ Listener	**add**(event.MouseMotionListener a, event.MouseMotionListener b)

❑	event.TextListener	**add**(event.TextListener a, event.TextListener b)
❑	event.WindowListener	**add**(event.WindowListener a, event.WindowListener b)
❑◆	java.util.EventListener	**addInternal**(java.util.EventListener a, java.util.EventListener b)
	void	**adjustmentValueChanged**(event.AdjustmentEvent e)
✳◆		**AWTEventMulticaster**(java.util.EventListener a, java.util.EventListener b)
◿●◆	java.util.EventListener	**b**
	void	**componentAdded**(event.ContainerEvent e)
	void	**componentHidden**(event.ComponentEvent e)
	void	**componentMoved**(event.ComponentEvent e)
	void	**componentRemoved**(event.ContainerEvent e)
	void	**componentResized**(event.ComponentEvent e)
	void	**componentShown**(event.ComponentEvent e)
	void	**focusGained**(event.FocusEvent e)
	void	**focusLost**(event.FocusEvent e)
	void	**itemStateChanged**(event.ItemEvent e)
	void	**keyPressed**(event.KeyEvent e)
	void	**keyReleased**(event.KeyEvent e)
	void	**keyTyped**(event.KeyEvent e)
	void	**mouseClicked**(event.MouseEvent e)
	void	**mouseDragged**(event.MouseEvent e)
	void	**mouseEntered**(event.MouseEvent e)
	void	**mouseExited**(event.MouseEvent e)
	void	**mouseMoved**(event.MouseEvent e)
	void	**mousePressed**(event.MouseEvent e)
	void	**mouseReleased**(event.MouseEvent e)
❑	event.ActionListener	**remove**(event.ActionListener l, event.ActionListener oldl)
❑	event.Adjustment¬Listener	**remove**(event.AdjustmentListener l, event.AdjustmentListener oldl)
❑	event.Component¬Listener	**remove**(event.ComponentListener l, event.ComponentListener oldl)
❑	event.Container¬Listener	**remove**(event.ContainerListener l, event.ContainerListener oldl)
◆	java.util.Event¬Listener	**remove**(java.util.EventListener oldl)
❑	event.FocusListener	**remove**(event.FocusListener l, event.FocusListener oldl)
❑	event.ItemListener	**remove**(event.ItemListener l, event.ItemListener oldl)
❑	event.KeyListener	**remove**(event.KeyListener l, event.KeyListener oldl)
❑	event.MouseListener	**remove**(event.MouseListener l, event.MouseListener oldl)
❑	event.MouseMotion¬Listener	**remove**(event.MouseMotionListener l, event.MouseMotionListener oldl)
❑	event.TextListener	**remove**(event.TextListener l, event.TextListener oldl)
❑	event.WindowListener	**remove**(event.WindowListener l, event.WindowListener oldl)
❑◆	java.util.Event¬Listener	**removeInternal**(java.util.EventListener l, java.util.EventListener oldl)

◻◆	void	**save**(java.io.ObjectOutputStream s, String k, java.util.EventListener l) *throws* java.io.IOException
◆	void	**saveInternal**(java.io.ObjectOutputStream s, String k) *throws* java.io.IOException
	void	**textValueChanged**(event.TextEvent e)
	void	**windowActivated**(event.WindowEvent e)
	void	**windowClosed**(event.WindowEvent e)
	void	**windowClosing**(event.WindowEvent e)
	void	**windowDeactivated**(event.WindowEvent e)
	void	**windowDeiconified**(event.WindowEvent e)
	void	**windowIconified**(event.WindowEvent e)
	void	**windowOpened**(event.WindowEvent e)

AWTException   **java.awt**

```
Object
  ➡Throwable                        java.io.Serializable
     ➡Exception
        ➡AWTException
```

1.0	✳	**AWTException**(String msg)

AWTPermission   **java.awt**

```
Object
  ➡java.security.Permission          java.security.Guard, java.io.Serializable
     ➡java.security.BasicPermission   java.io.Serializable
        ➡AWTPermission
```

✳	**AWTPermission**(String name)
✳	**AWTPermission**(String name, String actions)

BeanContext   **java.beans.beancontext**

BeanContext   BeanContextChild, java.util.Collection,
                                   java.beans.DesignMode, java.beans.Visibility

	void	**addBeanContextMembershipListener**(BeanContextMembershipListener bcml)
	java.net.URL	**getResource**(String name, BeanContextChild bcc) *throws* IllegalArgumentException
	java.io.InputStream	**getResourceAsStream**(String name,BeanContextChild bcc) *throws* IllegalArgumentException
◿◼	Object	**globalHierarchyLock**
	Object	**instantiateChild**(String beanName *throws* java.io.IOException, ClassNotFoundException
	void	**removeBeanContextMembershipListener**(BeanContextMembershipListener bcml)

BeanContextChild		**java.beans.beancontext**

BeanContextChild

void	**addPropertyChangeListener**(String name, java.beans.PropertyChangeListener pcl)
void	**addVetoableChangeListener**(String name, java.beans.VetoableChangeListener vcl)
BeanContext	**getBeanContext**()
void	**removePropertyChangeListener**(String name, java.beans.PropertyChangeListener pcl)
void	**removeVetoableChangeListener**(String name, java.beans.VetoableChangeListener vcl)
void	**setBeanContext**(BeanContext bc) *throws* java.beans.PropertyVetoException

BeanContextChildComponentProxy		**java.beans.beancontext**

BeanContextChildComponentProxy

java.awt.Component	**getComponent**()

BeanContextChildSupport		**java.beans.beancontext**

Object
➡ BeanContextChildSupport   BeanContextChild, BeanContextServicesListener,
                                    java.io.Serializable

	void	**addPropertyChangeListener**(String name, java.beans.PropertyChangeListener pcl)
	void	**addVetoableChangeListener**(String name, java.beans.VetoableChangeListener vcl)
⬒◆	BeanContext	**beanContext**
⬒	BeanContextChild	**beanContextChildPeer**
❋		**BeanContextChildSupport**()
❋		**BeanContextChildSupport**(BeanContextChild bcc)
	void	**firePropertyChange**(String name, Object oldValue, Object newValue)

	void	**fireVetoableChange**(String name, Object oldValue,
		      Object newValue)
		      throws java.beans.PropertyVetoException

	BeanContext	**getBeanContext**()
	BeanContextChild	**getBeanContextChildPeer**()
◆	void	**initializeBeanContextResources**()
	boolean	**isDelegated**()
⬒◆	java.beans.Property¬ ChangeSupport	**pcSupport**
⬒◆	boolean	**rejectedSetBCOnce**
◆	void	**releaseBeanContextResources**()
	void	**removePropertyChangeListener**(String name, java.beans.PropertyChangeListener pcl)

	void	**removeVetoableChangeListener**(String name, java.beans.VetoableChangeListener vcl)
	void	**serviceAvailable**(BeanContextServiceAvailableEvent bcsae)
	void	**serviceRevoked**(BeanContextServiceRevokedEvent bcsre)
	void	**setBeanContext**(BeanContext bc) *throws* java.beans.PropertyVetoException
	boolean	**validatePendingSetBeanContext**(BeanContext newValue)
✍◆	java.beans.Vetoable¬ ChangeSupport	**vcSupport**

BeanContextContainerProxy   java.beans.beancontext

BeanContextContainerProxy

java.awt.Container	**getContainer**()

BeanContextEvent   java.beans.beancontext

Object
  ➥java.util.EventObject   java.io.Serializable
    ➥BeanContextEvent

✳◆		**BeanContextEvent**(BeanContext bc)
	BeanContext	**getBeanContext**()
	BeanContext	**getPropagatedFrom**()
	boolean	**isPropagated**()
✍◆	BeanContext	**propagatedFrom**
	void	**setPropagatedFrom**(BeanContext bc)

BeanContextMembershipEvent   java.beans.beancontext

Object
  ➥java.util.EventObject   java.io.Serializable
    ➥BeanContextEvent
      ➥BeanContextMembershipEvent

✳		**BeanContextMembershipEvent**(BeanContext bc, java.util.Collection changes)
✳		**BeanContextMembershipEvent**(BeanContext bc, Object[] changes)
✍◆	java.util.Collection	**children**
	boolean	**contains**(Object child)
	java.util.Iterator	**iterator**()
	int	**size**()
	Object[]	**toArray**()

BeanContextMembershipListener	java.beans.beancontext
BeanContextMembershipListener	java.util.EventListener

	void	**childrenAdded**(BeanContextMembershipEvent bcme)
	void	**childrenRemoved**(BeanContextMembershipEvent bcme)

BeanContextProxy	java.beans.beancontext
BeanContextProxy	

	BeanContextChild	**getBeanContextProxy**()

BeanContextServiceAvailableEvent	java.beans.beancontext

Object
  ➥java.util.EventObject   java.io.Serializable
     ➥BeanContextEvent
        ➥BeanContextServiceAvailableEvent

	✳		**BeanContextServiceAvailableEvent**(
			BeanContextServices bcs, Class sc)
		java.util.Iterator	**getCurrentServiceSelectors**()
		Class	**getServiceClass**()
		BeanContextServices	**getSourceAsBeanContextServices**()
	✍◆	Class	**serviceClass**

BeanContextServiceProvider	java.beans.beancontext
BeanContextServiceProvider	

	java.util.Iterator	**getCurrentServiceSelectors**(BeanContextServices bcs,
		Class serviceClass)
	Object	**getService**(BeanContextServices bcs,
		Object requestor, Class serviceClass,
		Object serviceSelector)
	void	**releaseService**(BeanContextServices bcs,
		Object requestor, Object service)

BeanContextServiceProviderBeanInfo	java.beans.beancontext
BeanContextServiceProviderBeanInfo	java.beans.BeanInfo

	java.beans.BeanInfo[]	**getServicesBeanInfo**()

BeanContextServiceRevokedEvent	java.beans.beancontext

Object
  ➥java.util.EventObject   java.io.Serializable

➡BeanContextEvent
   ➡BeanContextServiceRevokedEvent

✳		**BeanContextServiceRevokedEvent(** BeanContextServices bcs, Class sc, boolean invalidate)
	Class	**getServiceClass()**
	BeanContextServices	**getSourceAsBeanContextServices()**
	boolean	**isCurrentServiceInvalidNow()**
	boolean	**isServiceClass(**Class service)
✍◆	Class	**serviceClass**

BeanContextServiceRevokedListener	**java.beans.beancontext**
BeanContextServiceRevokedListener	java.util.EventListener

void	**serviceRevoked(** BeanContextServiceRevokedEvent bcsre)

BeanContextServices	**java.beans.beancontext**
BeanContextServices	BeanContext, BeanContextServicesListener

void	**addBeanContextServicesListener(** BeanContextServicesListener bcsl)
boolean	**addService(**Class serviceClass, BeanContextServiceProvider serviceProvider)
java.util.Iterator	**getCurrentServiceClasses()**
java.util.Iterator	**getCurrentServiceSelectors(**Class serviceClass)
Object	**getService(**BeanContextChild child, Object requestor, Class serviceClass, Object serviceSelector, BeanContextServiceRevokedListener bcsrl) *throws* java.util.TooManyListenersException
boolean	**hasService(**Class serviceClass)
void	**releaseService(**BeanContextChild child, Object requestor, Object service)
void	**removeBeanContextServicesListener(** BeanContextServicesListener bcsl)
void	**revokeService(**Class serviceClass, BeanContextServiceProvider serviceProvider, boolean revokeCurrentServicesNow)

BeanContextServicesListener	**java.beans.beancontext**
BeanContextServicesListener	BeanContextServiceRevokedListener

void	**serviceAvailable(** BeanContextServiceAvailableEvent bcsae)

BeanContextServicesSupport	**java.beans.beancontext**

```
Object
    ➡BeanContextChildSupport              BeanContextChild,
                                          BeanContextServicesListener,
                                          java.io.Serializable
        ➡BeanContextSupport               BeanContext, java.io.Serializable,
                                          java.beans.PropertyChangeListener,
                                          java.beans.VetoableChangeListener
            ➡BeanContextServicesSupport   BeanContextServices
```

	void	**addBeanContextServicesListener(** BeanContextServicesListener bcsl**)**
	boolean	**addService(**Class serviceClass, BeanContextServiceProvider bcsp**)**
♦	boolean	**addService(**Class serviceClass, BeanContextServiceProvider bcsp, boolean fireEvent**)**
⚑♦	java.util.ArrayList	**bcsListeners**
♦	void	**bcsPreDeserializationHook(** java.io.ObjectInputStream ois**)** *throws* java.io.IOException, ClassNotFoundException
♦	void	**bcsPreSerializationHook(** java.io.ObjectOutputStream oos**)** *throws* java.io.IOException
✳		**BeanContextServicesSupport()**
✳		**BeanContextServicesSupport(** BeanContextServices peer**)**
✳		**BeanContextServicesSupport(** BeanContextServices peer, java.util.Locale lcle**)**
✳		**BeanContextServicesSupport(** BeanContextServices peer, java.util.Locale lcle, boolean dtime**)**
✳		**BeanContextServicesSupport(** BeanContextServices peer, java.util.Locale lcle, boolean dTime, boolean visible**)**
♦	void	**childJustRemovedHook(**Object child, BeanContextSupport.BCSChild bcsc**)**
♦	BeanContextSupport.¬ BCSChild	**createBCSChild(**Object targetChild, Object peer**)**
♦	BeanContextServices¬ Support.BCSSService¬ Provider	**createBCSSServiceProvider(**Class sc, BeanContextServiceProvider bcsp**)**
●♦	void	**fireServiceAdded(** BeanContextServiceAvailableEvent bcssae**)**
●♦	void	**fireServiceAdded(**Class serviceClass**)**
●♦	void	**fireServiceRevoked(** BeanContextServiceRevokedEvent bcsre**)**
●♦	void	**fireServiceRevoked(**Class serviceClass, boolean revokeNow**)**

	BeanContextServices	**getBeanContextServicesPeer**()
■♦	BeanContextServices¬ Listener	**getChildBeanContextServicesListener**(Object child)
	java.util.Iterator	**getCurrentServiceClasses**()
	java.util.Iterator	**getCurrentServiceSelectors**(Class serviceClass)

	Object	**getService**(BeanContextChild child,
		        Object requestor, Class serviceClass,
		        Object serviceSelector,
		        BeanContextServiceRevokedListener bcsrl)
		        throws java.util.TooManyListenersException

	boolean	**hasService**(Class serviceClass)
	void	**initialize**()
♦	void	**initializeBeanContextResources**()
✍♦	BeanContextServices¬ Support.BCSSProxy¬ ServiceProvider	**proxy**
♦	void	**releaseBeanContextResources**()
	void	**releaseService**(BeanContextChild child, Object requestor, Object service)
	void	**removeBeanContextServicesListener**(BeanContextServicesListener bcsl)

	void	**revokeService**(Class serviceClass,
		        BeanContextServiceProvider bcsp,
		        boolean revokeCurrentServicesNow)

✍♦	int	**serializable**
	void	**serviceAvailable**(BeanContextServiceAvailableEvent bcssae)
	void	**serviceRevoked**(BeanContextServiceRevokedEvent bcssre)
✍♦	java.util.HashMap	**services**

BeanContextServicesSupport.BCSSChild	**java.beans.beancontext**

Object
　➡BeanContextSupport.BCSChild   java.io.Serializable
　　　➡BeanContextServicesSupport.BCSSChild

BeanContextServicesSupport.¬ **BCSSProxyServiceProvider**	**java.beans.beancontext**

Object
　➡BeanContextServicesSupport.BCSSProxyServiceProvider   BeanContextService¬
　　　　　　　　　　　　　　　　　　　　　　　　　　　　　　Provider, BeanContext¬
　　　　　　　　　　　　　　　　　　　　　　　　　　　　　　ServiceRevokedListener

	java.util.Iterator	**getCurrentServiceSelectors**(BeanContextServices bcs, Class serviceClass)

	Object	**getService**(BeanContextServices bcs,
		        Object requestor, Class serviceClass,
		        Object serviceSelector)

	void	**releaseService**(BeanContextServices bcs, Object requestor, Object service)
	void	**serviceRevoked**(BeanContextServiceRevokedEvent bcsre)

BeanContextServicesSupport.¬ BCSSServiceProvider	**java.beans.beancontext**

Object
    ➡BeanContextServicesSupport.BCSSServiceProvider   java.io.Serializable

	BeanContextService¬ Provider	**getServiceProvider**()
🖉♦	BeanContextService¬ Provider	**serviceProvider**

BeanContextSupport	**java.beans.beancontext**

Object
    ➡BeanContextChildSupport   BeanContextChild, BeanContextServicesListener, java.io.Serializable
        ➡BeanContextSupport   BeanContext, java.io.Serializable, java.beans.PropertyChangeListener, java.beans.VetoableChangeListener

	boolean	**add**(Object targetChild)
	boolean	**addAll**(java.util.Collection c)
	void	**addBeanContextMembershipListener**(BeanContextMembershipListener bcml)
	boolean	**avoidingGui**()
🖉♦	java.util.ArrayList	**bcmListeners**
♦	java.util.Iterator	**bcsChildren**()
♦	void	**bcsPreDeserializationHook**(java.io.ObjectInputStream ois) *throws* java.io.IOException, ClassNotFoundException
♦	void	**bcsPreSerializationHook**(java.io.ObjectOutputStream oos) *throws* java.io.IOException
✳		**BeanContextSupport**()
✳		**BeanContextSupport**(BeanContext peer)
✳		**BeanContextSupport**(BeanContext peer, java.util.Locale lcle)
✳		**BeanContextSupport**(BeanContext peer, java.util.Locale lcle, boolean dtime)
✳		**BeanContextSupport**(BeanContext peer, java.util.Locale lcle, boolean dTime, boolean visible)
♦	void	**childDeserializedHook**(Object child, BeanContextSupport.BCSChild bcsc)

◆	void	**childJustAddedHook**(Object child, BeanContextSupport.BCSChild bcsc)
◆	void	**childJustRemovedHook**(Object child, BeanContextSupport.BCSChild bcsc)
⚙◆	java.util.HashMap	**children**
■◆	boolean	**classEquals**(Class first, Class second)
	void	**clear**()
	boolean	**contains**(Object o)
	boolean	**containsAll**(java.util.Collection c)
	boolean	**containsKey**(Object o)
●◆	Object[]	**copyChildren**()
◆	BeanContextSupport.¬ BCSChild	**createBCSChild**(Object targetChild, Object peer)
●◆	void	**deserialize**(java.io.ObjectInputStream ois, java.util.Collection coll) *throws* java.io.IOException, ClassNotFoundException
⚙◆	boolean	**designTime**
	void	**dontUseGui**()
●◆	void	**fireChildrenAdded**(BeanContextMembershipEvent bcme)
●◆	void	**fireChildrenRemoved**(BeanContextMembershipEvent bcme)
	BeanContext	**getBeanContextPeer**()
■◆	BeanContextChild	**getChildBeanContextChild**(Object child)
■◆	BeanContextMembership¬ Listener	**getChildBeanContextMembershipListener**(Object child)
■◆	java.beans.Property¬ ChangeListener	**getChildPropertyChangeListener**(Object child)
■◆	java.io.Serializable	**getChildSerializable**(Object child)
■◆	java.beans.Vetoable¬ ChangeListener	**getChildVetoableChangeListener**(Object child)
■◆	java.beans.Visibility	**getChildVisibility**(Object child)
	java.util.Locale	**getLocale**()
	java.net.URL	**getResource**(String name, BeanContextChild bcc)
	java.io.InputStream	**getResourceAsStream**(String name, BeanContextChild bcc)
◆	void	**initialize**()
	Object	**instantiateChild**(String beanName) *throws* java.io.IOException, ClassNotFoundException
	boolean	**isDesignTime**()
	boolean	**isEmpty**()
	boolean	**isSerializing**()
	java.util.Iterator	**iterator**()
⚙◆	java.util.Locale	**locale**
	boolean	**needsGui**()
⚙◆	boolean	**okToUseGui**
	void	**okToUseGui**()
	void	**propertyChange**(java.beans.PropertyChangeEvent pce)
●	void	**readChildren**(java.io.ObjectInputStream ois) *throws* java.io.IOException, ClassNotFoundException

	boolean	**remove**(Object targetChild)
♦	boolean	**remove**(Object targetChild, boolean callChildSetBC)
	boolean	**removeAll**(java.util.Collection c)
	void	**removeBeanContextMembershipListener**(
		BeanContextMembershipListener bcml)
	boolean	**retainAll**(java.util.Collection c)
●♦	void	**serialize**(java.io.ObjectOutputStream oos,
		java.util.Collection coll)
		throws java.io.IOException
	void	**setDesignTime**(boolean dTime)
	void	**setLocale**(java.util.Locale newLocale)
		throws java.beans.PropertyVetoException
	int	**size**()
	Object[]	**toArray**()
	Object[]	**toArray**(Object[] arry)
♦	boolean	**validatePendingAdd**(Object targetChild)
♦	boolean	**validatePendingRemove**(Object targetChild)
	void	**vetoableChange**(java.beans.PropertyChangeEvent pce)
		throws java.beans.PropertyVetoException
●	void	**writeChildren**(java.io.ObjectOutputStream oos)
		throws java.io.IOException

BeanContextSupport.BCSChild   java.beans.beancontext

Object
  ➥BeanContextSupport.BCSChild   java.io.Serializable

BeanContextSupport.BCSIterator   java.beans.beancontext

Object
  ➥BeanContextSupport.BCSIterator   java.util.Iterator

	boolean	**hasNext**()
	Object	**next**()
	void	**remove**()

BeanDescriptor   java.beans

Object
  ➥FeatureDescriptor
    ➥BeanDescriptor

✳		**BeanDescriptor**(Class beanClass)
✳		**BeanDescriptor**(Class beanClass,
		Class customizerClass)
	Class	**getBeanClass**()
	Class	**getCustomizerClass**()

BeanInfo		**java.beans**

BeanInfo

	BeanInfo[]	**getAdditionalBeanInfo**()
	BeanDescriptor	**getBeanDescriptor**()
	int	**getDefaultEventIndex**()
	int	**getDefaultPropertyIndex**()
	EventSetDescriptor[]	**getEventSetDescriptors**()
	java.awt.Image	**getIcon**(int iconKind)
	MethodDescriptor[]	**getMethodDescriptors**()
	PropertyDescriptor[]	**getPropertyDescriptors**()
⚒■	int	**ICON_COLOR_16x16**
⚒■	int	**ICON_COLOR_32x32**
⚒■	int	**ICON_MONO_16x16**
⚒■	int	**ICON_MONO_32x32**

Beans		**java.beans**

Object
  ➡Beans

✳		**Beans**()
❑	Object	**getInstanceOf**(Object bean, Class targetType)
❑	Object	**instantiate**(ClassLoader cls, String beanName)
		throws java.io.IOException,
		ClassNotFoundException
❑	Object	**instantiate**(ClassLoader cls, String beanName,
		beancontext.BeanContext beanContext)
		throws java.io.IOException,
		ClassNotFoundException
❑	Object	**instantiate**(ClassLoader cls, String beanName,
		beancontext.BeanContext beanContext,
		AppletInitializer initializer)
		throws java.io.IOException,
		ClassNotFoundException
❑	boolean	**isDesignTime**()
❑	boolean	**isGuiAvailable**()
❑	boolean	**isInstanceOf**(Object bean, Class targetType)
❑	void	**setDesignTime**(boolean isDesignTime)
		throws SecurityException
❑	void	**setGuiAvailable**(boolean isGuiAvailable)
		throws SecurityException

BigDecimal		**java.math**

Object
  ➡Number
    ➡BigDecimal

java.io.Serializable
Comparable

	BigDecimal	**abs**()
	BigDecimal	**add**(BigDecimal val)
*		**BigDecimal**(BigInteger val)
*		**BigDecimal**(BigInteger unscaledVal, int scale)
*		**BigDecimal**(double val)
*		**BigDecimal**(String val)
	int	**compareTo**(BigDecimal val)
1.2	int	**compareTo**(Object o)
	BigDecimal	**divide**(BigDecimal val, int roundingMode)
	BigDecimal	**divide**(BigDecimal val, int scale, int roundingMode)
	double	**doubleValue**()
	boolean	**equals**(Object x)
	float	**floatValue**()
	int	**hashCode**()
	int	**intValue**()
	long	**longValue**()
	BigDecimal	**max**(BigDecimal val)
	BigDecimal	**min**(BigDecimal val)
	BigDecimal	**movePointLeft**(int n)
	BigDecimal	**movePointRight**(int n)
	BigDecimal	**multiply**(BigDecimal val)
	BigDecimal	**negate**()
✎■	int	**ROUND_CEILING**
✎■	int	**ROUND_DOWN**
✎■	int	**ROUND_FLOOR**
✎■	int	**ROUND_HALF_DOWN**
✎■	int	**ROUND_HALF_EVEN**
✎■	int	**ROUND_HALF_UP**
✎■	int	**ROUND_UNNECESSARY**
✎■	int	**ROUND_UP**
	int	**scale**()
	BigDecimal	**setScale**(int scale)
	BigDecimal	**setScale**(int scale, int roundingMode)
	int	**signum**()
	BigDecimal	**subtract**(BigDecimal val)
	BigInteger	**toBigInteger**()
	String	**toString**()
1.2	BigInteger	**unscaledValue**()
❑	BigDecimal	**valueOf**(long val)
❑	BigDecimal	**valueOf**(long unscaledVal, int scale)

BigInteger   java.math

Object
  →Number
    →BigInteger

java.io.Serializable
Comparable

	BigInteger	**abs**()
	BigInteger	**add**(BigInteger)

```
      BigInteger  and(BigInteger )
      BigInteger  andNot(BigInteger )
                  BigInteger(byte[] )
                  BigInteger(int , byte[] )
                  BigInteger(int , int , java.util.Random )
                  BigInteger(int , java.util.Random )
                  BigInteger(String )
                  BigInteger(String , int )
             int  bitCount()
             int  bitLength()
      BigInteger  clearBit(int )
             int  compareTo(BigInteger )
             int  compareTo(Object )
      BigInteger  divide(BigInteger )
    BigInteger[]  divideAndRemainder(BigInteger )
          double  doubleValue()
         boolean  equals(Object )
      BigInteger  flipBit(int )
           float  floatValue()
      BigInteger  gcd(BigInteger )
             int  getLowestSetBit()
             int  hashCode()
             int  intValue()
         boolean  isProbablePrime(int )
            long  longValue()
      BigInteger  max(BigInteger )
      BigInteger  min(BigInteger )
      BigInteger  mod(BigInteger )
      BigInteger  modInverse(BigInteger )
      BigInteger  modPow(BigInteger , BigInteger )
      BigInteger  multiply(BigInteger )
      BigInteger  negate()
      BigInteger  not()
      BigInteger  ONE
      BigInteger  or(BigInteger )
      BigInteger  pow(int )
      BigInteger  remainder(BigInteger )
      BigInteger  setBit(int )
      BigInteger  shiftLeft(int )
      BigInteger  shiftRight(int )
             int  signum()
      BigInteger  subtract(BigInteger )
         boolean  testBit(int )
          byte[]  toByteArray()
          String  toString()
          String  toString(int )
      BigInteger  valueOf(long )
      BigInteger  xor(BigInteger )
      BigInteger  ZERO
```

BorderLayout   java.awt

Object
  ➡BorderLayout   LayoutManager2, java.io.Serializable

1.1		void	**addLayoutComponent**(Component comp, Object constraints)
		void	**addLayoutComponent**(String name, Component comp)
1.0	✳		**BorderLayout**()
1.0	✳		**BorderLayout**(int hgap, int vgap)
	⚠◼	String	**CENTER**
	⚠◼	String	**EAST**
1.1		int	**getHgap**()
		float	**getLayoutAlignmentX**(Container parent)
		float	**getLayoutAlignmentY**(Container parent)
1.1		int	**getVgap**()
		void	**invalidateLayout**(Container target)
1.0		void	**layoutContainer**(Container target)
		Dimension	**maximumLayoutSize**(Container target)
1.0		Dimension	**minimumLayoutSize**(Container target)
	⚠◼	String	**NORTH**
1.0		Dimension	**preferredLayoutSize**(Container target)
1.0		void	**removeLayoutComponent**(Component comp)
1.1		void	**setHgap**(int hgap)
1.1		void	**setVgap**(int vgap)
	⚠◼	String	**SOUTH**
1.0		String	**toString**()
	⚠◼	String	**WEST**

BufferedImage   java.awt.image

Object
  ➡java.awt.Image
    ➡BufferedImage

void	**coerceData**(boolean isAlphaPremultiplied)
void	**flush**()
ColorModel	**getColorModel**()
java.awt.Graphics	**getGraphics**()
int	**getHeight**()
int	**getHeight**(ImageObserver observer)
Object	**getProperty**(String name)
Object	**getProperty**(String name, ImageObserver observer)
String[]	**getPropertyNames**()
int	**getRGB**(int x, int y)
int[]	**getRGB**(int startX, int startY, int w, int h, int[] rgbArray, int offset, int scansize)
ImageProducer	**getSource**()
BufferedImage	**getSubimage**(int x, int y, int w, int h)
int	**getType**()
int	**getWidth**()
int	**getWidth**(ImageObserver observer)
boolean	**isAlphaPremultiplied**()
void	**setRGB**(int x, int y, int rgb)

		void	setRGB(int startX, int startY, int w, int h, int[] rgbArray, int offset, int scansize)
		String	toString()
	int	TYPE_3BYTE_BGR
	int	TYPE_4BYTE_ABGR
	int	TYPE_4BYTE_ABGR_PRE
	int	TYPE_BYTE_BINARY
	int	TYPE_BYTE_GRAY
	int	TYPE_BYTE_INDEXED
	int	TYPE_CUSTOM
	int	TYPE_INT_ARGB
	int	TYPE_INT_ARGB_PRE
	int	TYPE_INT_BGR
	int	TYPE_INT_RGB
	int	TYPE_USHORT_555_RGB
	int	TYPE_USHORT_565_RGB
	int	TYPE_USHORT_GRAY

Button   java.awt

Object
  ➡Component   image.ImageObserver, MenuContainer, java.io.Serializable
    ➡Button

1.1		void	addActionListener(event.ActionListener l)
1.0		void	addNotify()
1.0	❋		Button()
1.0	❋		Button(String label)
		String	getActionCommand()
1.0		String	getLabel()
1.0	◆	String	paramString()
1.1	◆	void	processActionEvent(event.ActionEvent e)
1.1	◆	void	processEvent(AWTEvent e)
1.1		void	removeActionListener(event.ActionListener l)
1.1		void	setActionCommand(String command)
1.0		void	setLabel(String label)

Canvas   java.awt

Object
  ➡Component   image.ImageObserver, MenuContainer, java.io.Serializable
    ➡Canvas

1.0		void	addNotify()
	❋		Canvas()
1.0		void	paint(Graphics g)

CardLayout   java.awt

Object
  ➡CardLayout   LayoutManager2, java.io.Serializable

1.0		void	addLayoutComponent(Component comp,
			Object constraints)
		void	addLayoutComponent(String name, Component comp)
1.0	✣		CardLayout()
1.0	✣		CardLayout(int hgap, int vgap)
1.0		void	first(Container parent)
1.1		int	getHgap()
		float	getLayoutAlignmentX(Container parent)
		float	getLayoutAlignmentY(Container parent)
		int	getVgap()
		void	invalidateLayout(Container target)
1.0		void	last(Container parent)
1.0		void	layoutContainer(Container parent)
		Dimension	maximumLayoutSize(Container target)
1.0		Dimension	minimumLayoutSize(Container parent)
1.0		void	next(Container parent)
1.0		Dimension	preferredLayoutSize(Container parent)
1.0		void	previous(Container parent)
1.0		void	removeLayoutComponent(Component comp)
1.1		void	setHgap(int hgap)
1.1		void	setVgap(int vgap)
1.0		void	show(Container parent, String name)
1.0		String	toString()

Checkbox   java.awt

```
Object
    ➡Component        image.ImageObserver, MenuContainer, java.io.Serializable
        ➡Checkbox     ItemSelectable
```

1.1		void	addItemListener(event.ItemListener l)
1.0		void	addNotify()
1.0	✣		Checkbox()
1.0	✣		Checkbox(String label)
1.0	✣		Checkbox(String label, boolean state)
1.1	✣		Checkbox(String label, boolean state,
			CheckboxGroup group)
	✣		Checkbox(String label, CheckboxGroup group,
			boolean state)
1.0		CheckboxGroup	getCheckboxGroup()
1.0		String	getLabel()
		Object[]	getSelectedObjects()
1.0		boolean	getState()
1.0	◆	String	paramString()
1.1	◆	void	processEvent(AWTEvent e)
1.1	◆	void	processItemEvent(event.ItemEvent e)
1.1		void	removeItemListener(event.ItemListener l)
1.0		void	setCheckboxGroup(CheckboxGroup g)
1.0		void	setLabel(String label)
1.0		void	setState(boolean state)

CheckboxGroup   java.awt

Object
➥CheckboxGroup   java.io.Serializable

1.0	✳		**CheckboxGroup**()
		Checkbox	**getCurrent**()
1.1		Checkbox	**getSelectedCheckbox**()
		void	**setCurrent**(Checkbox box)
1.1		void	**setSelectedCheckbox**(Checkbox box)
1.0		String	**toString**()

CheckboxMenuItem   java.awt

Object
➥MenuComponent   java.io.Serializable
➥MenuItem
➥CheckboxMenuItem   ItemSelectable

1.1		void	**addItemListener**(event.ItemListener l)
1.0		void	**addNotify**()
1.1	✳		**CheckboxMenuItem**()
1.0	✳		**CheckboxMenuItem**(String label)
1.1	✳		**CheckboxMenuItem**(String label, boolean state)
		Object[]	**getSelectedObjects**()
1.0		boolean	**getState**()
1.0		String	**paramString**()
1.1	♦	void	**processEvent**(AWTEvent e)
1.1	♦	void	**processItemEvent**(event.ItemEvent e)
1.1		void	**removeItemListener**(event.ItemListener l)
1.0		void	**setState**(boolean b)

Choice   java.awt

Object
➥Component   image.ImageObserver, MenuContainer, java.io.Serializable
➥Choice   ItemSelectable

1.1		void	**add**(String item)
		void	**addItem**(String item)
1.1		void	**addItemListener**(event.ItemListener l)
1.0		void	**addNotify**()
1.0	✳		**Choice**()
		int	**countItems**()
1.0		String	**getItem**(int index)
1.1		int	**getItemCount**()
		int	**getSelectedIndex**()
1.0		String	**getSelectedItem**()
		Object[]	**getSelectedObjects**()
		void	**insert**(String item, int index)
1.0	♦	String	**paramString**()

1.1	♦	void	**processEvent**(AWTEvent e)
1.1	♦	void	**processItemEvent**(event.ItemEvent e)
1.1		void	**remove**(int position)
1.1		void	**remove**(String item)
1.1		void	**removeAll**()
1.1		void	**removeItemListener**(event.ItemListener l)
1.0		void	**select**(int pos)
1.0		void	**select**(String str)

Clipboard   java.awt.datatransfer

Object
 ➠Clipboard

	✳		**Clipboard**(String name)
	🖉♦	Transferable	**contents**
		Transferable	**getContents**(Object requestor)
		String	**getName**()
	🖉♦	ClipboardOwner	**owner**
		void	**setContents**(Transferable contents, ClipboardOwner owner)

ClipboardOwner   java.awt.datatransfer

ClipboardOwner

		void	**lostOwnership**(Clipboard clipboard, Transferable contents)

Color   java.awt

Object
 ➠Color   java.io.Serializable

	🖉■	Color	**black**
	🖉■	Color	**blue**
1.0		Color	**brighter**()
1.0	✳		**Color**(float r, float g, float b)
1.0	✳		**Color**(int rgb)
1.0	✳		**Color**(int r, int g, int b)
	🖉■	Color	**cyan**
1.0		Color	**darker**()
	🖉■	Color	**darkGray**
1.1	❑	Color	**decode**(String nm) *throws* NumberFormatException
1.0		boolean	**equals**(Object obj)
1.0		int	**getBlue**()
1.0	❑	Color	**getColor**(String nm)
1.0	❑	Color	**getColor**(String nm, Color v)
1.0	❑	Color	**getColor**(String nm, int v)
1.0		int	**getGreen**()
1.0	❑	Color	**getHSBColor**(float h, float s, float b)
1.0		int	**getRed**()
1.0		int	**getRGB**()

	✍■	Color	gray
	✍■	Color	green
1.0		int	hashCode()
1.0	❏	int	HSBtoRGB(float hue, float saturation, float brightness)
	✍■	Color	lightGray
	✍■	Color	magenta
	✍■	Color	orange
	✍■	Color	pink
	✍▪	Color	red
1.0	❏	float[]	RGBtoHSB(int r, int g, int b, float[] hsbvals)
1.0		String	toString()
	✍■	Color	white
	✍■	Color	yellow

ColorModel   java.awt.image

Object
   ➡ColorModel

	✳		ColorModel(int bits)
		void	finalize()
	○	int	getAlpha(int pixel)
	○	int	getBlue(int pixel)
	○	int	getGreen(int pixel)
		int	getPixelSize()
	○	int	getRed(int pixel)
		int	getRGB(int pixel)
	❏	ColorModel	getRGBdefault()
	✍◆	int	pixel_bits

Component   java.awt

Object
   ➡Component   image.ImageObserver, MenuContainer, java.io.Serializable

		boolean	action(Event evt, Object what)
1.1		void	add(PopupMenu popup)
1.1		void	addComponentListener(event.ComponentListener l)
1.1		void	addFocusListener(event.FocusListener l)
1.1		void	addKeyListener(event.KeyListener l)
1.1		void	addMouseListener(event.MouseListener l)
1.1		void	addMouseMotionListener(event.MouseMotionListener l)
1.0		void	addNotify()
	✍■	float	BOTTOM_ALIGNMENT
		Rectangle	bounds()
	✍■	float	CENTER_ALIGNMENT
1.0		int	checkImage(Image image, image.ImageObserver observer)
1.0		int	checkImage(Image image, int width, int height, image.ImageObserver observer)
	✳◆		Component()

1.1		boolean	**contains**(int x, int y)
1.1		boolean	**contains**(Point p)
1.0		Image	**createImage**(image.ImageProducer producer)
1.0		Image	**createImage**(int width, int height)
		void	**deliverEvent**(Event e)
		void	**disable**()
1.1	●◆	void	**disableEvents**(long eventsToDisable)
	●	void	**dispatchEvent**(AWTEvent e)
		void	**doLayout**()
		void	**enable**()
		void	**enable**(boolean b)
1.1	●◆	void	**enableEvents**(long eventsToEnable)
		float	**getAlignmentX**()
		float	**getAlignmentY**()
1.0		Color	**getBackground**()
		Rectangle	**getBounds**()
1.0		image.ColorModel	**getColorModel**()
1.0		Component	**getComponentAt**(int x, int y)
1.1		Component	**getComponentAt**(Point p)
1.1		Cursor	**getCursor**()
1.0		Font	**getFont**()
1.0		FontMetrics	**getFontMetrics**(Font font)
1.0		Color	**getForeground**()
1.0		Graphics	**getGraphics**()
1.1		java.util.Locale	**getLocale**()
1.1		Point	**getLocation**()
		Point	**getLocationOnScreen**()
		Dimension	**getMaximumSize**()
		Dimension	**getMinimumSize**()
1.1		String	**getName**()
1.0		Container	**getParent**()
		peer.ComponentPeer	**getPeer**()
		Dimension	**getPreferredSize**()
1.1		Dimension	**getSize**()
1.0		Toolkit	**getToolkit**()
	●	Object	**getTreeLock**()
		boolean	**gotFocus**(Event evt, Object what)
		boolean	**handleEvent**(Event evt)
		void	**hide**()
1.0		boolean	**imageUpdate**(Image img, int flags, int x, int y, int w, int h)
		boolean	**inside**(int x, int y)
1.0		void	**invalidate**()
1.0		boolean	**isEnabled**()
1.1		boolean	**isFocusTraversable**()
1.0		boolean	**isShowing**()
1.0		boolean	**isValid**()
1.0		boolean	**isVisible**()
		boolean	**keyDown**(Event evt, int key)
		boolean	**keyUp**(Event evt, int key)
		void	**layout**()
	✍▪	float	**LEFT_ALIGNMENT**
1.0		void	**list**()

1.0		void	**list**(java.io.PrintStream out)
1.0		void	**list**(java.io.PrintStream out, int indent)
1.1		void	**list**(java.io.PrintWriter out)
1.1		void	**list**(java.io.PrintWriter out, int indent)
		Component	**locate**(int x, int y)
		Point	**location**()
		boolean	**lostFocus**(Event evt, Object what)
		Dimension	**minimumSize**()
		boolean	**mouseDown**(Event evt, int x, int y)
		boolean	**mouseDrag**(Event evt, int x, int y)
		boolean	**mouseEnter**(Event evt, int x, int y)
		boolean	**mouseExit**(Event evt, int x, int y)
		boolean	**mouseMove**(Event evt, int x, int y)
		boolean	**mouseUp**(Event evt, int x, int y)
		void	**move**(int x, int y)
		void	**nextFocus**()
1.0		void	**paint**(Graphics g)
1.0		void	**paintAll**(Graphics g)
1.0	♦	String	**paramString**()
		boolean	**postEvent**(Event e)
		Dimension	**preferredSize**()
1.0		boolean	**prepareImage**(Image image, image.ImageObserver observer)
1.0		boolean	**prepareImage**(Image image, int width, int height, image.ImageObserver observer)
1.0		void	**print**(Graphics g)
1.0		void	**printAll**(Graphics g)
1.1	♦	void	**processComponentEvent**(event.ComponentEvent e)
1.1	♦	void	**processEvent**(AWTEvent e)
1.1	♦	void	**processFocusEvent**(event.FocusEvent e)
1.1	♦	void	**processKeyEvent**(event.KeyEvent e)
1.1	♦	void	**processMouseEvent**(event.MouseEvent e)
1.1	♦	void	**processMouseMotionEvent**(event.MouseEvent e)
1.1		void	**remove**(MenuComponent popup)
1.1		void	**removeComponentListener**(event.ComponentListener l)
1.1		void	**removeFocusListener**(event.FocusListener l)
1.1		void	**removeKeyListener**(event.KeyListener l)
1.1		void	**removeMouseListener**(event.MouseListener l)
1.1		void	**removeMouseMotionListener**(event.MouseMotionListener l)
		void	**removeNotify**()
1.0		void	**repaint**()
1.0		void	**repaint**(int x, int y, int width, int height)
1.0		void	**repaint**(long tm)
1.0		void	**repaint**(long tm, int x, int y, int width, int height)
1.0		void	**requestFocus**()
		void	**reshape**(int x, int y, int width, int height)
		void	**resize**(Dimension d)
		void	**resize**(int width, int height)
	✍▪	float	**RIGHT_ALIGNMENT**
1.0		void	**setBackground**(Color c)
		void	**setBounds**(int x, int y, int width, int height)
1.1		void	**setBounds**(Rectangle r)

1.1		void	**setCursor**(Cursor cursor)
1.1		void	**setEnabled**(boolean b)
1.0		void	**setFont**(Font f)
1.0		void	**setForeground**(Color c)
1.1		void	**setLocale**(java.util.Locale l)
1.1		void	**setLocation**(int x, int y)
1.1		void	**setLocation**(Point p)
1.1		void	**setName**(String name)
1.1		void	**setSize**(Dimension d)
1.1		void	**setSize**(int width, int height)
1.1		void	**setVisible**(boolean b)
		void	**show**()
		void	**show**(boolean b)
		Dimension	**size**()
	⚠■	float	**TOP_ALIGNMENT**
1.0		String	**toString**()
1.1s		void	**transferFocus**()
1.0		void	**update**(Graphics g)
1.0		void	**validate**()

ComponentAdapter java.awt.event

Object
  ➡ComponentAdapter   ComponentListener

✳		**ComponentAdapter**()
	void	**componentHidden**(ComponentEvent e)
	void	**componentMoved**(ComponentEvent e)
	void	**componentResized**(ComponentEvent e)
	void	**componentShown**(ComponentEvent e)

ComponentEvent java.awt.event

Object
  ➡java.util.EventObject   java.io.Serializable
     ➡java.awt.AWTEvent
       ➡ComponentEvent

⚠■	int	**COMPONENT_FIRST**
⚠■	int	**COMPONENT_HIDDEN**
⚠■	int	**COMPONENT_LAST**
⚠■	int	**COMPONENT_MOVED**
⚠■	int	**COMPONENT_RESIZED**
⚠■	int	**COMPONENT_SHOWN**
✳		**ComponentEvent**(java.awt.Component source, int id)
	java.awt.Component	**getComponent**()
	String	**paramString**()

ComponentListener		java.awt.event
ComponentListener		java.util.EventListener

	void	componentHidden(ComponentEvent e)
	void	componentMoved(ComponentEvent e)
	void	componentResized(ComponentEvent e)
	void	componentShown(ComponentEvent e)

Container		java.awt

Object
  ➡Component   image.ImageObserver, MenuContainer, java.io.Serializable
    ➡Container

1.0		Component	**add**(Component comp)
1.0		Component	**add**(Component comp, int index)
1.1		void	**add**(Component comp, Object constraints)
		void	**add**(Component comp, Object constraints, int index)
		Component	**add**(String name, Component comp)
		void	**addContainerListener**(event.ContainerListener l)
1.1	♦	void	**addImpl**(Component comp, Object constraints, int index)
1.0		void	**addNotify**()
	✳♦		**Container**()
		int	**countComponents**()
		void	**deliverEvent**(Event e)
1.1		void	**doLayout**()
		float	**getAlignmentX**()
		float	**getAlignmentY**()
1.0		Component	**getComponent**(int n)
1.1		Component	**getComponentAt**(int x, int y)
1.1		Component	**getComponentAt**(Point p)
1.1		int	**getComponentCount**()
1.0		Component[]	**getComponents**()
1.1		Insets	**getInsets**()
1.0		LayoutManager	**getLayout**()
		Dimension	**getMaximumSize**()
1.1		Dimension	**getMinimumSize**()
1.0		Dimension	**getPreferredSize**()
		Insets	**insets**()
		void	**invalidate**()
1.1		boolean	**isAncestorOf**(Component c)
		void	**layout**()
		void	**list**(java.io.PrintStream out, int indent)
		void	**list**(java.io.PrintWriter out, int indent)
		Component	**locate**(int x, int y)
		Dimension	**minimumSize**()
		void	**paint**(Graphics g)
1.0		void	**paintComponents**(Graphics g)
1.0	♦	String	**paramString**()
		Dimension	**preferredSize**()

		void	**print**(Graphics g)
1.0		void	**printComponents**(Graphics g)
	◆	void	**processContainerEvent**(event.ContainerEvent e)
	◆	void	**processEvent**(AWTEvent e)
1.0		void	**remove**(Component comp)
1.1		void	**remove**(int index)
1.0		void	**removeAll**()
		void	**removeContainerListener**(event.ContainerListener l)
1.0		void	**removeNotify**()
1.1		void	**setCursor**(Cursor cursor)
1.0		void	**setLayout**(LayoutManager mgr)
		void	**update**(Graphics g)
1.0		void	**validate**()
	◆	void	**validateTree**()

ContainerAdapter   `java.awt.event`

Object
  ➥ContainerAdapter   ContainerListener

	void	**componentAdded**(ContainerEvent e)
	void	**componentRemoved**(ContainerEvent e)
✲		**ContainerAdapter**()

ContainerEvent   `java.awt.event`

Object
  ➥java.util.EventObject   java.io.Serializable
    ➥java.awt.AWTEvent
      ➥ComponentEvent
        ➥ContainerEvent

✍■		int	**COMPONENT_ADDED**
✍■		int	**COMPONENT_REMOVED**
✍■		int	**CONTAINER_FIRST**
✍■		int	**CONTAINER_LAST**
✲			**ContainerEvent**(java.awt.Component source, int id,
			java.awt.Component child)
	java.awt.Component	**getChild**()
	java.awt.Container	**getContainer**()
	String	**paramString**()

ContainerListener   `java.awt.event`

ContainerListener   java.util.EventListener

	void	**componentAdded**(ContainerEvent e)
	void	**componentRemoved**(ContainerEvent e)

CropImageFilter   java.awt.image

```
Object
    ➡ImageFilter                          ImageConsumer, Cloneable
        ➡CropImageFilter
```

✳		**CropImageFilter**(int x, int y, int w, int h)
	void	**setDimensions**(int w, int h)
	void	**setPixels**(int x, int y, int w, int h, ColorModel model, byte[] pixels, int off, int scansize)
	void	**setPixels**(int x, int y, int w, int h, ColorModel model, int[] pixels, int off, int scansize)
	void	**setProperties**(java.util.Hashtable props)

Cursor   java.awt

```
Object
    ➡Cursor                               java.io.Serializable
```

⚐■	int	**CROSSHAIR_CURSOR**
✳		**Cursor**(int type)
⚐■	int	**DEFAULT_CURSOR**
⚐■	int	**E_RESIZE_CURSOR**
❏	Cursor	**getDefaultCursor**()
❏	Cursor	**getPredefinedCursor**(int type)
	int	**getType**()
⚐■	int	**HAND_CURSOR**
⚐■	int	**MOVE_CURSOR**
⚐■	int	**N_RESIZE_CURSOR**
⚐■	int	**NE_RESIZE_CURSOR**
⚐■	int	**NW_RESIZE_CURSOR**
⚐❏◆	Cursor[]	**predefined**
⚐■	int	**S_RESIZE_CURSOR**
⚐■	int	**SE_RESIZE_CURSOR**
⚐■	int	**SW_RESIZE_CURSOR**
⚐■	int	**TEXT_CURSOR**
⚐■	int	**W_RESIZE_CURSOR**
⚐■	int	**WAIT_CURSOR**

Customizer   java.beans

```
Customizer
```

	void	**addPropertyChangeListener**(PropertyChangeListener listener)
	void	**removePropertyChangeListener**(PropertyChangeListener listener)
	void	**setObject**(Object bean)

DataFlavor   java.awt.datatransfer

```
Object
   ➡DataFlavor
```

✳		**DataFlavor**(Class representationClass, String humanPresentableName)
✳		**DataFlavor**(String mimeType, String humanPresentableName)
	boolean	**equals**(DataFlavor dataFlavor)
	String	**getHumanPresentableName**()
	String	**getMimeType**()
	Class	**getRepresentationClass**()
●	boolean	**isMimeTypeEqual**(DataFlavor dataFlavor)
	boolean	**isMimeTypeEqual**(String mimeType)
◆	String	**normalizeMimeType**(String mimeType)
◆	String	**normalizeMimeTypeParameter**(String parameterName, String parameterValue)
✐■	DataFlavor	**plainTextFlavor**
	void	**setHumanPresentableName**(String humanPresentableName)
✐■	DataFlavor	**stringFlavor**

DesignMode   java.beans

```
DesignMode
```

	boolean	**isDesignTime**()
✐■	String	**PROPERTYNAME**
	void	**setDesignTime**(boolean designTime)

Dialog   java.awt

```
Object
   ➡Component              image.ImageObserver, MenuContainer, java.io.Serializable
       ➡Container
           ➡Window
               ➡Dialog
```

1.0		void	**addNotify**()
1.0	✳		**Dialog**(Frame parent)
1.0	✳		**Dialog**(Frame parent, boolean modal)
1.0	✳		**Dialog**(Frame parent, String title)
1.0	✳		**Dialog**(Frame parent, String title, boolean modal)
1.0		String	**getTitle**()
1.0		boolean	**isModal**()
1.0		boolean	**isResizable**()
1.0	◆	String	**paramString**()
1.1		void	**setModal**(boolean modal)
1.0		void	**setResizable**(boolean resizable)
1.0		void	**setTitle**(String title)
1.0		void	**show**()

Dimension
`java.awt`

Object
➡Dimension   java.io.Serializable

1.0	✼		**Dimension**()
1.0	✼		**Dimension**(Dimension d)
1.0	✼		**Dimension**(int width, int height)
		boolean	**equals**(Object obj)
1.1		Dimension	**getSize**()
	✍	int	**height**
1.1		void	**setSize**(Dimension d)
1.1		void	**setSize**(int width, int height)
1.0		String	**toString**()
	✍	int	**width**

DirectColorModel
`java.awt.image`

Object
➡ColorModel
  ➡DirectColorModel

	✼		**DirectColorModel**(int bits, int rmask, int gmask, int bmask)
	✼		**DirectColorModel**(int bits, int rmask, int gmask, int bmask, int amask)
	●	int	**getAlpha**(int pixel)
	●	int	**getAlphaMask**()
	●	int	**getBlue**(int pixel)
	●	int	**getBlueMask**()
	●	int	**getGreen**(int pixel)
	●	int	**getGreenMask**()
	●	int	**getRed**(int pixel)
	●	int	**getRedMask**()
	●	int	**getRGB**(int pixel)

Event
`java.awt`

Object
➡Event   java.io.Serializable

1.0	✍■	int	**ACTION_EVENT**
1.0	✍■	int	**ALT_MASK**
1.0	✍	Object	**arg**
1.0	✍■	int	**BACK_SPACE**
1.0	✍■	int	**CAPS_LOCK**
1.0	✍	int	**clickCount**
1.0		boolean	**controlDown**()
1.0	✍■	int	**CTRL_MASK**
1.0	✍■	int	**DELETE**
1.0	✍■	int	**DOWN**
1.0	✍■	int	**END**
1.0	✍■	int	**ENTER**

1.0	⚠■		int	ESCAPE
1.0	✳			Event(Object target, int id, Object arg)
1.0	✳			Event(Object target, long when, int id, int x, int y, int key, int modifiers)
1.0	✳			Event(Object target, long when, int id, int x, int y, int key, int modifiers, Object arg)
1.0	⚠		Event	evt
1.0	⚠■		int	F1
1.0	⚠■		int	F10
1.0	⚠■		int	F11
1.0	⚠■		int	F12
1.0	⚠■		int	F2
1.0	⚠■		int	F3
1.0	⚠■		int	F4
1.0	⚠■		int	F5
1.0	⚠■		int	F6
1.0	⚠■		int	F7
1.0	⚠■		int	F8
1.0	⚠■		int	F9
1.0	⚠■		int	GOT_FOCUS
1.0	⚠■		int	HOME
1.0	⚠		int	id
1.0	⚠■		int	INSERT
1.0	⚠		int	key
1.0	⚠■		int	KEY_ACTION
1.0	⚠■		int	KEY_ACTION_RELEASE
1.0	⚠■		int	KEY_PRESS
1.0	⚠■		int	KEY_RELEASE
1.0	⚠■		int	LEFT
1.0	⚠■		int	LIST_DESELECT
1.0	⚠■		int	LIST_SELECT
1.0	⚠■		int	LOAD_FILE
1.0	⚠■		int	LOST_FOCUS
1.0	⚠■		int	META_MASK
1.0			boolean	metaDown()
1.0	⚠		int	modifiers
1.0	⚠■		int	MOUSE_DOWN
1.0	⚠■		int	MOUSE_DRAG
1.0	⚠■		int	MOUSE_ENTER
1.0	⚠■		int	MOUSE_EXIT
1.0	⚠■		int	MOUSE_MOVE
1.0	⚠■		int	MOUSE_UP
1.0	⚠■		int	NUM_LOCK
1.0	♦		String	paramString()
1.0	⚠■		int	PAUSE
1.0	⚠■		int	PGDN
1.0	⚠■		int	PGUP
1.0	⚠■		int	PRINT_SCREEN
1.0	⚠■		int	RIGHT
1.0	⚠■		int	SAVE_FILE
1.0	⚠■		int	SCROLL_ABSOLUTE
1.0	⚠■		int	SCROLL_BEGIN

1.0	⚠■	int	SCROLL_END
1.0	⚠■	int	SCROLL_LINE_DOWN
1.0	⚠■	int	SCROLL_LINE_UP
1.0	⚠■	int	SCROLL_LOCK
1.0	⚠■	int	SCROLL_PAGE_DOWN
1.0	⚠■	int	SCROLL_PAGE_UP
1.0	⚠■	int	SHIFT_MASK
1.0		boolean	shiftDown()
1.0	⚠■	int	TAB
1.0	⚠	Object	target
1.1		String	toString()
1.0		void	translate(int x, int y)
1.0	⚠■	int	UP
1.0	⚠	long	when
1.0	⚠■	int	WINDOW_DEICONIFY
1.0	⚠■	int	WINDOW_DESTROY
1.0	⚠■	int	WINDOW_EXPOSE
1.0	⚠■	int	WINDOW_ICONIFY
1.0	⚠■	int	WINDOW_MOVED
1.0	⚠	int	x
1.0	⚠	int	y

EventQueue   `java.awt`

Object
  ➥EventQueue

✳		EventQueue()
	AWTEvent	getNextEvent() *throws* InterruptedException
	AWTEvent	peekEvent()
	AWTEvent	peekEvent(int id)
	void	postEvent(AWTEvent theEvent)

EventSetDescriptor   `java.beans`

Object
  ➥FeatureDescriptor
    ➥EventSetDescriptor

| ✳ | | EventSetDescriptor(Class sourceClass, String eventSetName, Class listenerType, String listenerMethodName) *throws* IntrospectionException |
| ✳ | | EventSetDescriptor(Class sourceClass, String eventSetName, Class listenerType, String[] listenerMethodNames, String addListenerMethodName, String removeListenerMethodName) *throws* IntrospectionException |

✳		**EventSetDescriptor**(String eventSetName,
		Class listenerType,
		reflect.Method[] listenerMethods,
		reflect.Method addListenerMethod,
		reflect.Method removeListenerMethod)
		throws IntrospectionException
✳		**EventSetDescriptor**(String eventSetName,
		Class listenerType,
		MethodDescriptor[] listenerMethodDescriptors,
		reflect.Method addListenerMethod,
		reflect.Method removeListenerMethod)
		throws IntrospectionException
	reflect.Method	**getAddListenerMethod**()
	MethodDescriptor[]	**getListenerMethodDescriptors**()
	reflect.Method[]	**getListenerMethods**()
	Class	**getListenerType**()
	reflect.Method	**getRemoveListenerMethod**()
	boolean	**isInDefaultEventSet**()
	boolean	**isUnicast**()
	void	**setInDefaultEventSet**(boolean inDefaultEventSet)
	void	**setUnicast**(boolean unicast)

FeatureDescriptor   java.beans

Object
　　➡FeatureDescriptor

	java.util.Enumeration	**attributeNames**()
✳		**FeatureDescriptor**()
	String	**getDisplayName**()
	String	**getName**()
	String	**getShortDescription**()
	Object	**getValue**(String attributeName)
	boolean	**isExpert**()
	boolean	**isHidden**()
	boolean	**isPreferred**()
	void	**setDisplayName**(String displayName)
	void	**setExpert**(boolean expert)
	void	**setHidden**(boolean hidden)
	void	**setName**(String name)
	void	**setPreferred**(boolean preferred)
	void	**setShortDescription**(String text)
	void	**setValue**(String attributeName, Object value)

FileDialog   java.awt

Object
　　➡Component   image.ImageObserver, MenuContainer, java.io.Serializable
　　　➡Container
　　　　➡Window
　　　　　➡Dialog
　　　　　　➡FileDialog

		void	**addNotify**()
1.1	✳		**FileDialog**(Frame parent)
1.0	✳		**FileDialog**(Frame parent, String title)
1.0	✳		**FileDialog**(Frame parent, String title, int mode)
1.0		String	**getDirectory**()
1.0		String	**getFile**()
1.0		java.io.FilenameFilter	**getFilenameFilter**()
1.0		int	**getMode**()
1.0	⬛	int	**LOAD**
1.0	♦	String	**paramString**()
1.0	⬛	int	**SAVE**
1.0		void	**setDirectory**(String dir)
1.0		void	**setFile**(String file)
1.0		void	**setFilenameFilter**(java.io.FilenameFilter filter)
1.1		void	**setMode**(int mode)

FilteredImageSource   java.awt.image

Object
  ➡FilteredImageSource   ImageProducer

		void	**addConsumer**(ImageConsumer ic)
	✳		**FilteredImageSource**(ImageProducer orig, ImageFilter imgf)
		boolean	**isConsumer**(ImageConsumer ic)
		void	**removeConsumer**(ImageConsumer ic)
		void	**requestTopDownLeftRightResend**(ImageConsumer ic)
		void	**startProduction**(ImageConsumer ic)

FlowLayout   java.awt

Object
  ➡FlowLayout   LayoutManager, java.io.Serializable

1.0		void	**addLayoutComponent**(String name, Component comp)
1.0	⬛	int	**CENTER**
1.0	✳		**FlowLayout**()
1.0	✳		**FlowLayout**(int align)
1.0	✳		**FlowLayout**(int align, int hgap, int vgap)
1.1		int	**getAlignment**()
1.1		int	**getHgap**()
1.1		int	**getVgap**()
1.0		void	**layoutContainer**(Container target)
1.0	⬛	int	**LEFT**
1.0		Dimension	**minimumLayoutSize**(Container target)
1.0		Dimension	**preferredLayoutSize**(Container target)
1.0		void	**removeLayoutComponent**(Component comp)
1.0	⬛	int	**RIGHT**
1.1		void	**setAlignment**(int align)
1.1		void	**setHgap**(int hgap)
1.1		void	**setVgap**(int vgap)
1.0		String	**toString**()

FocusAdapter	java.awt.event

Object
   ➡FocusAdapter   FocusListener

✳		**FocusAdapter**()
	void	**focusGained**(FocusEvent e)
	void	**focusLost**(FocusEvent e)

FocusEvent	java.awt.event

Object
   ➡java.util.EventObject   java.io.Serializable
      ➡java.awt.AWTEvent
         ➡ComponentEvent
           ➡FocusEvent

◿■	int	**FOCUS_FIRST**
◿■	int	**FOCUS_GAINED**
◿■	int	**FOCUS_LAST**
◿■	int	**FOCUS_LOST**
✳		**FocusEvent**(java.awt.Component source, int id)
✳		**FocusEvent**(java.awt.Component source, int id,
		boolean temporary)
	boolean	**isTemporary**()
	String	**paramString**()

FocusListener	java.awt.event

FocusListener   java.util.EventListener

void	**focusGained**(FocusEvent e)
void	**focusLost**(FocusEvent e)

Font	java.awt

Object
   ➡Font   java.io.Serializable

1.0	◿■	int	**BOLD**
1.1	❑	Font	**decode**(String str)
1.0		boolean	**equals**(Object obj)
1.0	✳		**Font**(String name, int style, int size)
1.0		String	**getFamily**()
1.0	❑	Font	**getFont**(String nm)
1.0	❑	Font	**getFont**(String nm, Font font)
1.0		String	**getName**()
1.1		peer.FontPeer	**getPeer**()
1.0		int	**getSize**()
1.0		int	**getStyle**()
1.0		int	**hashCode**()
1.0		boolean	**isBold**()

1.0		boolean	isItalic()
1.0		boolean	isPlain()
1.0	✍■	int	ITALIC
1.0	✍◆	String	name
1.0	✍■	int	PLAIN
1.0	✍◆	int	size
	✍◆	int	style
1.0		String	toString()

FontMetrics   java.awt

Object
　➥FontMetrics   java.io.Serializable

1.0		int	bytesWidth(byte[] data, int off, int len)
1.0		int	charsWidth(char[] data, int off, int len)
1.0		int	charWidth(char ch)
1.0		int	charWidth(int ch)
1.0	✍◆	Font	font
1.0	✱◆		FontMetrics(Font font)
1.0		int	getAscent()
1.0		int	getDescent()
1.0		Font	getFont()
1.0		int	getHeight()
1.0		int	getLeading()
1.0		int	getMaxAdvance()
1.0		int	getMaxAscent()
		int	getMaxDescent()
1.0		int	getMaxDescent()
1.0		int[]	getWidths()
1.0		int	stringWidth(String str)
1.0.		String	toString()

Frame   java.awt

Object
　➥Component   image.ImageObserver, MenuContainer, java.io.Serializable
　　➥Container
　　　➥Window
　　　　➥Frame   MenuContainer

1.0		void	addNotify()
	✍■	int	CROSSHAIR_CURSOR
	✍■	int	DEFAULT_CURSOR
1.0		void	dispose()
	✍■	int	E_RESIZE_CURSOR
1.0	✱		Frame()
1.0	✱		Frame(String title)
		int	getCursorType()
1.2	❑	Frame[]	getFrames()
1.0		Image	getIconImage()
1.0		MenuBar	getMenuBar()

1.0		String	getTitle()
	⚠■	int	HAND_CURSOR
1.0		boolean	isResizable()
	⚠■	int	MOVE_CURSOR
	⚠■	int	N_RESIZE_CURSOR
	⚠■	int	NE_RESIZE_CURSOR
	⚠■	int	NW_RESIZE_CURSOR
	◆	String	paramString()
1.0		void	remove(MenuComponent m)
	⚠■	int	S_RESIZE_CURSOR
	⚠■	int	SE_RESIZE_CURSOR
		void	setCursor(int cursorType)
1.0		void	setIconImage(Image image)
1.0		void	setMenuBar(MenuBar mb)
1.0		void	setResizable(boolean resizable)
1.0		void	setTitle(String title)
	⚠■	int	SW_RESIZE_CURSOR
	⚠■	int	TEXT_CURSOR
	⚠■	int	W_RESIZE_CURSOR
	⚠■	int	WAIT_CURSOR

Graphics   java.awt

Object
   ➥Graphics

1.0	○	void	clearRect(int x, int y, int width, int height)
	○	void	clipRect(int x, int y, int width, int height)
1.0	○	void	copyArea(int x, int y, int width, int height, int dx, int dy)
1.0	○	Graphics	create()
1.0	○	Graphics	create(int x, int y, int width, int height)
1.0		void	dispose()
1.0		void	draw3DRect(int x, int y, int width, int height, boolean raised)
1.0		void	drawArc(int x, int y, int width, int height, int startAngle, int arcAngle)
1.0		void	drawBytes(byte[] data, int offset, int length, int x, int y)
1.0		void	drawChars(char[] data, int offset, int length, int x, int y)
1.0	○	boolean	drawImage(Image img, int x, int y, Color bgcolor, image.ImageObserver observer)
1.0	○	boolean	drawImage(Image img, int x, int y, image.ImageObserver observer)
1.0	○	boolean	drawImage(Image img, int x, int y, int width, int height, Color bgcolor, image.ImageObserver observer)
1.0	○	boolean	drawImage(Image img, int x, int y, int width, int height, image.ImageObserver observer)
1.1	○	boolean	drawImage(Image img, int dx1, int dy1, int dx2, int dy2, int sx1, int sy1, int sx2, int sy2, Color bgcolor, image.ImageObserver observer)

1.1	○	boolean	**drawImage**(Image img, int dx1, int dy1, int dx2, int dy2, int sx1, int sy1, int sx2, int sy2, image.ImageObserver observer)
1.0	○	void	**drawLine**(int x1, int y1, int x2, int y2)
1.0	○	void	**drawOval**(int x, int y, int width, int height)
1.0	○	void	**drawPolygon**(int[] xPoints, int[] yPoints, int nPoints)
1.0		void	**drawPolygon**(Polygon p)
1.1	○	void	**drawPolyline**(int[] xPoints, int[] yPoints, int nPoints)
1.0		void	**drawRect**(int x, int y, int width, int height)
1.0	○	void	**drawRoundRect**(int x, int y, int width, int height, int arcWidth, int arcHeight)
1.0	○	void	**drawString**(String str, int x, int y)
1.0		void	**fill3DRect**(int x, int y, int width, int height, boolean raised)
1.0	○	void	**fillArc**(int x, int y, int width, int height, int startAngle, int arcAngle)
1.0	○	void	**fillOval**(int x, int y, int width, int height)
1.0	○	void	**fillPolygon**(int[] xPoints, int[] yPoints, int nPoints)
1.0		void	**fillPolygon**(Polygon p)
1.0	○	void	**fillRect**(int x, int y, int width, int height)
1.0	○	void	**fillRoundRect**(int x, int y, int width, int height, int arcWidth, int arcHeight)
1.0		void	**finalize**()
1.1	○	Shape	**getClip**()
1.1	○	Rectangle	**getClipBounds**()
		Rectangle	**getClipRect**()
1.0	○	Color	**getColor**()
1.0	○	Font	**getFont**()
1.0		FontMetrics	**getFontMetrics**()
1.0	○	FontMetrics	**getFontMetrics**(Font f)
1.0	✳◆		**Graphics**()
1.1	○	void	**setClip**(int x, int y, int width, int height)
1.1	○	void	**setClip**(Shape clip)
1.0	○	void	**setColor**(Color c)
1.0	○	void	**setFont**(Font font)
1.0	○	void	**setPaintMode**()
1.0	○	void	**setXORMode**(Color c1)
1.0		String	**toString**()
1.0	○	void	**translate**(int x, int y)

GridBagConstraints   `java.awt`

Object
  ➡GridBagConstraints   Cloneable, java.io.Serializable

1.0	⬚	int	**anchor**
1.0	⬚■	int	**BOTH**
1.0	⬚■	int	**CENTER**
1.0		Object	**clone**()
1.0	⬚■	int	**EAST**

1.0	✍	int	`fill`
1.0	✳		`GridBagConstraints()`
1.0	✍	int	`gridheight`
1.0	✍	int	`gridwidth`
1.0	✍	int	`gridx`
1.0	✍	int	`gridy`
1.0	✍■	int	`HORIZONTAL`
1.0	✍	Insets	`insets`
1.0	✍	int	`ipadx`
1.0	✍	int	`ipady`
1.0	✍■	int	`NONE`
1.0	✍■	int	`NORTH`
1.0	✍■	int	`NORTHEAST`
1.0	✍■	int	`NORTHWEST`
1.0	✍■	int	`RELATIVE`
1.0	✍■	int	`REMAINDER`
1.0	✍■	int	`SOUTH`
1.0	✍■	int	`SOUTHEAST`
1.0	✍■	int	`SOUTHWEST`
1.0	✍■	int	`VERTICAL`
1.0	✍	double	`weightx`
1.0	✍	double	`weighty`
1.0	✍■	int	`WEST`

GridBagLayout			**java.awt**

Object
   ➡GridBagLayout   LayoutManager2, java.io.Serializable

1.0		void	`addLayoutComponent(Component comp,` `    Object constraints)`
1.0		void	`addLayoutComponent(String name, Component comp)`
	♦	void	`AdjustForGravity(GridBagConstraints constraints,` `    Rectangle r)`
	♦	void	`ArrangeGrid(Container parent)`
	✍	double[]	`columnWeights`
	✍	int[]	`columnWidths`
	✍♦	java.util.Hashtable	`comptable`
	✍♦	GridBagConstraints	`defaultConstraints`
1.0		GridBagConstraints	`getConstraints(Component comp)`
		float	`getLayoutAlignmentX(Container parent)`
		float	`getLayoutAlignmentY(Container parent)`
1.1		int[][]	`getLayoutDimensions()`
	♦	GridBagLayoutInfo	`GetLayoutInfo(Container parent, int sizeflag)`
1.1		Point	`getLayoutOrigin()`
1.1		double[][]	`getLayoutWeights()`
	♦	Dimension	`GetMinSize(Container parent, GridBagLayoutInfo info)`
1.0	✳		`GridBagLayout()`
		void	`invalidateLayout(Container target)`
1.0		void	`layoutContainer(Container parent)`
	✍♦	GridBagLayoutInfo	`layoutInfo`
1.1		Point	`location(int x, int y)`
1.0	♦	GridBagConstraints	`lookupConstraints(Component comp)`

1.0	✍■◆	int	**MAXGRIDSIZE**
		Dimension	**maximumLayoutSize**(Container target)
1.0		Dimension	**minimumLayoutSize**(Container parent)
1.0	✍■◆	int	**MINSIZE**
1.0		Dimension	**preferredLayoutSize**(Container parent)
	✍■◆	int	**PREFERREDSIZE**
1.0		void	**removeLayoutComponent**(Component comp)
	✍	int[]	**rowHeights**
	✍	double[]	**rowWeights**
1.0		void	**setConstraints**(Component comp, GridBagConstraints constraints)
1.0		String	**toString**()

GridLayout   java.awt

Object
  ➥GridLayout   LayoutManager, java.io.Serializable

1.0		void	**addLayoutComponent**(String name, Component comp)
1.1		int	**getColumns**()
1.1		int	**getHgap**()
1.1		int	**getRows**()
1.1		int	**getVgap**()
1.1	❊		**GridLayout**()
1.0	❊		**GridLayout**(int rows, int cols)
1.0	❊		**GridLayout**(int rows, int cols, int hgap, int vgap)
1.0		void	**layoutContainer**(Container parent)
1.0		Dimension	**minimumLayoutSize**(Container parent)
1.0		Dimension	**preferredLayoutSize**(Container parent)
1.0		void	**removeLayoutComponent**(Component comp)
1.1		void	**setColumns**(int cols)
1.1		void	**setHgap**(int hgap)
1.1		void	**setRows**(int rows)
1.1		void	**setVgap**(int vgap)
1.0		String	**toString**()

IllegalComponentStateException   java.awt

Object
  ➥Throwable   java.io.Serializable
    ➥Exception
      ➥RuntimeException
        ➥IllegalStateException
          ➥IllegalComponentStateException

❊		**IllegalComponentStateException**()
❊		**IllegalComponentStateException**(String s)

Image   java.awt

Object
  ➥Image

1.0	○	void	**flush**()
1.0	○	Graphics	**getGraphics**()
1.0	○	int	**getHeight**(image.ImageObserver observer)
1.0	○	Object	**getProperty**(String name,
			image.ImageObserver observer)
1.1		Image	**getScaledInstance**(int width, int height, int hints)
	○	image.ImageProducer	**getSource**()
1.0	○	int	**getWidth**(image.ImageObserver observer)
	✳		**Image**()
1.1	⟁■	int	**SCALE_AREA_AVERAGING**
1.1	⟁■	int	**SCALE_DEFAULT**
1.1	⟁■	int	**SCALE_FAST**
1.1	⟁■	int	**SCALE_REPLICATE**
1.1	⟁■	int	**SCALE_SMOOTH**
1.0	⟁■	Object	**UndefinedProperty**

ImageConsumer   java.awt.image

ImageConsumer

⟁■	int	**COMPLETESCANLINES**
⟁■	int	**IMAGEABORTED**
	void	**imageComplete**(int status)
⟁■	int	**IMAGEERROR**
⟁■	int	**RANDOMPIXELORDER**
	void	**setColorModel**(ColorModel model)
	void	**setDimensions**(int width, int height)
	void	**setHints**(int hintflags)
	void	**setPixels**(int x, int y, int w, int h,
		ColorModel model, byte[] pixels, int off,
		int scansize)
	void	**setPixels**(int x, int y, int w, int h,
		ColorModel model, int[] pixels, int off,
		int scansize)
	void	**setProperties**(java.util.Hashtable props)
⟁■	int	**SINGLEFRAME**
⟁■	int	**SINGLEFRAMEDONE**
⟁■	int	**SINGLEPASS**
⟁■	int	**STATICIMAGEDONE**
⟁■	int	**TOPDOWNLEFTRIGHT**

ImageFilter   java.awt.image

Object
    ➥ImageFilter   ImageConsumer, Cloneable

	Object	**clone**()
⟁◆	ImageConsumer	**consumer**
	ImageFilter	**getFilterInstance**(ImageConsumer ic)
	void	**imageComplete**(int status)
✳		**ImageFilter**()

```
        void  resendTopDownLeftRight(ImageProducer ip)
        void  setColorModel(ColorModel model)
        void  setDimensions(int width, int height)
        void  setHints(int hints)
        void  setPixels(int x, int y, int w, int h,
                  ColorModel model, byte[] pixels, int off,
                  int scansize)
        void  setPixels(int x, int y, int w, int h,
                  ColorModel model, int[] pixels, int off,
                  int scansize)
        void  setProperties(java.util.Hashtable props)
```

ImageObserver   java.awt.image

ImageObserver

```
         int  ABORT
         int  ALLBITS
         int  ERROR
         int  FRAMEBITS
         int  HEIGHT
     boolean  imageUpdate(java.awt.Image img, int infoflags,
                  int x, int y, int width, int height)
         int  PROPERTIES
         int  SOMEBITS
         int  WIDTH
```

ImageProducer   java.awt.image

ImageProducer

```
        void  addConsumer(ImageConsumer ic)
     boolean  isConsumer(ImageConsumer ic)
        void  removeConsumer(ImageConsumer ic)
        void  requestTopDownLeftRightResend(ImageConsumer ic)
        void  startProduction(ImageConsumer ic)
```

IndexColorModel   java.awt.image

Object
  ➥ColorModel
    ➥IndexColorModel

```
         int  getAlpha(int pixel)
        void  getAlphas(byte[] a)
         int  getBlue(int pixel)
        void  getBlues(byte[] b)
         int  getGreen(int pixel)
        void  getGreens(byte[] g)
         int  getMapSize()
         int  getRed(int pixel)
```

●	void	**getReds**(byte[] r)
●	int	**getRGB**(int pixel)
●	int	**getTransparentPixel**()
❋		**IndexColorModel**(int bits, int size, byte[] r, byte[] g, byte[] b)
❋		**IndexColorModel**(int bits, int size, byte[] r, byte[] g, byte[] b, byte[] a)
❋		**IndexColorModel**(int bits, int size, byte[] r, byte[] g, byte[] b, int trans)
❋		**IndexColorModel**(int bits, int size, byte[] cmap, int start, boolean hasalpha)
❋		**IndexColorModel**(int bits, int size, byte[] cmap, int start, boolean hasalpha, int trans)

IndexedPropertyDescriptor   java.beans

```
Object
   ➥FeatureDescriptor
      ➥PropertyDescriptor
         ➥IndexedPropertyDescriptor
```

	Class	**getIndexedPropertyType**()
	reflect.Method	**getIndexedReadMethod**()
	reflect.Method	**getIndexedWriteMethod**()
❋		**IndexedPropertyDescriptor**(String propertyName, Class beanClass) *throws* IntrospectionException
❋		**IndexedPropertyDescriptor**(String propertyName, Class beanClass, String getterName, String setterName, String indexedGetterName, String indexedSetterName) *throws* IntrospectionException
❋		**IndexedPropertyDescriptor**(String propertyName, reflect.Method getter, reflect.Method setter, reflect.Method indexedGetter, reflect.Method indexedSetter) *throws* IntrospectionException
	void	**setIndexedReadMethod**(reflect.Method getter) *throws* IntrospectionException
	void	**setIndexedWriteMethod**(reflect.Method setter) *throws* IntrospectionException

InputEvent   java.awt.event

```
Object
   ➥java.util.EventObject              java.io.Serializable
      ➥java.awt.AWTEvent
         ➥ComponentEvent
            ➥InputEvent
```

◢■	int	**ALT_GRAPH_MASK**
◢■	int	**ALT_MASK**
◢■	int	**BUTTON1_MASK**

		int	BUTTON2_MASK
✍■		int	BUTTON2_MASK
✍■		int	BUTTON3_MASK
		void	consume()
✍■		int	CTRL_MASK
		int	getModifiers()
		long	getWhen()
		boolean	isAltDown()
		boolean	isAltGraphDown()
		boolean	isConsumed()
		boolean	isControlDown()
		boolean	isMetaDown()
		boolean	isShiftDown()
✍■		int	META_MASK
✍■		int	SHIFT_MASK

Insets   java.awt

Object
  ➡Insets   Cloneable, java.io.Serializable

1.0	✍	int	bottom
1.0		Object	clone()
1.1		boolean	equals(Object obj)
1.0	✳		Insets(int top, int left, int bottom, int right)
1.0	✍	int	left
1.0	✍	int	right
1.0	✍	int	top
1.0		String	toString()

IntrospectionException   java.beans

Object
  ➡Throwable   java.io.Serializable
    ➡Exception
      ➡IntrospectionException

✳		IntrospectionException(String mess)

Introspector   java.beans

Object
  ➡Introspector

❑		String	decapitalize(String name)
❑		void	flushCaches()
❑		void	flushFromCaches(Class clz)
❑		BeanInfo	getBeanInfo(Class beanClass)
			throws IntrospectionException
❑		BeanInfo	getBeanInfo(Class beanClass, Class stopClass)
			throws IntrospectionException

❑	BeanInfo	**getBeanInfo**(Class beanClass, int flags)
		throws IntrospectionException
❑	String[]	**getBeanInfoSearchPath**()
▵■	int	**IGNORE_ALL_BEANINFO**
▵■	int	**IGNORE_IMMEDIATE_BEANINFO**
❑	void	**setBeanInfoSearchPath**(String[] path)
▵■	int	**USE_ALL_BEANINFO**

InvocationEvent — java.awt.event

```
Object
   ➥java.util.EventObject              java.io.Serializable
      ➥java.awt.AWTEvent
         ➥InvocationEvent              java.awt.peer.ActiveEvent
```

▵◆	boolean	**catchExceptions**
	void	**dispatch**()
	Exception	**getException**()
▵■	int	**INVOCATION_DEFAULT**
▵■	int	**INVOCATION_FIRST**
▵■	int	**INVOCATION_LAST**
✳◆		**InvocationEvent**(Object source, int id,
		Runnable runnable, Object notifier,
		boolean catchExceptions)
✳		**InvocationEvent**(Object source, Runnable runnable)
✳		**InvocationEvent**(Object source, Runnable runnable,
		Object notifier, boolean catchExceptions)
▵◆	Object	**notifier**
	String	**paramString**()
▵◆	Runnable	**runnable**

ItemEvent — java.awt.event

```
Object
   ➥java.util.EventObject              java.io.Serializable
      ➥java.awt.AWTEvent
         ➥ItemEvent
```

▵■	int	**DESELECTED**
	Object	**getItem**()
	java.awt.ItemSelectable	**getItemSelectable**()
	int	**getStateChange**()
▵■	int	**ITEM_FIRST**
▵■	int	**ITEM_LAST**
▵■	int	**ITEM_STATE_CHANGED**
✳		**ItemEvent**(java.awt.ItemSelectable source, int id,
		Object item, int stateChange)
	String	**paramString**()
▵■	int	**SELECTED**

ItemListener   java.awt.event

ItemListener   java.util.EventListener

	void	itemStateChanged(ItemEvent e)

ItemSelectable   java.awt

ItemSelectable

	void	addItemListener(event.ItemListener l)
	Object[]	getSelectedObjects()
	void	removeItemListener(event.ItemListener l)

KeyAdapter   java.awt.event

Object
➤KeyAdapter   KeyListener

✳		KeyAdapter()
	void	keyPressed(KeyEvent e)
	void	keyReleased(KeyEvent e)
	void	keyTyped(KeyEvent e)

KeyEvent   java.awt.event

Object
➤java.util.EventObject   java.io.Serializable
  ➤java.awt.AWTEvent
   ➤ComponentEvent
    ➤InputEvent
     ➤KeyEvent

⌂■	char	CHAR_UNDEFINED
	char	getKeyChar()
	int	getKeyCode()
❑	String	getKeyModifiersText(int modifiers)
❑	String	getKeyText(int keyCode)
	boolean	isActionKey()
⌂■	int	KEY_FIRST
⌂■	int	KEY_LAST
⌂■	int	KEY_PRESSED
⌂■	int	KEY_RELEASED
⌂■	int	KEY_TYPED
✳		KeyEvent(java.awt.Component source, int id, long when, int modifiers, int keyCode)
✳		KeyEvent(java.awt.Component source, int id, long when, int modifiers, int keyCode, char keyChar)
	String	paramString()
	void	setKeyChar(char keyChar)
	void	setKeyCode(int keyCode)

		void	**setModifiers**(int modifiers)
		void	**setSource**(Object newSource)
	✎▪	int	**VK_0**
	✎▪	int	**VK_1**
	✎▪	int	**VK_2**
	✎▪	int	**VK_3**
	✎▪	int	**VK_4**
	✎▪	int	**VK_5**
	✎▪	int	**VK_6**
	✎▪	int	**VK_7**
	✎▪	int	**VK_8**
	✎▪	int	**VK_9**
	✎▪	int	**VK_A**
	✎▪	int	**VK_ACCEPT**
	✎▪	int	**VK_ADD**
1.2	✎▪	int	**VK_AGAIN**
1.2	✎▪	int	**VK_ALL_CANDIDATES**
1.2	✎▪	int	**VK_ALPHANUMERIC**
	✎▪	int	**VK_ALT**
1.2	✎▪	int	**VK_ALT_GRAPH**
1.2	✎▪	int	**VK_AMPERSAND**
1.2	✎▪	int	**VK_ASTERISK**
1.2	✎▪	int	**VK_AT**
	✎▪	int	**VK_B**
	✎▪	int	**VK_BACK_QUOTE**
	✎▪	int	**VK_BACK_SLASH**
	✎▪	int	**VK_BACK_SPACE**
1.2	✎▪	int	**VK_BRACELEFT**
1.2	✎▪	int	**VK_BRACERIGHT**
	✎▪	int	**VK_C**
	✎▪	int	**VK_CANCEL**
	✎▪	int	**VK_CAPS_LOCK**
1.2	✎▪	int	**VK_CIRCUMFLEX**
	✎▪	int	**VK_CLEAR**
	✎▪	int	**VK_CLOSE_BRACKET**
1.2	✎▪	int	**VK_CODE_INPUT**
1.2	✎▪	int	**VK_COLON**
	✎▪	int	**VK_COMMA**
1.2	✎▪	int	**VK_COMPOSE**
	✎▪	int	**VK_CONTROL**
	✎▪	int	**VK_CONVERT**
1.2	✎▪	int	**VK_COPY**
1.2	✎▪	int	**VK_CUT**
	✎▪	int	**VK_D**
1.2	✎▪	int	**VK_DEAD_ABOVEDOT**
1.2	✎▪	int	**VK_DEAD_ABOVERING**
1.2	✎▪	int	**VK_DEAD_ACUTE**
1.2	✎▪	int	**VK_DEAD_BREVE**
1.2	✎▪	int	**VK_DEAD_CARON**
1.2	✎▪	int	**VK_DEAD_CEDILLA**
1.2	✎▪	int	**VK_DEAD_CIRCUMFLEX**
1.2	✎▪	int	**VK_DEAD_DIAERESIS**
1.2	✎▪	int	**VK_DEAD_DOUBLEACUTE**

1.2	int	VK_DEAD_GRAVE
1.2	int	VK_DEAD_IOTA
1.2	int	VK_DEAD_MACRON
1.2	int	VK_DEAD_OGONEK
1.2	int	VK_DEAD_SEMIVOICED_SOUND
1.2	int	VK_DEAD_TILDE
1.2	int	VK_DEAD_VOICED_SOUND
	int	VK_DECIMAL
	int	VK_DELETE
	int	VK_DIVIDE
1.2	int	VK_DOLLAR
	int	VK_DOWN
	int	VK_E
	int	VK_END
	int	VK_ENTER
	int	VK_EQUALS
	int	VK_ESCAPE
1.2	int	VK_EURO_SIGN
1.2	int	VK_EXCLAMATION_MARK
	int	VK_F
	int	VK_F1
	int	VK_F10
	int	VK_F11
	int	VK_F12
1.2	int	VK_F13
1.2	int	VK_F14
1.2	int	VK_F15
1.2	int	VK_F16
1.2	int	VK_F17
1.2	int	VK_F18
1.2	int	VK_F19
	int	VK_F2
1.2	int	VK_F20
1.2	int	VK_F21
1.2	int	VK_F22
1.2	int	VK_F23
1.2	int	VK_F24
	int	VK_F3
	int	VK_F4
	int	VK_F5
	int	VK_F6
	int	VK_F7
	int	VK_F8
	int	VK_F9
	int	VK_FINAL
1.2	int	VK_FIND
1.2	int	VK_FULL_WIDTH
	int	VK_G
1.2	int	VK_GREATER
	int	VK_H
1.2	int	VK_HALF_WIDTH
	int	VK_HELP
1.2	int	VK_HIRAGANA

		int	VK_HOME
		int	VK_I
1.3		int	VK_INPUT_METHOD_ON_OFF
		int	VK_INSERT
1.2		int	VK_INVERTED_EXCLAMATION_MARK
		int	VK_J
1.2		int	VK_JAPANESE_HIRAGANA
1.2		int	VK_JAPANESE_KATAKANA
1.2		int	VK_JAPANESE_ROMAN
		int	VK_K
		int	VK_KANA
1.3		int	VK_KANA_LOCK
		int	VK_KANJI
1.2		int	VK_KATAKANA
1.2		int	VK_KP_DOWN
1.2		int	VK_KP_LEFT
1.2		int	VK_KP_RIGHT
1.2		int	VK_KP_UP
		int	VK_L
		int	VK_LEFT
1.2		int	VK_LEFT_PARENTHESIS
1.2		int	VK_LESS
		int	VK_M
		int	VK_META
1.2		int	VK_MINUS
		int	VK_MODECHANGE
		int	VK_MULTIPLY
		int	VK_N
		int	VK_NONCONVERT
		int	VK_NUM_LOCK
1.2		int	VK_NUMBER_SIGN
		int	VK_NUMPAD0
		int	VK_NUMPAD1
		int	VK_NUMPAD2
		int	VK_NUMPAD3
		int	VK_NUMPAD4
		int	VK_NUMPAD5
		int	VK_NUMPAD6
		int	VK_NUMPAD7
		int	VK_NUMPAD8
		int	VK_NUMPAD9
		int	VK_O
		int	VK_OPEN_BRACKET
		int	VK_P
		int	VK_PAGE_DOWN
		int	VK_PAGE_UP
1.2		int	VK_PASTE
		int	VK_PAUSE
		int	VK_PERIOD
1.2		int	VK_PLUS
1.2		int	VK_PREVIOUS_CANDIDATE
		int	VK_PRINTSCREEN
1.2		int	VK_PROPS

	🔒■	int	**VK_Q**
	🔒■	int	**VK_QUOTE**
1.2	🔒■	int	**VK_QUOTEDBL**
	🔒■	int	**VK_R**
	🔒■	int	**VK_RIGHT**
1.2	🔒■	int	**VK_RIGHT_PARENTHESIS**
1.2	🔒■	int	**VK_ROMAN_CHARACTERS**
	🔒■	int	**VK_S**
	🔒■	int	**VK_SCROLL_LOCK**
	🔒■	int	**VK_SEMICOLON**
	🔒■	int	**VK_SEPARATER**
	🔒■	int	**VK_SHIFT**
	🔒■	int	**VK_SLASH**
	🔒■	int	**VK_SPACE**
1.2	🔒■	int	**VK_STOP**
	🔒■	int	**VK_SUBTRACT**
	🔒■	int	**VK_T**
	🔒■	int	**VK_TAB**
	🔒■	int	**VK_U**
	🔒■	int	**VK_UNDEFINED**
1.2	🔒■	int	**VK_UNDERSCORE**
1.2	🔒■	int	**VK_UNDO**
	🔒■	int	**VK_UP**
	🔒■	int	**VK_V**
	🔒■	int	**VK_W**
	🔒■	int	**VK_X**
	🔒■	int	**VK_Y**
	🔒■	int	**VK_Z**

KeyListener   `java.awt.event`

KeyListener   java.util.EventListener

		void	**keyPressed**(KeyEvent e)
		void	**keyReleased**(KeyEvent e)
		void	**keyTyped**(KeyEvent e)

Label   `java.awt`

Object
➡Component
➡Label   image.ImageObserver, MenuContainer, java.io.Serializable

		void	**addNotify**()
1.0	🔒■	int	**CENTER**
1.0		int	**getAlignment**()
1.0		String	**getText**()
1.0	❋		**Label**()
1.0	❋		**Label**(String text)
1.0	❋		**Label**(String text, int alignment)
1.0	🔒■	int	**LEFT**
1.0	◆	String	**paramString**()

1.0t.		int	RIGHT
1.0		void	setAlignment(int alignment)
1.0		void	setText(String text)

LayoutManager   java.awt

LayoutManager

	void	addLayoutComponent(String name, Component comp)
	void	layoutContainer(Container parent)
	Dimension	minimumLayoutSize(Container parent)
	Dimension	preferredLayoutSize(Container parent)
	void	removeLayoutComponent(Component comp)

LayoutManager2   java.awt

LayoutManager2   LayoutManager

	void	addLayoutComponent(Component comp, Object constraints)
	float	getLayoutAlignmentX(Container target)
	float	getLayoutAlignmentY(Container target)
	void	invalidateLayout(Container target)
	Dimension	maximumLayoutSize(Container target)

List   java.awt

Object
➡Component   image.ImageObserver, MenuContainer, java.io.Serializable
➡List   ItemSelectable

1.1		void	add(String item)
1.1		void	add(String item, int index)
1.1		void	addActionListener(event.ActionListener l)
		void	addItem(String item)
		void	addItem(String item, int index)
1.1		void	addItemListener(event.ItemListener l)
		void	addNotify()
		boolean	allowsMultipleSelections()
		void	clear()
		int	countItems()
		void	delItem(int position)
		void	delItems(int start, int end)
1.0		void	deselect(int index)
1.0		String	getItem(int index)
1.0		int	getItemCount()
1.1		String[]	getItems()
1.1		Dimension	getMinimumSize()
1.1		Dimension	getMinimumSize(int rows)
1.1		Dimension	getPreferredSize()
1.1		Dimension	getPreferredSize(int rows)
1.0		int	getRows()

1.0		int	**getSelectedIndex**()
1.0		int[]	**getSelectedIndexes**()
1.0		String	**getSelectedItem**()
1.0		String[]	**getSelectedItems**()
		Object[]	**getSelectedObjects**()
1.0		int	**getVisibleIndex**()
1.1		boolean	**isIndexSelected**(int index)
1.1		boolean	**isMultipleMode**()
		boolean	**isSelected**(int index)
1.0	✳		**List**()
1.1	✳		**List**(int rows)
1.0	✳		**List**(int rows, boolean multipleMode)
1.0		void	**makeVisible**(int index)
		Dimension	**minimumSize**()
		Dimension	**minimumSize**(int rows)
1.0	♦	String	**paramString**()
		Dimension	**preferredSize**()
		Dimension	**preferredSize**(int rows)
1.1	♦	void	**processActionEvent**(event.ActionEvent e)
1.1	♦	void	**processEvent**(AWTEvent e)
1.1	♦	void	**processItemEvent**(event.ItemEvent e)
1.1		void	**remove**(int position)
1.1		void	**remove**(String item)
1.1		void	**removeActionListener**(event.ActionListener l)
1.1		void	**removeAll**()
1.1		void	**removeItemListener**(event.ItemListener l)
		void	**removeNotify**()
1.0		void	**replaceItem**(String newValue, int index)
1.0		void	**select**(int index)
1.1		void	**setMultipleMode**(boolean b)
		void	**setMultipleSelections**(boolean b)

MediaTracker   java.awt

Object
　➡MediaTracker   java.io.Serializable

1.0	✍▪	int	**ABORTED**
1.0		void	**addImage**(Image image, int id)
1.0		void	**addImage**(Image image, int id, int w, int h)
1.0		boolean	**checkAll**()
1.0		boolean	**checkAll**(boolean load)
1.0		boolean	**checkID**(int id)
1.0		boolean	**checkID**(int id, boolean load)
1.0	✍▪	int	**COMPLETE**
1.0	✍▪	int	**ERRORED**
1.0		Object[]	**getErrorsAny**()
1.0		Object[]	**getErrorsID**(int id)
1.0		boolean	**isErrorAny**()
1.0		boolean	**isErrorID**(int id)
1.0	✍▪	int	**LOADING**
1.0	✳		**MediaTracker**(Component comp)
1.1		void	**removeImage**(Image image)

1.1	void	**removeImage**(Image image, int id)
1.1	void	**removeImage**(Image image, int id, int width, int height)
1.0	int	**statusAll**(boolean load)
1.0	int	**statusID**(int id, boolean load)
1.0	void	**waitForAll**() *throws* InterruptedException
1.0	boolean	**waitForAll**(long ms) *throws* InterruptedException
1.0	void	**waitForID**(int id) *throws* InterruptedException
1.0	boolean	**waitForID**(int id, long ms) *throws* InterruptedException

---

MemoryImageSource   **java.awt.image**

Object
   ➡MemoryImageSource   ImageProducer

	void	**addConsumer**(ImageConsumer ic)
	boolean	**isConsumer**(ImageConsumer ic)
✳		**MemoryImageSource**(int w, int h, ColorModel cm, byte[] pix, int off, int scan)
✳		**MemoryImageSource**(int w, int h, ColorModel cm, byte[] pix, int off, int scan, java.util.Hashtable props)
✳		**MemoryImageSource**(int w, int h, ColorModel cm, int[] pix, int off, int scan)
✳		**MemoryImageSource**(int w, int h, ColorModel cm, int[] pix, int off, int scan, java.util.Hashtable props)
✳		**MemoryImageSource**(int w, int h, int[] pix, int off, int scan)
✳		**MemoryImageSource**(int w, int h, int[] pix, int off, int scan, java.util.Hashtable props)
	void	**newPixels**()
	void	**newPixels**(byte[] newpix, ColorModel newmodel, int offset, int scansize)
	void	**newPixels**(int[] newpix, ColorModel newmodel, int offset, int scansize)
	void	**newPixels**(int x, int y, int w, int h)
	void	**newPixels**(int x, int y, int w, int h, boolean framenotify)
	void	**removeConsumer**(ImageConsumer ic)
	void	**requestTopDownLeftRightResend**(ImageConsumer ic)
	void	**setAnimated**(boolean animated)
	void	**setFullBufferUpdates**(boolean fullbuffers)
	void	**startProduction**(ImageConsumer ic)

Menu   **java.awt**

Object
   ➡MenuComponent   java.io.Serializable
      ➡MenuItem
         ➡Menu   MenuContainer

1.0		MenuItem	**add**(MenuItem mi)
1.0		void	**add**(String label)
		void	**addNotify**()
1.0		void	**addSeparator**()
		int	**countItems**()
1.0		MenuItem	**getItem**(int index)
1.1		int	**getItemCount**()
1.1		void	**insert**(MenuItem menuitem, int index)
1.1		void	**insert**(String label, int index)
1.1		void	**insertSeparator**(int index)
1.0		boolean	**isTearOff**()
1.1	❊		**Menu**()
1.0	❊		**Menu**(String label)
1.0.	❊		**Menu**(String label, boolean tearOff)
1.0u.		String	**paramString**()
1.0		void	**remove**(int index)
1.0		void	**remove**(MenuComponent item)
1.0.		void	**removeAll**()
		void	**removeNotify**()

MenuBar   `java.awt`

Object
  ➥MenuComponent   java.io.Serializable
    ➥MenuBar   MenuContainer

1.0		Menu	**add**(Menu m)
		void	**addNotify**()
		int	**countMenus**()
1.1		void	**deleteShortcut**(MenuShortcut s)
1.0		Menu	**getHelpMenu**()
1.0		Menu	**getMenu**(int i)
1.1		int	**getMenuCount**()
1.1		MenuItem	**getShortcutMenuItem**(MenuShortcut s)
1.0	❊		**MenuBar**()
1.0		void	**remove**(int index)
1.0		void	**remove**(MenuComponent m)
		void	**removeNotify**()
1.0		void	**setHelpMenu**(Menu m)
1.1		java.util.Enumeration	**shortcuts**()

MenuComponent   `java.awt`

Object
  ➥MenuComponent   java.io.Serializable

	●	void	**dispatchEvent**(AWTEvent e)
1.0		Font	**getFont**()
1.1		String	**getName**()
1.0		MenuContainer	**getParent**()
		peer.MenuComponentPeer	**getPeer**()
	●◆	Object	**getTreeLock**()
	❊		**MenuComponent**()

1.0	♦	String	**paramString**()
1.0		boolean	**postEvent**(Event evt)
1.1	♦	void	**processEvent**(AWTEvent e)
		void	**removeNotify**()
1.0		void	**setFont**(Font f)
1.1		void	**setName**(String name)
1.0		String	**toString**()

MenuContainer   java.awt

MenuContainer

Font	**getFont**()
boolean	**postEvent**(Event evt)
void	**remove**(MenuComponent comp)

MenuItem   java.awt

Object
  ➡MenuComponent   java.io.Serializable
     ➡MenuItem

1.1		void	**addActionListener**(event.ActionListener l)
		void	**addNotify**()
1.1		void	**deleteShortcut**()
		void	**disable**()
1.1	●♦	void	**disableEvents**(long eventsToDisable)
		void	**enable**()
		void	**enable**(boolean b)
1.1	●♦	void	**enableEvents**(long eventsToEnable)
1.1		String	**getActionCommand**()
1.0		String	**getLabel**()
1.1		MenuShortcut	**getShortcut**()
1.0		boolean	**isEnabled**()
1.1	✳		**MenuItem**()
1.0	✳		**MenuItem**(String label)
1.1	✳		**MenuItem**(String label, MenuShortcut s)
1.0		String	**paramString**()
1.1	♦	void	**processActionEvent**(event.ActionEvent e)
1.1	♦	void	**processEvent**(AWTEvent e)
1.1		void	**removeActionListener**(event.ActionListener l)
1.1		void	**setActionCommand**(String command)
1.1		void	**setEnabled**(boolean b)
1.0		void	**setLabel**(String label)
1.1		void	**setShortcut**(MenuShortcut s)

MenuShortcut   java.awt

Object
  ➡MenuShortcut   java.io.Serializable

	boolean	**equals**(MenuShortcut s)
	int	**getKey**()
✻		**MenuShortcut**(int key)
✻		**MenuShortcut**(int key, boolean useShiftModifier)
◆	String	**paramString**()
	String	**toString**()
	boolean	**usesShiftModifier**()

MethodDescriptor   `java.beans`

Object
➥FeatureDescriptor
  ➥MethodDescriptor

	reflect.Method	**getMethod**()
	ParameterDescriptor[]	**getParameterDescriptors**()
✻		**MethodDescriptor**(reflect.Method method)
✻		**MethodDescriptor**(reflect.Method method,
		ParameterDescriptor[] parameterDescriptors)

MouseAdapter   `java.awt.event`

Object
➥MouseAdapter   MouseListener

✻		**MouseAdapter**()
	void	**mouseClicked**(MouseEvent e)
	void	**mouseEntered**(MouseEvent e)
	void	**mouseExited**(MouseEvent e)
	void	**mousePressed**(MouseEvent e)
	void	**mouseReleased**(MouseEvent e)

MouseEvent   `java.awt.event`

Object
➥java.util.EventObject   java.io.Serializable
  ➥java.awt.AWTEvent
    ➥ComponentEvent
      ➥InputEvent
        ➥MouseEvent

	int	**getClickCount**()
	java.awt.Point	**getPoint**()
	int	**getX**()
	int	**getY**()
	boolean	**isPopupTrigger**()
⟑■	int	**MOUSE_CLICKED**
⟑■	int	**MOUSE_DRAGGED**
⟑■	int	**MOUSE_ENTERED**
⟑■	int	**MOUSE_EXITED**

	int	MOUSE_FIRST
	int	MOUSE_LAST
	int	MOUSE_MOVED
	int	MOUSE_PRESSED
	int	MOUSE_RELEASED
		MouseEvent(java.awt.Component source, int id, long when, int modifiers, int x, int y, int clickCount, boolean popupTrigger)
	String	**paramString**()
	void	**translatePoint**(int x, int y)

MouseListener   java.awt.event

MouseListener   java.util.EventListener

	void	**mouseClicked**(MouseEvent e)
	void	**mouseEntered**(MouseEvent e)
	void	**mouseExited**(MouseEvent e)
	void	**mousePressed**(MouseEvent e)
	void	**mouseReleased**(MouseEvent e)

MouseMotionAdapter   java.awt.event

Object
⮕MouseMotionAdapter   MouseMotionListener

	void	**mouseDragged**(MouseEvent e)
		MouseMotionAdapter()
	void	**mouseMoved**(MouseEvent e)

MouseMotionListener   java.awt.event

MouseMotionListener   java.util.EventListener

	void	**mouseDragged**(MouseEvent e)
	void	**mouseMoved**(MouseEvent e)

PaintEvent   java.awt.event

Object
⮕java.util.EventObject   java.io.Serializable
  ⮕java.awt.AWTEvent
    ⮕ComponentEvent
      ⮕PaintEvent

	java.awt.Rectangle	**getUpdateRect**()
	int	**PAINT**
	int	**PAINT_FIRST**
	int	**PAINT_LAST**

✳		**PaintEvent**(java.awt.Component source, int id, java.awt.Rectangle updateRect)
	String	**paramString**()
	void	**setUpdateRect**(java.awt.Rectangle updateRect)
🖉▪	int	**UPDATE**

Panel   java.awt

Object
➡Component   image.ImageObserver, MenuContainer, java.io.Serializable
    ➡Container
        ➡Panel

	void	**addNotify**()
1.0 ✳		**Panel**()
1.1 ✳		**Panel**(LayoutManager layout)

ParameterDescriptor   java.beans

Object
➡FeatureDescriptor
    ➡ParameterDescriptor

✳	**ParameterDescriptor**()

PixelGrabber   java.awt.image

Object
➡PixelGrabber   ImageConsumer

	void	**abortGrabbing**()
	ColorModel	**getColorModel**()
	int	**getHeight**()
	Object	**getPixels**()
	int	**getStatus**()
	int	**getWidth**()
	boolean	**grabPixels**() *throws* InterruptedException
	boolean	**grabPixels**(long ms) *throws* InterruptedException
	void	**imageComplete**(int status)
✳		**PixelGrabber**(java.awt.Image img, int x, int y, int w, int h, boolean forceRGB)
✳		**PixelGrabber**(java.awt.Image img, int x, int y, int w, int h, int[] pix, int off, int scansize)
✳		**PixelGrabber**(ImageProducer ip, int x, int y, int w, int h, int[] pix, int off, int scansize)
	void	**setColorModel**(ColorModel model)
	void	**setDimensions**(int width, int height)
	void	**setHints**(int hints)

	void	**setPixels**(int srcX, int srcY, int srcW, int srcH,
		    ColorModel model, byte[] pixels, int srcOff,
		    int srcScan)

		void	**setPixels**(int srcX, int srcY, int srcW, int srcH, ColorModel model, int[] pixels, int srcOff, int srcScan)
		void	**setProperties**(java.util.Hashtable props)
		void	**startGrabbing**()
		int	**status**()

Point   java.awt

Object
➡Point   java.io.Serializable

1.0		boolean	**equals**(Object obj)
1.1		Point	**getLocation**()
1.0		int	**hashCode**()
1.0		void	**move**(int x, int y)
1.1	✳		**Point**()
1.0	✳		**Point**(int x, int y)
1.1	✳		**Point**(Point p)
1.1		void	**setLocation**(int x, int y)
1.1		void	**setLocation**(Point p)
1.0		String	**toString**()
1.0		void	**translate**(int x, int y)
1.0	✍	int	**x**
1.0	✍	int	**y**

Polygon   java.awt

Object
➡Polygon   Shape, java.io.Serializable

1.0		void	**addPoint**(int x, int y)
	✍◆	Rectangle	**bounds**
1.1		boolean	**contains**(int x, int y)
		boolean	**contains**(Point p)
		Rectangle	**getBoundingBox**()
1.1		Rectangle	**getBounds**()
		boolean	**inside**(int x, int y)
1.0	✍	int	**npoints**
1.0	✳		**Polygon**()
1.0	✳		**Polygon**(int[] xpoints, int[] ypoints, int npoints)
1.1		void	**translate**(int deltaX, int deltaY)
1.0	✍	int[]	**xpoints**
1.0	✍	int[]	**ypoints**

PopupMenu   java.awt

Object
➡MenuComponent   java.io.Serializable

```
➥MenuItem
   ➥Menu                              MenuContainer
      ➥PopupMenu
```

※	void	**addNotify**()
※		**PopupMenu**()
		PopupMenu(String label)
	void	**show**(Component origin, int x, int y)

PrintGraphics · java.awt

PrintGraphics

	PrintJob	**getPrintJob**()

PrintJob · java.awt

```
Object
   ➥PrintJob
```

○	void	**end**()
	void	**finalize**()
○	Graphics	**getGraphics**()
○	Dimension	**getPageDimension**()
○	int	**getPageResolution**()
○	boolean	**lastPageFirst**()
※		**PrintJob**()

PropertyChangeEvent · java.beans

```
Object
   ➥java.util.EventObject            java.io.Serializable
      ➥PropertyChangeEvent
```

	Object	**getNewValue**()
	Object	**getOldValue**()
	Object	**getPropagationId**()
	String	**getPropertyName**()
※		**PropertyChangeEvent**(Object source, String propertyName, Object oldValue, Object newValue)
	void	**setPropagationId**(Object propagationId)

PropertyChangeListener · java.beans

PropertyChangeListener   java.util.EventListener

	void	**propertyChange**(PropertyChangeEvent evt)

PropertyChangeSupport		java.beans

Object
  ➡PropertyChangeSupport   java.io.Serializable

void	**addPropertyChangeListener**(	
	PropertyChangeListener listener)	
void	**addPropertyChangeListener**(String propertyName,	
	PropertyChangeListener listener)	
void	**firePropertyChange**(PropertyChangeEvent evt)	
void	**firePropertyChange**(String propertyName,	
	boolean oldValue, boolean newValue)	
void	**firePropertyChange**(String propertyName,	
	int oldValue, int newValue)	
void	**firePropertyChange**(String propertyName,	
	Object oldValue, Object newValue)	
boolean	**hasListeners**(String propertyName)	
✳	**PropertyChangeSupport**(Object sourceBean)	
void	**removePropertyChangeListener**(	
	PropertyChangeListener listener)	
void	**removePropertyChangeListener**(String propertyName,	
	PropertyChangeListener listener)	

PropertyDescriptor		java.beans

Object
  ➡FeatureDescriptor
    ➡PropertyDescriptor

Class	**getPropertyEditorClass**()	
Class	**getPropertyType**()	
reflect.Method	**getReadMethod**()	
reflect.Method	**getWriteMethod**()	
boolean	**isBound**()	
boolean	**isConstrained**()	
✳	**PropertyDescriptor**(String propertyName,	
	Class beanClass) *throws* IntrospectionException	
✳	**PropertyDescriptor**(String propertyName,	
	Class beanClass, String getterName,	
	String setterName)	
	throws IntrospectionException	
✳	**PropertyDescriptor**(String propertyName,	
	reflect.Method getter, reflect.Method setter)	
	throws IntrospectionException	
void	**setBound**(boolean bound)	
void	**setConstrained**(boolean constrained)	
void	**setPropertyEditorClass**(Class propertyEditorClass)	
void	**setReadMethod**(reflect.Method getter)	
	throws IntrospectionException	
void	**setWriteMethod**(reflect.Method setter)	
	throws IntrospectionException	

PropertyEditor — java.beans

PropertyEditor

```
                void  addPropertyChangeListener(
                          PropertyChangeListener listener)
              String  getAsText()
 java.awt.Component  getCustomEditor()
              String  getJavaInitializationString()
            String[]  getTags()
              Object  getValue()
             boolean  isPaintable()
                void  paintValue(java.awt.Graphics gfx,
                          java.awt.Rectangle box)
                void  removePropertyChangeListener(
                          PropertyChangeListener listener)
                void  setAsText(String text)
                          throws IllegalArgumentException
                void  setValue(Object value)
             boolean  supportsCustomEditor()
```

PropertyEditorManager — java.beans

Object
  ➥PropertyEditorManager

```
❑   PropertyEditor  findEditor(Class targetType)
❑         String[]  getEditorSearchPath()
✳                   PropertyEditorManager()
❑             void  registerEditor(Class targetType, Class editorClass)
❑             void  setEditorSearchPath(String[] path)
```

PropertyEditorSupport — java.beans

Object
  ➥PropertyEditorSupport   PropertyEditor

```
                 void  addPropertyChangeListener(
                           PropertyChangeListener listener)
                 void  firePropertyChange()
               String  getAsText()
  java.awt.Component  getCustomEditor()
               String  getJavaInitializationString()
             String[]  getTags()
               Object  getValue()
              boolean  isPaintable()
                 void  paintValue(java.awt.Graphics gfx,
                           java.awt.Rectangle box)
✳◆                    PropertyEditorSupport()
✳◆                    PropertyEditorSupport(Object source)
                 void  removePropertyChangeListener(
                           PropertyChangeListener listener)
```

		void	setAsText(String text)
			throws IllegalArgumentException
		void	setValue(Object value)
		boolean	supportsCustomEditor()

PropertyVetoException   java.beans

```
Object
  ➥Throwable                              java.io.Serializable
     ➥Exception
        ➥PropertyVetoException
```

	PropertyChangeEvent	getPropertyChangeEvent()
❊		PropertyVetoException(String mess,
		PropertyChangeEvent evt)

Rectangle   java.awt

```
Object
  ➥Rectangle                             Shape, java.io.Serializable
```

		void	add(int newx, int newy)
1.0		void	add(int newx, int newy)
1.0		void	add(Point pt)
1.0		void	add(Rectangle r)
1.1		boolean	contains(int x, int y)
1.1		boolean	contains(Point p)
1.0		boolean	equals(Object obj)
1.1		Rectangle	getBounds()
1.1		Point	getLocation()
1.1		Dimension	getSize()
1.0		void	grow(int h, int v)
1.0		int	hashCode()
1.0	✍	int	height
		boolean	inside(int x, int y)
1.0		Rectangle	intersection(Rectangle r)
1.0		boolean	intersects(Rectangle r)
1.0		boolean	isEmpty()
		void	move(int x, int y)
1.0	❊		Rectangle()
1.0	❊		Rectangle(Dimension d)
1.0	❊		Rectangle(int width, int height)
1.0	❊		Rectangle(int x, int y, int width, int height)
1.0	❊		Rectangle(Point p)
1.0	❊		Rectangle(Point p, Dimension d)
1.1	❊		Rectangle(Rectangle r)
		void	reshape(int x, int y, int width, int height)
		void	resize(int width, int height)
1.1		void	setBounds(int x, int y, int width, int height)
1.1		void	setBounds(Rectangle r)
1.1		void	setLocation(int x, int y)

1.1		void	**setLocation**(Point p)
1.1		void	**setSize**(Dimension d)
1.1		void	**setSize**(int width, int height)
1.0		String	**toString**()
1.0		void	**translate**(int x, int y)
1.0		Rectangle	**union**(Rectangle r)
1.0.	✍	int	**width**
1.0	✍	int	**x**
1.0	✍	int	**y**

ReplicateScaleFilter   java.awt.image

```
Object
  ➥ImageFilter                          ImageConsumer, Cloneable
      ➥ReplicateScaleFilter
```

✍♦	int	**destHeight**
✍♦	int	**destWidth**
✍♦	Object	**outpixbuf**
✳		**ReplicateScaleFilter**(int width, int height)
	void	**setDimensions**(int w, int h)
	void	**setPixels**(int x, int y, int w, int h, ColorModel model, byte[] pixels, int off, int scansize)
	void	**setPixels**(int x, int y, int w, int h, ColorModel model, int[] pixels, int off, int scansize)
	void	**setProperties**(java.util.Hashtable props)
✍♦	int[]	**srccols**
✍♦	int	**srcHeight**
✍♦	int[]	**srcrows**
✍♦	int	**srcWidth**

RGBImageFilter   java.awt.image

```
Object
  ➥ImageFilter                          ImageConsumer, Cloneable
      ➥RGBImageFilter
```

✍♦	boolean	**canFilterIndexColorModel**
	IndexColorModel	**filterIndexColorModel**(IndexColorModel icm)
○	int	**filterRGB**(int x, int y, int rgb)
	void	**filterRGBPixels**(int x, int y, int w, int h, int[] pixels, int off, int scansize)
✍♦	ColorModel	**newmodel**
✍♦	ColorModel	**origmodel**
✳		**RGBImageFilter**()
	void	**setColorModel**(ColorModel model)
	void	**setPixels**(int x, int y, int w, int h, ColorModel model, byte[] pixels, int off, int scansize)

		void	setPixels(int x, int y, int w, int h, ColorModel model, int[] pixels, int off, int scansize)
		void	substituteColorModel(ColorModel oldcm, ColorModel newcm)

Scrollbar — java.awt

Object
➡ Component   image.ImageObserver, MenuContainer, java.io.Serializable
  ➡ Scrollbar   Adjustable

1.1		void	addAdjustmentListener(event.AdjustmentListener l)
		void	addNotify()
1.1		int	getBlockIncrement()
		int	getLineIncrement()
1.0		int	getMaximum()
1.0		int	getMinimum()
1.0		int	getOrientation()
		int	getPageIncrement()
1.1		int	getUnitIncrement()
1.0		int	getValue()
		int	getVisible()
1.1		int	getVisibleAmount()
1.0	⏴▣	int	HORIZONTAL
1.0	◆	String	paramString()
1.1	◆	void	processAdjustmentEvent(event.AdjustmentEvent e)
1.1	◆	void	processEvent(AWTEvent e)
1.1		void	removeAdjustmentListener(event.AdjustmentListener l)
1.0	✳		Scrollbar()
1.0	✳		Scrollbar(int orientation)
1.0	✳		Scrollbar(int orientation, int value, int visible, int minimum, int maximum)
1.1		void	setBlockIncrement(int v)
		void	setLineIncrement(int v)
1.1		void	setMaximum(int newMaximum)
1.1		void	setMinimum(int newMinimum)
1.1		void	setOrientation(int orientation)
		void	setPageIncrement(int v)
1.1		void	setUnitIncrement(int v)
1.0		void	setValue(int newValue)
1.0		void	setValues(int value, int visible, int minimum, int maximum)
1.1		void	setVisibleAmount(int newAmount)
1.0	⏴▣	int	VERTICAL

ScrollPane — java.awt

Object
➡ Component   image.ImageObserver, MenuContainer, java.io.Serializable

➡Container
   ➡ScrollPane

●◆	void	**addImpl**(Component comp, Object constraints, int index)
	void	**addNotify**()
	void	**doLayout**()
	Adjustable	**getHAdjustable**()
	int	**getHScrollbarHeight**()
	int	**getScrollbarDisplayPolicy**()
	Point	**getScrollPosition**()
	Adjustable	**getVAdjustable**()
	Dimension	**getViewportSize**()
	int	**getVScrollbarWidth**()
	void	**layout**()
	String	**paramString**()
	void	**printComponents**(Graphics g)
✐■	int	**SCROLLBARS_ALWAYS**
✐■	int	**SCROLLBARS_AS_NEEDED**
✐■	int	**SCROLLBARS_NEVER**
✳		**ScrollPane**()
✳		**ScrollPane**(int scrollbarDisplayPolicy)
●	void	**setLayout**(LayoutManager mgr)
	void	**setScrollPosition**(int x, int y)
	void	**setScrollPosition**(Point p)

Shape   java.awt

Shape

Rectangle	**getBounds**()

SimpleBeanInfo   java.beans

Object
   ➡SimpleBeanInfo   BeanInfo

	BeanInfo[]	**getAdditionalBeanInfo**()
	BeanDescriptor	**getBeanDescriptor**()
	int	**getDefaultEventIndex**()
	int	**getDefaultPropertyIndex**()
	EventSetDescriptor[]	**getEventSetDescriptors**()
	java.awt.Image	**getIcon**(int iconKind)
	MethodDescriptor[]	**getMethodDescriptors**()
	PropertyDescriptor[]	**getPropertyDescriptors**()
	java.awt.Image	**loadImage**(String resourceName)
✳		**SimpleBeanInfo**()

StringSelection   java.awt.datatransfer

Object
   ➡StringSelection   Transferable, ClipboardOwner

	Object	**getTransferData**(DataFlavor flavor)
		throws UnsupportedFlavorException,
		java.io.IOException
	DataFlavor[]	**getTransferDataFlavors**()
	boolean	**isDataFlavorSupported**(DataFlavor flavor)
	void	**lostOwnership**(Clipboard clipboard,
		Transferable contents)
✱		**StringSelection**(String data)

SystemColor	java.awt

Object
  ➡Color   java.io.Serializable
      ➡SystemColor   java.io.Serializable

△■	int	**ACTIVE_CAPTION**
△■	int	**ACTIVE_CAPTION_BORDER**
△■	int	**ACTIVE_CAPTION_TEXT**
△■	SystemColor	**activeCaption**
△■	SystemColor	**activeCaptionBorder**
△■	SystemColor	**activeCaptionText**
△■	SystemColor	**control**
△■	int	**CONTROL**
△■	int	**CONTROL_DK_SHADOW**
△■	int	**CONTROL_HIGHLIGHT**
△■	int	**CONTROL_LT_HIGHLIGHT**
△■	int	**CONTROL_SHADOW**
△■	int	**CONTROL_TEXT**
△■	SystemColor	**controlDkShadow**
△■	SystemColor	**controlHighlight**
△■	SystemColor	**controlLtHighlight**
△■	SystemColor	**controlShadow**
△■	SystemColor	**controlText**
△■	SystemColor	**desktop**
△■	int	**DESKTOP**
	int	**getRGB**()
△■	int	**INACTIVE_CAPTION**
△■	int	**INACTIVE_CAPTION_BORDER**
△■	int	**INACTIVE_CAPTION_TEXT**
△■	SystemColor	**inactiveCaption**
△■	SystemColor	**inactiveCaptionBorder**
△■	SystemColor	**inactiveCaptionText**
△■	SystemColor	**info**
△■	int	**INFO**
△■	int	**INFO_TEXT**
△■	SystemColor	**infoText**
△■	SystemColor	**menu**
△■	int	**MENU**
△■	int	**MENU_TEXT**
△■	SystemColor	**menuText**
△■	int	**NUM_COLORS**

✍■	SystemColor	**scrollbar**
✍■	int	**SCROLLBAR**
✍■	SystemColor	**text**
✍■	int	**TEXT**
✍■	int	**TEXT_HIGHLIGHT**
✍■	int	**TEXT_HIGHLIGHT_TEXT**
✍■	int	**TEXT_INACTIVE_TEXT**
✍■	int	**TEXT_TEXT**
✍■	SystemColor	**textHighlight**
✍■	SystemColor	**textHighlightText**
✍■	SystemColor	**textInactiveText**
✍■	SystemColor	**textText**
	String	**toString**()
✍■	SystemColor	**window**
✍■	int	**WINDOW**
✍■	int	**WINDOW_BORDER**
✍■	int	**WINDOW_TEXT**
✍■	SystemColor	**windowBorder**
✍■	SystemColor	**windowText**

TextArea   java.awt

```
Object
    ➡Component                image.ImageObserver, MenuContainer, java.io.Serializable
        ➡TextComponent
            ➡TextArea
```

		void	**addNotify**()
		void	**append**(String str)
		void	**appendText**(String str)
1.0		int	**getColumns**()
1.1		Dimension	**getMinimumSize**()
1.1		Dimension	**getMinimumSize**(int rows, int columns)
1.1		Dimension	**getPreferredSize**()
1.1		Dimension	**getPreferredSize**(int rows, int columns)
1		int	**getRows**()
1.1		int	**getScrollbarVisibility**()
1.1		void	**insert**(String str, int pos)
		void	**insertText**(String str, int pos)
		Dimension	**minimumSize**()
		Dimension	**minimumSize**(int rows, int columns)
1.0	◆	String	**paramString**()
		Dimension	**preferredSize**()
		Dimension	**preferredSize**(int rows, int columns)
1.1		void	**replaceRange**(String str, int start, int end)
		void	**replaceText**(String str, int start, int end)
1.1	✍■	int	**SCROLLBARS_BOTH**
1.1	✍■	int	**SCROLLBARS_HORIZONTAL_ONLY**
1.1	✍■	int	**SCROLLBARS_NONE**
1.1	✍■	int	**SCROLLBARS_VERTICAL_ONLY**

1.1		void	**setColumns**(int columns)
1.1		void	**setRows**(int rows)
1.0	❊		**TextArea**()
	❊		**TextArea**(int rows, int columns)
1.0	❊		**TextArea**(String text)
1.0	❊		**TextArea**(String text, int rows, int columns)
1.1	❊		**TextArea**(String text, int rows, int columns, int scrollbars)

TextComponent · java.awt

Object
→Component   image.ImageObserver, MenuContainer, java.io.Serializable
→TextComponent

		void	**addTextListener**(event.TextListener l)
1.1		int	**getCaretPosition**()
1.0		String	**getSelectedText**()
1.0		int	**getSelectionEnd**()
1.0		int	**getSelectionStart**()
1.0		String	**getText**()
1ble		boolean	**isEditable**()
1.0	◆	String	**paramString**()
	◆	void	**processEvent**(AWTEvent e)
	◆	void	**processTextEvent**(event.TextEvent e)
		void	**removeNotify**()
		void	**removeTextListener**(event.TextListener l)
1.0		void	**select**(int selectionStart, int selectionEnd)
1.0		void	**selectAll**()
1.1		void	**setCaretPosition**(int position)
1.0		void	**setEditable**(boolean b)
1.1		void	**setSelectionEnd**(int selectionEnd)
1.1		void	**setSelectionStart**(int selectionStart)
1.0		void	**setText**(String t)
	✍◆	event.TextListener	**textListener**

TextEvent · java.awt.event

Object
→java.util.EventObject   java.io.Serializable
→java.awt.AWTEvent
→TextEvent

		String	**paramString**()
	✍■	int	**TEXT_FIRST**
	✍■	int	**TEXT_LAST**
	✍■	int	**TEXT_VALUE_CHANGED**
	❊		**TextEvent**(Object source, int id)

TextField   java.awt

```
Object
    ➡Component              image.ImageObserver, MenuContainer, java.io.Serializable
        ➡TextComponent
            ➡TextField
```

1.1		void	**addActionListener**(event.ActionListener l)
		void	**addNotify**()
1.0		boolean	**echoCharIsSet**()
1.1ld		int	**getColumns**()
1.0		char	**getEchoChar**()
1.1		Dimension	**getMinimumSize**()
1.1		Dimension	**getMinimumSize**(int columns)
1.1		Dimension	**getPreferredSize**()
1.1		Dimension	**getPreferredSize**(int columns)
		Dimension	**minimumSize**()
		Dimension	**minimumSize**(int columns)
1.0	♦	String	**paramString**()
		Dimension	**preferredSize**()
		Dimension	**preferredSize**(int columns)
1.1	♦	void	**processActionEvent**(event.ActionEvent e)
1.1	♦	void	**processEvent**(AWTEvent e)
1.1		void	**removeActionListener**(event.ActionListener l)
1.1		void	**setColumns**(int columns)
1.1		void	**setEchoChar**(char c)
		void	**setEchoCharacter**(char c)
1.0	✳		**TextField**()
	✳		**TextField**(int columns)
1.0	✳		**TextField**(String text)
1.0	✳		**TextField**(String text, int columns)

TextListener   java.awt.event

```
TextListener                              java.util.EventListener
```

	void	**textValueChanged**(TextEvent e)

Toolkit   java.awt

```
Object
    ➡Toolkit
```

1.1	○	void	**beep**()
1.0	○	int	**checkImage**(Image image, int width, int height, image.ImageObserver observer)
1.0	○♦	peer.ButtonPeer	**createButton**(Button target)
1.0	○♦	peer.CanvasPeer	**createCanvas**(Canvas target)

1.0	○♦	peer.CheckboxPeer	**createCheckbox**(Checkbox target)
1.0	○♦	peer.CheckboxMenu¬ ItemPeer	**createCheckboxMenuItem**(CheckboxMenuItem target)
1.0	○♦	peer.ChoicePeer	**createChoice**(Choice target)
	♦	peer.LightweightPeer	**createComponent**(Component target)
1.0	○♦	peer.DialogPeer	**createDialog**(Dialog target)
1.0	○♦	peer.FileDialogPeer	**createFileDialog**(FileDialog target)
1.0	○♦	peer.FramePeer	**createFrame**(Frame target)
1.1		Image	**createImage**(byte[] imagedata)
1.1	○	Image	**createImage**(byte[] imagedata, int imageoffset, int imagelength)
1.0	○	Image	**createImage**(image.ImageProducer producer)
	○	Image	**createImage**(String filename)
	○	Image	**createImage**(java.net.URL url)
1.0	○♦	peer.LabelPeer	**createLabel**(Label target)
1.0	○♦	peer.ListPeer	**createList**(List target)
1.0	○♦	peer.MenuPeer	**createMenu**(Menu target)
1.0	○♦	peer.MenuBarPeer	**createMenuBar**(MenuBar target)
1.0	○♦	peer.MenuItemPeer	**createMenuItem**(MenuItem target)
1.0	○♦	peer.PanelPeer	**createPanel**(Panel target)
1.1	○♦	peer.PopupMenuPeer	**createPopupMenu**(PopupMenu target)
1.0	○♦	peer.ScrollbarPeer	**createScrollbar**(Scrollbar target)
1.1	○♦	peer.ScrollPanePeer	**createScrollPane**(ScrollPane target)
1.0	○♦	peer.TextAreaPeer	**createTextArea**(TextArea target)
1.0	○♦	peer.TextFieldPeer	**createTextField**(TextField target)
1.0	○♦	peer.WindowPeer	**createWindow**(Window target)
1.0	○	image.ColorModel	**getColorModel**()
1.0	❑	Toolkit	**getDefaultToolkit**()
1.0	○	String[]	**getFontList**()
1.0	○	FontMetrics	**getFontMetrics**(Font font)
1.0	○♦	peer.FontPeer	**getFontPeer**(Font target)
	○	Image	**getImage**(String filename)
	○	Image	**getImage**(java.net.URL url)
1.1		int	**getMenuShortcutKeyMask**()
	❑♦	Container	**getNativeContainer**(Component c)
1.1	○	PrintJob	**getPrintJob**(Frame frame, String jobtitle, java.util.Properties props)
	❑	String	**getProperty**(String key, String defaultValue)
1.0	○	int	**getScreenResolution**()
1.0	○	Dimension	**getScreenSize**()
1.1	○	datatransfer.Clipboard	**getSystemClipboard**()
	●	EventQueue	**getSystemEventQueue**()
	○♦	EventQueue	**getSystemEventQueueImpl**()
1.1	♦	void	**loadSystemColors**(int[] systemColors)
1.0	○	boolean	**prepareImage**(Image image, int width, int height, image.ImageObserver observer)
1.0	○	void	**sync**()
	✹		**Toolkit**()

Transferable · java.awt.datatransfer

Transferable

Object	**getTransferData**(DataFlavor flavor) *throws* UnsupportedFlavorException, java.io.IOException
DataFlavor[]	**getTransferDataFlavors**()
boolean	**isDataFlavorSupported**(DataFlavor flavor)

UnsupportedFlavorException · java.awt.datatransfer

Object
→Throwable   java.io.Serializable
  →Exception
    →UnsupportedFlavorException

✳	**UnsupportedFlavorException**(DataFlavor flavor)

VetoableChangeListener · java.beans

VetoableChangeListener   java.util.EventListener

void	**vetoableChange**(PropertyChangeEvent evt) *throws* PropertyVetoException

VetoableChangeSupport · java.beans

Object
→VetoableChangeSupport   java.io.Serializable

void	**addVetoableChangeListener**(String propertyName, VetoableChangeListener listener)
void	**addVetoableChangeListener**(VetoableChangeListener listener)
void	**fireVetoableChange**(PropertyChangeEvent evt) *throws* PropertyVetoException
void	**fireVetoableChange**(String propertyName, boolean oldValue, boolean newValue) *throws* PropertyVetoException
void	**fireVetoableChange**(String propertyName, int oldValue, int newValue) *throws* PropertyVetoException
void	**fireVetoableChange**(String propertyName, Object oldValue, Object newValue) *throws* PropertyVetoException
boolean	**hasListeners**(String propertyName)
void	**removeVetoableChangeListener**(String propertyName, VetoableChangeListener listener)

		void	removeVetoableChangeListener(
			VetoableChangeListener listener)
❄			VetoableChangeSupport(Object sourceBean)

Visibility   java.beans

Visibility

		boolean	avoidingGui()
		void	dontUseGui()
		boolean	needsGui()
		void	okToUseGui()

Window   java.awt

Object
➡Component   image.ImageObserver, MenuContainer, java.io.Serializable
    ➡Container
        ➡Window

		void	addNotify()
		void	addWindowListener(event.WindowListener l)
1.0		void	dispose()
		Component	getFocusOwner()
1.1		java.util.Locale	getLocale()
1.0		Toolkit	getToolkit()
1.0	●	String	getWarningString()
		boolean	isShowing()
1.0		void	pack()
		boolean	postEvent(Event e)
	♦	void	processEvent(AWTEvent e)
	♦	void	processWindowEvent(event.WindowEvent e)
		void	removeWindowListener(event.WindowListener l)
1.1		void	setCursor(Cursor cursor)
1.0		void	show()
1.0		void	toBack()
1.0		void	toFront()
1.0	❄		Window(Frame parent)

WindowAdapter   java.awt.event

Object
➡WindowAdapter   WindowListener

		void	windowActivated(WindowEvent e)
❄			WindowAdapter()
		void	windowClosed(WindowEvent e)
		void	windowClosing(WindowEvent e)
		void	windowDeactivated(WindowEvent e)
		void	windowDeiconified(WindowEvent e)

void	**windowIconified**(WindowEvent e)	
void	**windowOpened**(WindowEvent e)	

WindowEvent   java.awt.event

```
Object
  ➥java.util.EventObject          java.io.Serializable
      ➥java.awt.AWTEvent
          ➥ComponentEvent
              ➥WindowEvent
```

	java.awt.Window	**getWindow**()
	String	**paramString**()
✍■	int	**WINDOW_ACTIVATED**
✍■	int	**WINDOW_CLOSED**
✍■	int	**WINDOW_CLOSING**
✍■	int	**WINDOW_DEACTIVATED**
✍■	int	**WINDOW_DEICONIFIED**
✍■	int	**WINDOW_FIRST**
✍■	int	**WINDOW_ICONIFIED**
✍■	int	**WINDOW_LAST**
✍■	int	**WINDOW_OPENED**
✳		**WindowEvent**(java.awt.Window source, int id)

WindowListener   java.awt.event

WindowListener   java.util.EventListener

void	**windowActivated**(WindowEvent e)	
void	**windowClosed**(WindowEvent e)	
void	**windowClosing**(WindowEvent e)	
void	**windowDeactivated**(WindowEvent e)	
void	**windowDeiconified**(WindowEvent e)	
void	**windowIconified**(WindowEvent e)	
void	**windowOpened**(WindowEvent e)	

Index

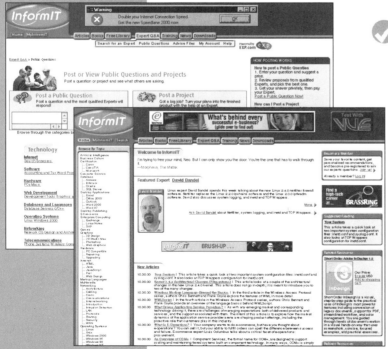